A MIND
THAT FEEDS
UPON INFINITY

A MIND THAT FEEDS UPON INFINITY

The Deep Self in English Romantic Poetry

Jean Hall

Rutherford • Madison • Teaneck
Fairleigh Dickinson University Press
London and Toronto: Associated University Presses

Associated University Presses
440 Forsgate Drive
Cranbury, NJ 08512

Associated University Presses
25 Sicilian Avenue
London WC1A 2QH, England

Associated University Presses
P.O. Box 39, Clarkson Pstl. Stn.
Mississauga, Ontario,
L5J 3X9 Canada

The paper used in this publication meets the requirements of the American National Standard for Permanence of Paper for Printed Library Materials Z39.48-1984.

Library of Congress Cataloging-in-Publication Data

Hall, Jean, 1941–
  A mind that feeds upon infinity : the deep self in English romantic poetry / Jean Hall.
    p.   cm.
  Includes bibliographical references and index.
  ISBN 0-8386-3430-3
  1. English poetry—19th century—History and criticism.
  2. Romanticism—Great Britain.   3. Infinite in literature.   4. Self in literature.   I. Title.
PR590.H29   1991   90-55871
                                                             CIP

To Will and Molly Jones
with Affection and Respect

CONTENTS

ACKNOWLEDGMENTS

My special thanks goes to Paul A. Cantor, who read my manuscript in an early version and offered helpful, astute criticisms which led me to entirely refocus the work. I am also grateful for the sensible suggestions he made at later stages of the writing.

Thanks also to my good friends Will Jones and Carol Collins, who read some of my first drafts and continued to be interested in this project over the years. It's a pleasure to also acknowledge the help of Christine Gallant, Rhoda Rand Codner, JoAnn Gora, Bettyann Kevles, Margaret J. Osler, and Barbara Buhler Lynes. I am grateful to the American Council of Learned Societies for a fellowship which enabled me to begin work on the book.

Finally, thanks to my husband, Jim, the computer whiz, who patiently introduced me to the world of word processing—and devoted a great deal of his time to formatting and printing various versions of the manuscript.

A MIND
THAT FEEDS
UPON INFINITY

1

INTRODUCTION
Routes to Infinity

In the letter of 14 February–3 May 1819 to his brother and
sister-in-law, Keats outlines "a grander system of salvation
than the chryst<e>ian religion"—his now famous remarks
on the world as "The value of Soul-making." He begins by
differentiating "Soul as distinguished from an Intelligence—
There may be intelligences or sparks of the divinity in mil-
lions—but they are not Souls <the> till they acquire identities, till each one is personally itself." For Keats, individual
identity depends on one's emotional response to his or her own
experience. He asks, "Do you not see how necessary a World of
Pains and troubles is to school an Intelligence and make it a
soul? A Place where the heart must feel and suffer in a thousand diverse ways!" His image of the soul's education is of the
world as "a School instituted for the purpose of teaching little
children to read—I will call the *human heart* the *horn Book*
used in that School—and I will call the *Child able to read*, the
Soul made from that *school* and its *hornbook*."[1]

The unformed human being is made into an individual person by learning to read his or her own heart—by coming to
understand the meaning of his or her own feelings. Interpretation, in the form of an ever-renewed inward gaze or self-reflexive reading and rereading, schools the human "Intelligence"
and renders it a "Soul." Keats's hornbook image identifies interpretation as the hermeneutical process which creates the
ever-growing "Soul," an entity more individualized than mere
"Intelligence" because of its wisdom—its centered capacity to
understand profoundly the significance of its own experience.
The deep self becomes a humane presence that lives and continually grows through self-interpretive acts.

As Clifford Siskin argues in his *The Historicity of Romantic
Discourse*, the Romantics naturalized this "modern psychol-

13

ogized subject: a mind, capable of limitless growth, that takes itself to be the primary object of its own inquiries."[2] But what the Romantics present as psychologized and naturalized, Siskin views as constructed. For if Keats takes his own image of the heart as hornbook metaphorically, Siskin suggests that the deep self's lyrical acts of self-interpretation actually do depend on reading and writing—on processes of literary transformation rather than visionary transcendence. The deep self is written up and continually needs to be rewritten and reread. If this persona is not natural, then it also is not inevitable; and so Siskin's demystifying analysis leads us to inquire into the reasons why the deep self is made. Why should a soul necessarily be profound, and why should the heart's feelings inevitably become deep? The answer obviously implied by Keats's metaphor of the hornbook is that growing souls become continually wiser and more humane as they deepen themselves through their continually renewed acts of self-transcendence. But if this model of naturalized visionary transcendence provides one rationale for depth, I shall argue that conflict furnishes another (and often unacknowledged) motive. The deep self is constructed not only to foster growth but also to provide a retreat, a place of defense and protection, against the threat posed by aggressive impulses.

In advancing this speculation I do not want to confuse my approach with the literary treatment of aggression advanced in Harold Bloom's theory of poetic precursors, in which the ephebe inevitably struggles with the anxiety of influence.[3] This book is a study not of literary visions but of the imagination's social dreamings—its potential relations with selves beyond its own soul, its accommodation to the human world in which it must forge its individual identity.

My title is drawn from the climactic experience of *The Prelude*, Wordsworth's ascent of Snowden. Here Wordsworth gives us a version of the deep self as godlike, as participating in the metamorphic powers of nature. The mountaintops wreathed in seas of fog and resounding to the voices of subterranean waters become "The perfect image of a mighty mind, / Of one that feeds upon infinity."[4] Wordsworth celebrates the soul's capacity for growth, construing the visionary poet's appetite for unlimited acts of self-transcendence as the human version of infinity. Our minds desire infinity, and continually must feed upon it in workings that incessantly deepen the self. But if Wordsworth ascends Snowden with a climbing party, he experiences his vision in isolation—and his celebration of the deep self's enactment of infinity carries anti-social undertones. Although the imaginative mind is godlike, Wordsworth's description also makes it sound rather Napoleonic.[5] In his vision Nature, like the human imagination, moulds the fog in a "domination which she oftentimes / Exerts upon the outward face of things, . . . Doth make one object so impress itself / Upon all others, and pervades them so, / That even the grossest minds must see and hear, / And cannot chuse but feel" (77–84). This language conveys not only the transforming capacity of the imagination but also its coercive power. An implication of Wordsworth's words is that the imagination may feed upon infinity not only through incessant self-transcendence, but also in ever-renewed attempts to dominate, manipulate, overcome, everything outside itself. Perhaps the self can be formed not only by making worlds but also by conquering them. Romantic soul-making, then, involves a profound duality of purpose and tends to move between polarities of harmony and conflict. The meditative self, the deep Wordsworthian soul, always is potentially an imperial self too—for the capacity for self-knowledge and self-mastery is linked to the social possibility of conquest. In this volume I emphasize the dimension of conflict and its relation to the poets' social sense, their realization that they must make themselves within a human world—a world of others.

The social dimension of Romantic soul-making is the subject of Charles J. Rzepka's suggestive study, *The Self as Mind*. In his formulation, the duality of the deep self becomes a movement between what he calls the disembodied pole of "visionary solipsism," the "poet's tendency to identify solely with mind, and thus to make the perceived world something unreal, something lacking substantiality apart from the mind," and the opposite embodied pole of social confrontation, involving the "ambivalent need for definitive self-recognition from others who are either sympathetic or are to be made, somehow, nonthreatening."[6] By encountering another, the poetic self confronts its "fear of not properly belonging to the world" and "attempts to make a place for itself among others, but on the poet's own terms . . . the poet seeks to identify himself by redefining the circumstances, and even the audience, in or before which his identity becomes concrete."[7] For the most part Rzepka sees the poet's presentation of himself to the world as a process of allaying his own anxieties, confirming his sense of self, and identifying with some authority outside the self as a mind which can validate his attempts at growth and maturation. What I propose to do is intensify Rzepka's scenario of social confrontation into a description of conflict, by showing the way that poetic selves-as-minds in their deep and retired state tend to imagine not only visions of infinite harmony but also of hyperbolically intensified aggression.

And indeed, the tendency to engage conflict as a vital element in soul-making can be seen as characteristic of the Romantic historical moment. As Rzepka observes, in late eighteenth and early nineteenth-century England, "Greater social mobility, mass urbanization, the disappearance of sumptuary laws, all had the general effect of making England an island of strangers. It became increasingly difficult for the self to find a recognizable place in English society, harder to tell if what others saw was the true self, or if the self was being compromised, made false, taken away from its 'owner' by more fluid and less dependable categories of public identification."[8] The destabilization of traditional social categories which Rzepka refers to indeed did make the attribution of individual identity difficult, on a widespread scale. During this period the older ideology of a stable, hierarchical society vanished in the dawning self-consciousness of separate social classes, which came into being as a function of the conflict of interests created by the new political and economic conditions of the French and Industrial Revolutions.[9]

If the individual found himself or herself estranged in Rzepka's "island of strangers," stripped of traditional social identification and compelled to make his or her own identity, it is also true that whole groups of people began to reforge their sense of social identity. And just as class consciousness emerged as a function of class conflict, the Romantic deep self emerged as a function of conflicting elements—of the imagination's infinite desires versus the claims of other people, and even, within the individual poetic soul, of the competing claims exerted by different parts of the self. Wordsworth's Snowden meditation suggests a model of soul-making as self-reflexive conflict, when he describes how imagination dominates mundane perception so "That even the grossest minds must see and hear, / And cannot chuse but feel." Here one part of the self pits itself against another; and it is by such acts of self-mastery than an ever-deeper and more resonant identity constantly is remade.

The deep self, then, emerges as radically ambiguous. Its attempts at soul-making promise to create a profoundly humane persona, but this consciousness must be born in conflict—and is generated as a function of the imagination's infinite, imperialistic desire. The ambivalent, unstable nature of a self constructed on such foundations is a subject of intense concern for the poets studied in this volume. A brief analysis of Blake's way of dealing with the dilemma may clarify my point, for his is perhaps the paradigm case, which I describe in my first chapter.

In the masterwork of Blake's early career, *Songs of Innocence*, the reader's mind is made to feed upon infinity by participating in the lyric visions of Blake's innocents. These beings are wholly candid—they reveal themselves in their expressions, which take for granted a loving relationship between the innocents and all other things in the world. They are exactly what they appear to be, for they have nothing to hide and no need to defend themselves against anyone or anything. I shall call their condition superficial, in the most affirmative sense—they are creatures of the surface because for them depths are both nonexistent and unnecessary. Blake's paradise of innocence is a socialized state that I term open expressiveness, the condition in which every person reveals the self spontaneously and unreservedly. But when Blake added the *Songs of Experience* to *Songs of Innocence*, he created a new class of characters who are creatures with depth because they construct surface appearances to disguise their motives, a procedure that allows them to mislead and manipulate others, and even themselves. In Experience the imagination waxes imperialistic, thirsting for possession and domination—and so the self closes itself off, retreating from the surface which it uses as a disguise, in order to work out its own obscure purposes in the depths.

Taken together, *Songs of Innocence and of Experience* creates a formidable problem for Blake: he would like to affirm innocence, with its great ideal of open expressiveness, but to do so while ignoring the human potential for selfishness and manipulation would be naive. His solution, worked out in the series of his prophecies, is what I shall call the translucent deep self—a being that has looked into its depths and struggled to work through its own dark impulses, so that at last it becomes profound yet also utterly clear. In contrast to the children and childlike adults of *Songs of Innocence*, the redeemed Albion of

Jerusalem becomes a being not only of surface, but also of depth—a candid yet resonant and deep self. He is capable in a way the innocents cannot be, for he is able to defend against dark impulses—whether his own or those of other, experienced selves—and can do so without resorting to the disguises of the experienced. For Albion, open expressiveness involves the values of courageous strength, clearsighted honesty, and wisdom, qualities not developed in the surface life of the innocents. By imagining the translucent deep self Blake redeems inwardness, works through the depths, shows us a way to cope with the obscure menace of our subterranean infinities.

The Blakean deep self thus stages its act of transcendence as the growth of the poet's mind—but this typically Romantic narrative of self-development proceeds not autonomously but within an environment of aggression. For the self is not simply self-referential, and its feedings upon infinity do not always occur in isolation. The acts of mind that produce growth must be conducted in an awareness of the competing powers of other people. Indeed, if these potential conflicts did not exist there would be no reason for the Blakean child to grow up: his surface perfection would comprise the ideal human state. It is conflict which necessitates depth and its attendant qualities, penetration and complexity. The great Romantic ideal of the deep self—the humane, profound, ever-evolving soul that constantly resonates itself in acts of imaginative transcendence—cannot be entirely self-born. In its social aspect, it is generated as a function of conflict. So after the *Songs*, when Blake writes his great prophetic books that enact the deep self's development, he adopts a mythological approach which arrays the individual soul as a social world. Microcosm and macrocosm become dual aspects of a unity wherein spiritual self-development results from the interaction of competing forces. The Blakean imagination fosters formations which simultaneously become conflicting characters and various aspects of the deepening self. For Blake, then, the deep self emerges as a dialectical interplay of the individual and the social.

In my chapter on Blake, which I have just summarized, I have told a story of self-development, the tale of how one version of the deep self was imagined as a response to one poet's special feeling for aggression. But in telling Blake's story, and the stories of the other poets related in this volume, I do not want to foster the mistaken impression that I am treating the Romantic self as a natural presence. Our contemporary criticism has decentered the self and called the authority of subjective transcendence into question far too successfully to permit another naturalistic account of the Romantic imagination.[10] In particular, the new historicist critique has questioned subjectivity by reminding us of the material and social considerations involved in poetic creation, and suggesting that imaginative transcendence may serve ideological ends by idealizing social conflicts. As Jerome McGann puts it in *The Romantic Ideology:*

> Romantic poetry pursued the illusions of its own ideas and Ideals in order to avoid facing the truths of immediate history. . . . When reading Romantic poems, then, we are to remember that their ideas—for example, ideas about the creativity of Imagination, about the centrality of the Self, about the organic and processive structure of social life, and so forth—are all historically specific. . . . In the Romantic Age these and similar ideas are represented as trans-historical—eternal truths which wake to perish never. The very belief that transcendental categories can provide a permanent ground for culture becomes, in the Romantic Age, an ideological formation—another illusion raised up to hold back an awareness of the contradictions inherent in contemporary social structures and the relations they support.[11]

McGann demystifies Romantic writing but does not debunk it; his aim is to show the contemporary social pressures that underwrite the poets' imaginations of transcendence, and to reveal how their hard-won visions emerge out of difficulties which are embedded but not really eradicated in the poetry itself. This is the spirit in which Marjorie Levinson excavates "Tintern Abbey" to reveal the historical losses that Wordsworth transcendentalizes as spiritual gains,[12] and in which Jon Klancher deconstructs the universalized voices of early nineteenth-century mass periodicals to reveal the class conflicts which such articulations were meant to transcend.[13]

Recently Marlon B. Ross has extended the historicist analysis to the question of gender, in his *The Contours of Masculine Desire.* He finds the major English Romantic poets—of course, all male—wrote a poetry "not *intrinsically* masculine, but . . . *sociohistorically* masculine," as a response to the increasing number of women poets and readers, who were rapidly feminizing the literary market.[14] Ross sees the male poets' response as hyperbolically masculinized, an exaggeration of gender difference motivated by their suppressed fears of feminization and marginalization. The male Romantics transcendentalize the problem of audience possession by redefining it as a question of self-possession, a shift which removes poetry from the sordid, feminized, material conditions of the marketplace to enthrone it spiritually as the eternal masculine quest for self identity. Where women disperse selfhood in the softness of feeling, the male poet will utilize his feelings as an occasion for self-possession—rather than being overcome by emotion, he will become its master. Naturally, Ross's self-imperializing deep self views his relations with the world antagonistically. Poetry "becomes chivalric jousting transformed to meet the conditions of a social system in which power manifests itself no longer in physical strength but in the strength of various kinds of cognitive and metaphorical exchanges . . . the individual or society that devises ways of establishing and sustaining mental influence becomes the strongest and rules the world."[15]

Although the present volume is not a work of feminist criticism, I have not been blind to how frequently the Romantic poets regard woman as an object of possession, and hence, an occasion for self-possession. When Blake's Los excludes Enitharmon from the conversational communion of universal manhood at the end of *Jerusalem*, when Coleridge displaces his own conflicts onto Christabel, the infinitely open woman who infinitely submits, or when Keats selects Lamia as the most extreme embodiment of a problem of mixed motives from which he himself suffers, I have noted a dubious centering of woman that ultimately leads to the marginalization of the feminine.

Nevertheless, my view of the Romantic poets' aggressiveness is, as it were, mild in comparison to Ross's. For him they are often obnoxiously macho; while I share in that perception, I also am struck by the moments in which they are amazingly afraid of their own fearfulness. For example, my account of Wordsworth reveals a poet so dismayed by his own aggressiveness that he will go absolutely to any lengths to suppress it; and my analysis of Coleridge concerns a bard who must murder his conscious self before he can release his emotional powers. Perhaps the terrible extremity of these visions might elicit our sympathy, as well as our irritation.

In this volume I have displayed the Romantic deep self as six selves—six formations that enact selfhood as the transcendence of inward and social conflict. My effort has been to set the poets in dialectical relation with each other, so that this

general movement of transcendence can be viewed not as
monolithic but as a series of variations, an array of possibilities. By engaging Wordsworth in a dialogue with Coleridge and Byron, and Byron in a conversation with Shelley and
Keats, I have tried to open up the Romantic self—to show how
similar assumptions can lead to diverse routes, varying con-
structions. These differences among the poets lead back to a
recognition of their similarities—but then, their similarities
return to breed difference. The self becomes neither self-contained nor naturally inevitable, but instead can be considered
as a deployment of options. By thus interweaving the poets I
have attempted my own revision of the deep self. Mindful of
Bakhtin's fundamental postulation of the other, which makes
identity a function of evolving dialogue rather than deep interior monologue, I have sought to bring these writers out into an
illuminating conversational society.[16]

A brief rehearsal of this volume's scenario perhaps can con-
vey its dialogic qualities. After developing the argument about
Blake summarized above, I turn to Wordsworth, who fears
becoming a man of action because he suspects men of the
world exercise their will to power through repeated acts of
destruction. He creates the character of Rivers in his early
drama *The Borderers* to exorcise his own desire for activity in
the world and later develops a view of meditation as a species
of purified action, which leads to his notion of the spirit's
growth as an inner experience. By withdrawing from the
worldly surface to establish himself in meditative depths
Wordsworth redeems the inner darkness, and creates an infinite attitude, tranquillity, which subsumes and harmonizes
the imagination's impulses. Having transformed worldly action into spiritual meditation, the Wordsworthian self can conceive of social harmony as a matter of communication—the
poetic communion developed by a community of constantly
developing minds.

Coleridge's history initially resembles Wordsworth's; he rejects activity in the world from the time of his boyhood, retreating from the arena of childhood games and sports to
create his own inner realm. The dream-poems he eventually
writes out of this world are powered by infinitely obscure
aggressiveness, centering on the murder of the ego and acts of
power. Unlike Wordsworth, he cannot purify the depths. Instead, he sacrifices his conscious self to them, creating the
sublimely powerful but potentially anti-social figure of the

possessed bard. The social harmonization implied by the Wordsworthian project of self-development is replaced by Coleridgean ambivalence, in which poetic acts of communication constantly threaten to become imperialistic acts of domination.

Keats begins with a longing for heroic activity in the world but as he grows he discovers that his desire for experience is also a lust for power, an almost Coleridgean need to possess and manipulate others. To compensate for these imperialistic urges he backgrounds the Wordsworthian egotistical sublime to develop its seeming opposite, the invisible poet, that selfless self or figure of negative capability who works unseen and disinterestedly in the world. But when he at last realizes that true disinterest is impossible for him, the Keats of the Odes turns to his inner world as a way of defusing his manipulative energies, of deploying them upon himself rather than other human beings. He stages a new, creative act of the imagination: the development of the deep, resonant, humane self. Like the Wordsworthian self of *The Prelude*, this Keatsian persona speaks for society by becoming the voice of the cultural community; but like the Wordsworthian self, the Keatsian deep self of the Odes comes into being and is most at home in an attitude of isolation.

Although Byron distinguishes himself from all these poets by denying the existence of inwardness and depth, his claim that surface is the sole reality becomes an inversion, and therefore a variant, of the normal Romantic defenses. The worldly poet of *Don Juan* moves to the outside to avoid the clandestine manipulations of the Laker poets of depth, proposing that if life must be a struggle at least it should be fought openly and fairly, not behind a poetic smoke screen of pseudo-profundities. He openly baits his audience, but if his antagonistic model of audience relations inverts Wordsworth's sympathetic model of audience communion, nevertheless these opposing attitudes further the same end—the promotion of social harmony through imaginative transformation of aggressive impulses.

The young Shelley of *Alastor* experiences the inspirational power of poetry as the capacity to cast oneself into the depths, where as an imaginative isolate one dies in the fruitless search for meaning. For Shelley, aggression registers primarily as the impulse toward self-destruction, and so like Byron, he turns from the depths outward toward the surface—but unlike Byron, he tries to convert surface into a transformed version of depth by linking the evolution of the self's meaning to the gathering coherence of the world, an unfolding harmony that in the last Act of *Prometheus Unbound* redeems the isolate self through a vision of universal social concord.

As these preliminary descriptions suggest, I shall view the Romantic tendency to write a poetry of imaginative self-development as the poets' attempt to socialize their own imaginations, which in themselves pose the possibilities of obscure threat as well as of profound wisdom. These poets sense the danger as well as the glory that lies within, and so they all must struggle to redeem the imagination. For them, growth and defense become intertwined. But paradoxically, in working toward socialization the poets find themselves developing a new isolate state as deep selves, and this dialectical recoil often sets them radically apart from others and redoubles the force of the imagination's anti-social, imperialistic desires. So the story of the deep self as told in this volume will be the story of unattainable transcendence, of incessant Romantic process. Certainly it would be possible to unmask the inglorious elements in this seemingly eternal quest, but like Jerome McGann, I tend both to sympathize with the Romantic project and also note that it is not the only or the inevitable human endeavor. I shall begin the Romantic dialogue with Blake, who in a long lifetime of poetry strove to construct the deep self as a vision of open and translucent expressiveness capable of uniting all individuals within a great poetic Man.

2

BLAKE

The Translucent Man

Blake's earliest illuminated work, the companion tracts *There is No Natural Religion* and *All Religions are One*, reveal him as a mind hungering for infinity. "Less than All cannot satisfy Man," proclaims the first tract: and because man desires infinitely Blake concludes that his "possession is Infinite & himself Infinite." In making this flat assertion Blake sets himself against Lockean rationalistic sensationalism and the tradition of British Empirical philosophy that followed from it. What Blake terms Natural Religion, the eighteenth-century religious sensibility derived from Empiricism, has reduced the human body to a merely natural self, limiting each person's scope to the range of his physical senses. In this state of stifling restriction man becomes "only a natural organ subject to Sense"—a strictly local being, a small part of the world deprived of ability to comprehend the whole. Indeed, he does not even conceive of wholeness; since natural "Mans desires are limited by his perceptions," his small physical size and sensory capacities produce a restricted soul—a spiritless presence closed to all sense of wonder.[1]

To unveil infinity, Blake therefore must begin by redeeming our perception of the human body. In place of the Lockean or merely physical self he advances his notion of the poetic body, which is the human form understood not rationalistically but symbolically.[2] His second tract, *All Religions are One*, defines the human form as an identity-in-difference. Just "As all men are alike (tho' infinitely various) So all Religions & as all similars have one source." The suggestion is that each person is a body at once particular and general, in that we are ourselves but we also display universal or generic form—our features, coloring, presence, attest both to our individual identity and our membership in the human race. If body manifests identity

24

in difference, then soul must do the same: so all religions become one—simultaneously expressions of individual inspiration and universal human spirituality. The symbolic principle of identity in difference allows Blake to see mankind as one and many, here and everywhere, himself and infinity: "The true Man is the source he being the Poetic Genius."[3]

Blake's infinity is based in the human body, and as such it perforce becomes a social form. Where the Lockean body is a system of sense organs that gathers in knowledge, Blake's poetic body knows and is known through its expansive expressiveness—its voice, attitudes, gestures, which exist not for themselves but as communications to others. Open expressiveness becomes Blake's great ideal: poetry and society are identified—All Religions are One. In his early prophecy the *Visions of the Daughters of Albion* this social vision is expressed through his heroine Oothoon's hyperbolic eroticism. She proclaims herself as "Open to joy and to delight where ever beauty appears / If in the morning sun I find it: there my eyes are fix'd / In happy copulation: if in evening mild. wearied with work; / Sit on a bank and draw the pleasures of this free born joy" (6.22–23; 7.1–2). For Oothoon infinity is comprehended through total openness: she draws in not Lockean sensory information but tremendous feelings of beauty and joy, which prompt her to ecstatic expressions.[4] This paradisiacal openness, this eroticized intensity of her relationships, so permeates her being that she becomes at once a distinctive poetic voice and a portion of the world's universal delight. For Blake, individuality makes sense only as an aspect of generality—to properly be herself, Oothoon must be in unrestricted relationship to the world.

The *Songs of Innocence* become Blake's most successful early depiction of open expressiveness. Here the perhaps forced tone of Oothoon's eroticism is modulated to the naturalistic expressions of Blake's innocents, children and childlike adults who are utterly open and trusting toward the world. These characters truly are naive poets, for as innocents they live in a pre-reflective state, the period when one has not learned to be conscious of oneself. At this time everything is on the surface, for no sooner is an impulse felt than it is expressed. Hence, relationship in the state of innocence is instantaneous—these speakers are intuitively social beings. Where Oothoon elaborately argues for her eroticized vision, the children of *Songs of Innocence* simply say poetically. They are superficial in the best sense—for they experience themselves as an unconflicted unity, an untrammeled flow of generous expressive energy that does not harbor contradictory depths. As they are they see, and they say. These innocents become a prime example of Blake's "true Man" because in naively expressing the impulse to relationship they embody the divinity in humankind.

"The Lamb" is a Song worth remarking, for it reveals what this childish poetry leads to with exceptional clarity. Here Blake shows a child catechizing his pet lamb, asking the creature if it knows who brought it into the gentle and hospitable world where it enjoys its existence. Who "Gave thee clothing of delight, / Softest clothing wooly bright; / Gave thee such a tender voice, / Making all the vales rejoice!" That the lamb cannot answer is no hindrance, for the child is perfectly ready to speak the self-evident reply for him: "Little Lamb I'll tell thee." The child knows clearly that the lamb's maker "is called by thy name, / For he calls himself a Lamb." This child's superficial understanding of the catechism, which leads him to identify his pet with the Lamb of God, emphatically is not shallow—for the emotion conveyed is relational: the child loves both lamb and God, and connects them in open equivalence. This is an instinctively loving speaker, and so when he continues his equivalences by adding that his God "is meek & he is mild, / He became a little child: / I a child & thou a lamb, / We are called by his name," we are prepared to accept his assertion not as evidence of egotism in elevating himself to divinity but as a mark of an unself-conscious generosity which speaks the truth about itself unawares. For indeed the lamb, the child, and Christ become an identity in difference, distinctive forms that share a spiritual unity. The effect of "The Lamb" is to incarnate divinity—to bring it to earth in the bodily forms of the child and the lamb. That is the way the child himself sees and knows, and his guileless and confident song persuades the reader of "The Lamb" that this innocent speaks a profound truth.

And in this way the other *Songs of Innocence* also tend to strike the reader as childish assertions that harbor deep verities. Each speaker in Blake's collection of *Songs* speaks locally, as an individual—but because the attitude of these innocents is utterly loving and open their speech constantly tends to build relationships between the human and the divine. The collective impact of the *Songs of Innocence* is to suggest a compound vision of the world's innocents as an identity in difference—a group of individuals whose expressions of loving relationships converge in the intuition of God. At its full reach, the *Songs of Innocence* expresses God through the innocents by showing that the speech of these characters inhabits particular times and places and yet transcends them unawares, through the religious humanity of the speakers' generous impulses. These characters preserve the concrete locality of the Lockean body, but by their energetic feeling they also go beyond it, to achieve universal scope. They remain themselves, but at the same time they also express infinity.[5]

And so "The Divine Image," which affirms the identity of the human and divine forms, becomes more than a figurative assertion. When the speaker says that "all must love the human form, / In heathen, turk or jew. / Where Mercy Love & Pity dwell, / There God is dwelling too," he suggests that in order to exist, God must live within the human body. So the *Songs of Innocence* becomes a Romantic version of the Christian doctrine of incarnation, in which God is brought into our world through the power of poetic open expressiveness. For Blake infinity can exist only as it is seen in the human image; soul can come into being only as the song of the body. The human form becomes an expressive vehicle that acts out God.

But where the notion of incarnation pervades the *Songs of Innocence*, the story of the Fall shadows *Songs of Experience*. For after Adam and Eve disobey God by eating the fruit of the tree of knowledge, they suddenly understand they are naked. In Blakean terms, they are converted from innocents to experienced individuals by becoming aware of their bodies. Where Innocence is pure surface, the unreflective condition of perfect expressiveness that lives through the body without seeing itself, Experience becomes a contrary awareness of one's own display. In the experienced state expressiveness functions not to reveal the individual unawares in all the forms he or she sees, but to turn the person's vision inward, to compel the study of his or her own body. Then the poetic songs of innocence become corrupted into self-dramatization. Innocent artlessness becomes experienced artfulness. Where Blake's innocents are pure surface, the primal unity of expressive openness, his experienced speakers are divided between their surfaces and their depths—for they present an appearance to the world and close themselves within it as a disguise. This disjunction between the displayed and hidden selves allows them to become manipulative. The corrupted theater of Experience becomes a deceptive performance, a misleading surface that dupes the audience and allows the concealed agent to maneuver for power behind the scenes.

If Innocence is expressive openness, the display of the whole self through its unreflective surface, then Experience is the state of closure, the creation of a boundary between surface and depth that sets the stage for manipulation. Expression and manipulation become the great contrary human powers, and they achieve their force through contrary processes. Expression joyfully incarnates infinity through the open affirmation of relationship, whereas manipulation bases its power on the denial of relationship. It rejects the aggregate humanity, the human form divine, in order to establish the dominance of the individual. So the individualist shows energy not in the form of God's indwelling, but in the contrary power—to make himself or herself into a god, to seize the world and become its ruler. Expressiveness projects infinity, but manipulation tries to possess it.

And so the dramas of *Songs of Experience* are all founded on self-interest, which is the natural consequence of the self-awareness initiated by the experienced condition. The experienced speakers remain adamantly within themselves, and in their strictly local focus they display the worst implications of the Lockean or merely natural state. Their concentration on self materializes the human condition, manifests consciousness of body as a passion for possession. These characters have destroyed the poetic unity of body and spirit, turning their humanity into a state of nature that echoes Hobbes more closely than Locke. The visionary sociability of Innocence is transformed into the defensive, anti-social posturing of Experience.

Hobbes's man yearns for personal power, but at the same time, as an isolated individualist he finds life to be "solitary, poor, nasty, brutish, and short."[6] The same is generally true of Blake's experienced people. They manipulate for power, but since any power they gain must be at the cost of others, they usually disguise their intentions through a show of harmlessness. So in Experience the aggressive thrust of manipulation comes cloaked in the mask of impotence. The manipulator diminishes his surface, demeans his own body, so it will not frighten others. For example, the self-aware chimney sweep depicts himself as "A little black thing among the snow: / Crying weep, weep, in notes of woe!" By reducing himself in order to gain his audience's pity, the child transforms the relational qualities of pity into possessive ones. Pity becomes not the projective power of infinity, the ability to feel for others, but a kind of emotional capital that one constantly seeks to appropriate for oneself.

However, the theatrics of Experience make it likely that this emotional robbery will occur at the actor's own cost. For manipulation is a deceptive act that merges insensibly into self-deception; the individual who assumes a demeaning disguise soon comes to believe in his or her own performance. So the experienced chimney sweep appropriates pity at the cost of projecting a pitiful and impoverished world—a world in which emotion is atrophied, and not really worth the taking. The poetics of Experience aspires to wealth and possession but ends in the creation of spiritual poverty.

But if Experience cannot achieve the human wealth of Innocence, nevertheless it does have the power to destroy it. For the innocent are pure surface; they live in trust, unable to imagine an inwardness that could lurk behind surface and use it for ulterior motives. They accept everything they see at face value, which means they can be easily duped by the experienced. Innocence is all surface and no depth, a poem not a poet, an unself-conscious vision. In creating his experienced characters Blake implicitly has suggested the flaw in his perfect innocents: the paradise of utter surface, of open and untrammeled expressiveness, cannot defend itself if a defense becomes necessary. Under some circumstances perfection is rendered helpless. This limitation of the innocents implies the necessity for a new kind of personality, one not completely superficial and yet not corrupted in its interior as are the experienced. It will be necessary to see into people, to know one's own depths and the depths of others, in order to defend innocence. But if the depths can be seen and dealt with clearly enough, perhaps the ideal of open expressiveness still can be maintained. Taken together, the *Songs of Innocence and of Experience* imply the necessity for an open but self-conscious personality. If the innocents are a poem not a poet, then Blake must produce the poet capable of both imagining and protecting innocence.

In the *Songs*, the reader begins to play this role. It is possible to read *Songs of Innocence and of Experience* as an innocent child would, completely as poetry of the surface; but most adult readers would agree that such a reading does not do full justice to the profundity of Blake's creation. Implicitly, the reader of Blake's *Songs* is invited to grow up by learning to see into the depths of these simple lyrics, to render readings that are progressively more adequate. Maturity and process are linked in the Blakean capable reader, for reading turns out to be an openly evolving activity that continually enables the reader to see and cope with more.

Some things apt to impress the growing reader merit special mention here. First, the self-dramatizations of both the innocent and the experienced speakers—their way of making their worlds through the nature of their speech—suggests that we are at least to a great extent free to choose our modes of being. Just as *There is No Natural Religion* and *All Religions are One* presented opposed world visions founded on the rival grounding intuitions of Lockean reductionism and Blakean poetry, so the *Songs* involve a large number of contrary song pairings in which similar situations are dramatized through opposing lyrical responses. As we compare the worlds of the Piper and the Bard, the innocent and the experienced chimney sweeps, the innocent and the experienced nurses, and so forth, we begin to see that these lives are governed by dramatic rather than by natural necessity. As in Blake's tracts on religion, life is seen to be an affair of competing intuitions; and implicitly we are invited to choose those that best satisfy our heart's desire.

But such a choice involves responsibility. For if we are free to choose our own responses, nevertheless we always must respond to the situations in which we find ourselves. In the *Songs* many of the speakers are oppressed—victims of an unjust society or a tyrannical family; and when the reader begins to understand the suppressions inflicted on many of the innocents and the self-suppressions imposed by the experienced, he reacts in anger. The innocents are perfect because they are unaware of such feelings; they transcend their situations by accepting them and simply being what they are. The experienced are hardly innocent, but in deluding themselves, often they have denied responsibility for their lives and attributed it to their situations. But to grow up is to become aware of one's situation and also to realize that one has the power to alter it. Anger becomes a response crucial to the reader's maturing vision, for it can spring from a reflective perception of situation that opens the way to change.

This kind of anger, which is so different from the covert aggressiveness of Blake's manipulative speakers, has the potential not only to reform the reader's life but to initiate social transformations—to help create a human order better than the worlds depicted in the *Songs of Experience.* Blake's lyrics suggest the necessity for a new form of openness: honest and clearsighted indignation. Such emotion would be generated in reflectiveness but expressed on the surface. It would dialectically link the individual's self-assertion to the project of social transformation by recreating the reflective reader as prophetic poet—the voice of honest indignation that in expressing the self simultaneously articulates a social vision. Aggressiveness thus could be redeemed, becoming not the energy fuelling self-interest but the power capable of revolutionizing human life.

But *The Book of Urizen* chronicles the failure to achieve this revolutionary anger. It is of special interest among the group of Blake's Lambeth prophecies because it reworks the issues of the *Songs of Experience,* using a mythic mode to investigate the problems of personality surface and depth, the boundaries of the self, and the drives to anger and manipulation. At the beginning of *Urizen* the world is boundless and infinite, transcending personality in the simple presence of the undefined "Immortal," which "expanded / Or contracted his all flexible senses" in absolute freedom (II. 1. 37–38). This paradisiacal unity, which is related to the vision of infinity achieved by the speakers of *Songs of Innocence,* is broken by the appearance of Urizen. He arises as a separate personality by constructing a body to house himself—a body whose primal form is spherical, an enclosure which suggests a head, a womb, a heart, an embryonic world.

Body and boundary are created simultaneously, and they come into existence as an attempt at self-definition. Ordinarily we are inclined to regard the struggle to define self rather positively, but in *The Book of Urizen* this is not the case. Here self-definition is prompted by negative emotions, beginning with Urizen's feeling of being "Self-closd, all-repelling" (I. 1. 3). Like the speakers of the *Songs of Experience,* Urizen rejects the innocent impulse to open, expressive relationship, preferring to turn inward and close himself off. But the individuality created by such closure is not coherent; instead of defining him, Urizen's boundary creates an inner being "Unknown, unprolific," an "abdominable void / This soul-shudd'ring vacuum" (I. 1. 2–5). His depths come into existence as a dark chaotic void, an empty yet obscurely threatening space. To establish control Urizen proclaims a new kind of boundary—

the law. It calls for "One command, one joy, one desire, / One curse, one weight, one measure / One King, one God" (II. 8. 38–40). Like Moses he unfolds his "Book / Of eternal brass, written in my solitude" (II. 7. 32–33). Instead of the Blakean symbolic principle of identity in difference, which constitutes the one "true Man" as the aggregate humanity, the god in us all, Urizen proclaims a oneness that achieves unity by excluding differences. Urizen's body therefore becomes not the human form divine but the closed form of his solitary self—a kind of armor that at once defines and protects him.

And indeed, he immediately does need protection—for his closure rends the fabric of eternity and provokes a cataclysmic anger in the Immortal. Outside of himself Urizen's proclamation of oneness is received as a tyrannical imposition, and "Rage siez'd the strong / Rage, fury, intense indignation" (III. 1. 44; 2. 45). The result is the shattering of relationship; the void within Urizen now is matched by the void outside him created by the immortal fury: "Eternity roll'd wide apart . . . Leaving ruinous fragments of life . . . An ocean of voidness unfathomable" (III. 3. 5–11). In *The Book of Urizen* anger has tragic results: instead of functioning as honest indignation, the revolutionary emotion that could renovate eternity, anger separates the Immortal into beings surrounded by voids. Just as Urizen rejected relationship by imposing the tyranny of his one law, the Immortal furiously rejects Urizen, and in so doing destroys the very principle of relationship.

Now Los enters the poem, a new individual who must cope with the threatening Urizen. Anger has arisen in the world and it is swiftly followed by terror: Los looks on the primitive form of Urizen and is "affrighted / At the formless unmeasurable death" (III. 14. 8–9). Urizen seems to him a threat to eternity's very existence, a formless menace that promises to infect all things. Therefore he joins Urizen in the effort to create body. They labor together to bring forth Urizen's physical form—which Urizen regards as his protective enclosure and Los sees as the prison which will isolate Urizen from eternity.

These desperate attempts to define by establishing physical boundaries are ironic; for as flesh and bone become more and more solid, soul becomes increasingly vague. An implication of *Songs of Innocence and of Experience* was that in a dangerous world perfect surface might not be enough; innocence would have to be protected by the capacity to see into the depths. But none of the characters in *The Book of Urizen* are able to do this.

Their vision, nurtured by the impulse to separation, remains relentlessly on the surface of things. The Immortal reacts against Urizen in blind fury—not clearsighted indignation—failing completely to see into Urizen and understand the fears and uncertainties that motivate his tyrannical pronunciations. Urizen creates depths in himself by proclaiming his bodily boundary but since he acts in the spirit of closure, he cannot see into his own obscure interior—and so his darkness becomes threatening not only to the Immortal but even to himself. And finally, Los cannot see that in erecting a physical boundary to protect eternity he himself is acting in the spirit of separation and therefore is collaborating with Urizen rather than opposing him. Los never enters into Urizen's heart, as he enters Albion's bosom later, in *Jerusalem*—and by remaining outside Urizen he also remains outside himself. He desperately wants his prophetic forge and his chains and rivets of poetry to be different from Urizen's book of brass and his line and plummet; but in *The Book of Urizen* the defining capacity of poetry is irresistibly perverted into the fixed and deathly law of tyranny. In striving to be different from Urizen Los becomes the same; the perception of identity in difference that opened out infinity in *Songs of Innocence* now leads to a dreadful chaotic merger of selves, a parody of socialization. At the moment they complete creation of Urizen's body, that moment when they should be completely isolated from each other, Los drops his hammer and "A nerveless silence, his prophetic voice / Seiz'd; a cold solitude & dark void / The Eternal Prophet & Urizen clos'd" (V. 4. 38–40). In laboring to create difference, Los inadvertently has enacted his identity with Urizen.[7]

The next individual to appear is Los's lover Enitharmon, and she arises from Los's appalled vision of Urizen: "He saw Urizen deadly black, / In his chains bound, & Pity began" (V. 6. 50–51), which leads to the extrusion of a blood globe from Los's bosom that grows into Enitharmon, "the first female form now separate / They call'd her Pity" (V. 10. 15–16). Normally we think of pity as a positive emotion, an evidence of ability to love and sympathize with others. But Los's pity for Urizen is hardly sympathetic: it is a self-deception, since it is Los himself who created the chains in which Urizen lies bound. As "The Human Abstract" of *Songs of Experience* proclaims, "Pity would be no more, / If we did not make somebody poor." The pity Blake condemns is the kind that creates separations and then indulges in the sentimental luxury of being distressed by them.

This pity is a muddled emotion, one that depends on a blindness to one's own obscure motives. It is a specious softness that originates in a hidden hardness of heart.

Ostensibly Los loves Enitharmon; where he went to great lengths to separate himself from Urizen, he immediately makes passionate love to her. His sexual act manifests his desire for complete merger, but the version of relationship suggested here is hardly the open, generous expressiveness of *Songs of Innocence:* "He embrac'd her, she wept, she refus'd / In perverse and cruel delight / She fled from his arms, yet he followd" (VI. 1. 11–13). Here love becomes a contest of wills, so that sexual participation is not a giving of the self but rather, the act of possessing the other. The seeming softness of love conceals a drive to domination—sexuality becomes manipulative. Therefore, "Eternity shudder'd when they saw, / Man begetting his likeness, / On his own divided image" (Plate 19, 14–16). In attempting reunion with himself Los has not explored his depths in an effort at self-understanding. Quite the contrary: he has let his impulses become alienated so that they appear in separation from himself—a separation he then attempts to overcome by acts of power. The result of his grotesque love is legion: Los and Enitharmon produce the human family as a repeated attempt at self-possession which invariably is doomed to failure. Their children become the race of reductive Lockean man, each person isolated in the prison of his or her body, forever closed off from expression, relation, the poetry of the world.

The Book of Urizen creates a mythic cosmos whose ur-principle is separation—a world founded on the spirit of closure dramatized in *Songs of Experience.* In his late prophetic works Blake struggles to create worlds embodying the opposite principle, relationship. These prophecies are related to *Songs of Innocence,* for they continue to advocate open expressiveness as the Blakean ideal. However, unlike *Innocence,* they cannot be works of the surface; for in them Blake must cope with the disruptive elements he has discovered in his worlds of separation—with closure, aggression, manipulation. *Jerusalem* perhaps is his most successful and comprehensive attempt in this vein. Repeatedly he announces that this poem is about "forgiveness," and a look at the dialogue between Joseph and Mary in Chapter 3 will show why this is so.

When Joseph learns Mary is pregnant, at first he wants to separate himself from her. Blake's Mary very clearly has not experienced immaculate conception but a human lover, and she knows she needs Joseph's forgiveness. She tells him, "if I were pure, never could I taste the sweets / Of the Forgive[ne]ss of Sins! if I were holy! I never could behold the tears / Of love! of him who loves me in the midst of his anger in furnace of fire" (3. 61. 11–13). What Mary affirms is Joseph's mixed emotions— she knows that he is angry and yet he still loves her. His feelings are inconsistent, but she begs him not to acknowledge one at the expense of the other. She wants him to experience his anger, but also to experience his love. Mary does not want a mild hypocritical forgiveness that would suppress rage but allow it to survive and emerge later in disguised forms. She prefers to walk through the furnace of Joseph's anger, to openly and passionately experience the emotion together with him. Joseph replies that he has heard the divine voice telling him "There is none that liveth & Sinneth not! And this is the Covenant / Of Jehovah: If you Forgive one-another, so shall Jehovah Forgive You: / That He Himself may Dwell among You" (3. 61. 24–26). He sees that the human condition is mixed—there is none that liveth and sinneth not—and that true holiness is not purity but the inclusive power of relationship. He must live not by casting out but by including. For if he takes everything into himself, is able to live through and forgive all, then God will forgive him and dwell within him. Mary replies, "O Forgiveness & Pity & Compassion! If I were Pure I should never / Have known Thee" (3. 61. 44–46). She rejoices in not being one of Blake's innocents, those surface beings who have known only joy and relationship—for the innocents take relationship for granted and in this sense do not really understand it. To truly know relationship one must fall away from it. In loss one develops self-conscious awareness of what one has had and determination to recreate it.

Blake's treatment of the Mary and Joseph episode suggests why in *Jerusalem* he struggles to create a personality type capable of including absolutely everything. We must not cast out; we must take everything that exists into our hearts and live through it, in order to develop a resonant deep self that knows and rightly values itself. Blake does not want the interior darkness and vacancy of Urizen to be the human lot. As an advance upon the perfect innocents, the later prophecies propose the inclusively deep self—the impure person who loses the surface perfection of innocence but takes everything into his or her depths, and in bravely seeing and experiencing all, develops visionary profundity.[8] Like his Mary and Joseph Blake also is "perhaps the most sinful of men! I pretend not to holiness! yet I pretend to love, to see, to converse with daily, as man with man, & the more to have an interest in the Friend of Sinners" (145). The Jesus of *Jerusalem* is indeed the friend of sinners—the god who does not separate himself from man but abides within us, constantly experiencing our impurities and forgiving them so that we are not lost to our own darkness. Blake's Jesus is the embodied principle of relationship.

It must be added that this Blakean project of inclusiveness is staggeringly ambitious. The focus of the present chapter is personality formation, but my psychologizing emphasis represents only one facet of Blake's interests. From the beginning— or at least from the period of his tracts on religion—his fundamental concerns were articulated through the fulcrum of his symbolic theory, which constituted the "true Man" as an interplay of local man and infinity, here and everywhere, difference and identity. *Jerusalem* therefore centers on the body of Albion, who is Britain incarnated but stretching into greater inclusiveness, also the incarnation of humankind and its history, the earth, and even the cosmos. In making these multiple identifications Blake commits himself to the poem as heterocosm.

The ensuing difficulties are easy enough to note, as any reader of the later prophecies can testify. In order to capture the everythingness of time Blake dismembers narrative and replaces it with the necessity to read his poem less successively than synchronically. The systematic overtones of *Songs of Innocence and of Experience*, which also called for rereading and synchronic vision, for the reader's absorption of the various individual songs into an embracing systematic totality that could reveal the identity implicit in difference, are exaggerated immensely in the dense textures of *Jerusalem*.[9] But the difficulty of this technique must be balanced against some compensating rewards. As we read the poem we begin to see that Blake really does view difference and identity as interpenetrating: for him, personality is not the character or presence of individual human beings, as we usually tend to think of it, but a momentary attitude or aspect of everything. The speakers of *Songs of Innocence and of Experience* articulated moments of perception that suggested their characteristic attitudes toward life, and in a much more exaggerated form the characters of *Jerusalem* speak for attitudes which are momentary perspectives on cosmic totality. Self and society, personality and human world, are envisioned as fundamentally interdependent in Blake's later prophecies.

The vision of *Jerusalem* is radically open: when we read this poem we will not encounter personality as we know it or world as we know it, for the prophetic eye is not bounded by the sphere of self but sees everywhere and into everything. Consequently, *Jerusalem* is not the kind of solipsistic poem that might be made by Urizen, who would want to possess the world and encapsulate it within himself. In breaking open the boundary of personality Blake allows his poem from one perspective to be about the self, but from others to be about other people and other societies. The moments of being and perspectives embodied in the poem could be parts of an individual's interior history, or they equally well could depict an interaction between persons, a political situation, or a social history. Blake's aspiration to utterly open expressiveness leads to the constitution of *Jerusalem* as an encyclopedic form, a radically inclusive Poem of Everything.

What immediately emerges in Chapter 1 of *Jerusalem* is Blake's desire to replay the mythos of separation expressed by *The Book of Urizen* in order to build a contrary vision of relationship. Where Urizen and Los labored to separate themselves into self-contained personalities in *Urizen*, now Los confronts his friend Albion, who like Urizen, wants to turn away and separate himself. In the first passages of the poem Albion denounces the Blakean symbolic principle of identity in difference, saying to Los, "[*We are not One: we are Many, thou most simulative*] / Phantom of the overheated brain! shadow of immortality! / Seeking to keep my soul a victim to thy Love! which binds / Man the enemy of man into deceitful friendships" (1. 4. 23–26).

But if Albion sees all friendship as deceit, as the presentation of a hypocritical surface that conceals antagonistic depths, Los labors in Chapter 1 to overcome that charge. He recognizes Albion's friendship has been precisely of this sort but instead of trying to bind Albion, as Los does Urizen in *The Book of Urizen*, Los directs his attention not to the exterior threat but to the menace within—to the aspects of himself that replicate Albion's antagonism. These aggressive feelings are given a body in Blake's myth, extruding from Los's back in a painful birth agony and appearing before him as his Spectre. Not only does this alienated part of himself entertain murderous thoughts

against Albion, he also wants to devour Los himself, "Watching
his time with glowing eyes to leap upon his prey" (1. 8. 22).
Although he is deathliness itself, the Spectre cloaks his arguments in exactly the kind of deceitful friendship of which he
accuses Albion. His views are half-truths, citations of Albion's
perfidiousness designed to provoke the same kind of behavior
in Los. But Los sees through the Spectre's performance, ex-
claiming, "Thou art my Pride & Self-righteousness: I have
found thee out" (1. 8. 30).

His treatment of the Spectre is severe. Where in *The Book of
Urizen* Los forged chains to bind Urizen, now he opens his
furnace and threatens to cast his own Spectre within: "I will
break thee into shivers! & melt thee in the furnaces of death; / I
will cast thee into forms of abhorrence & torment if thou /
Desist not from thine own will, & obey not my stern command!" (1. 8. 10–12). Although Los is firm with his Spectre,
emphasizing the necessity to bend his own aggressiveness to
his will, it should be emphasized that he does not cast out this
aspect of himself. Instead, he commands the Spectre, "Take
thou this Hammer & in patience heave the thundering Bellows
/ Take thou these Tongs: Strike thou alternate with me: labour
obedient" (1. 8. 39–40). Los is forging an inclusive personality
that acknowledges its own antagonistic energies and deliberately converts them to positive ends. This is why Los is a
creator, an artist: he lives in the fallen condition that Blake
says we all share, but he looks within himself, struggling to
recognize what is there and redeem it. Los's furnaces recast
aggression into prophetic energy.

The deathliness infecting Los's Spectre is shared by Albion;
and indeed, in his fallen condition he is the very embodiment
of deathliness itself. For Albion, like Urizen, is committed to
the principle of separation. But where Blake refrained from
exploring Urizen's interior in *The Book of Urizen*, merely suggesting that it was a dark chaotic void, he gives us an inner
vision of Albion in Chapter 1 of *Jerusalem*. It is libidinal energies that prove Albion's downfall: the beloved of Jerusalem, he
also pursues and loves Vala but then is appalled at his own
expression of sexuality, declaring that "The disease of Shame
covers me from head to feet: I have no hope / Every boil upon
my body is a separate & deadly Sin" (1. 21. 3–4). Albion casts
out his own acts, branding them sin and shame; and in doing
so he divides himself. Blake suggests that the primal separation is self-murder, the refusal to include everything one is in
the acknowledged version of oneself.

Secrecy arises in Albion's world as the necessity to hide himself from himself. Rejecting Jerusalem, he disembodies her, commanding her to "Hide thou Jerusalem in impalpable voidness, not to be / Touchd by the hand nor seen with the eye: O Jerusalem / Would thou wert not" (1. 22. 26–28). His dismissal of Jerusalem's body is reinforced by his affirmation of Vala as a "Scarlet Tabernacle" in which he may "hide" (1. 22. 30). The open relationship of bodies, the communion of touch and sight, is to be replaced by a religious formalism that conceals the dark sinful self behind a surface of holiness. Albion firmly separates sin from purity, rejecting the one and affirming the other as his ideal—but since he knows he has sinned, his only recourse is to offer penance by sacrificing himself. He entreats, "come O Vala with knife & cup: drain my blood / To the last drop!" (1. 22. 29–30). Where Los firmly commands his Spectre to labor alongside him in the furnaces to redeem the self, Albion engages in a futile attempt to purify himself by casting out and sacrificing his own unassimilable aspects.

He invites Los to join in this sacrifice as a test of friendship, crying, "Will none accompany me in my death? or be a Ransom for me / In that dark Valley?" Los replies, "Must the Wise die for an Atonement? Does Mercy endure Atonement? / No! It is Moral Severity, & destroys Mercy in its Victim" (2. 35[39]. 19–26). Los sees that Albion's vision of friendship is a parody of Jesus' passion and crucifixion; for in the guise of love the deathly Albion seeks to kill his friend. Instead of replying in kind, as he does in *The Book of Urizen,* Los counters the threat of Albion by seeing through his hypocrisies and learning to understand Albion much better than Albion does himself. By constantly struggling to penetrate Albion's self-righteous surface Los learns about the true deathly threat lurking within and is better able to defend himself against it; but he also can see Albion's inner suffering and feel for it in a way that Albion, the deluded self-victimizer, cannot. And so Los becomes capable of both firm resistance and sympathetic identification. He is a true friend to Albion because his dealings with him are based on a clearsighted understanding that frees him to both love and differ with Albion rightly. Patience and perception become the keynotes of *Jerusalem:* Los stands his protective watch over the world, explores Albion's bosom with his globe of fire, and builds the redemptive structures of Golgonooza, living through the times of Albion's trial until Albion himself can cleanse his inner vision and arise self-renewed. Blake suggests that it is necessary for each person to deal with his own

inner depths, but that if we cannot save others at least we can
contain destructiveness and preserve the possibility of salvation by faithfully acting in true friendship.

The first three Chapters of *Jerusalem* show Los laboring to
preserve life while Albion pursues his works of deathliness. In
particular, Chapter 3, with its panoramic historical visions of
Albion's sacrificial rites, reveals the libidinal origins of Albion's aggressiveness. *The Book of Urizen* had suggested that
sexual relations, as practiced by Los and Enitharmon, could be
a manipulative performance in which the will to dominate
came cloaked in the guise of love. Since Enitharmon was an
aspect of Los himself, Blake's further suggestion was that sexuality can constitute a grotesque form of self-love, the forceful
and blinded attempt of the self to reunite with itself. Although
the purity-obsessed Albion abjures sex in *Jerusalem*, preferring
to remain relentlessly chaste, he does constantly offer himself
up for sacrifice. His bloody altars become the symbolic coun-
terpart to the prophetic furnaces where Los forges his self-
redemption. Blake portrays Albion's sacrifices as Druid cere-
monies performed by priestesses, who bind down men and cut
out their hearts. These gruesome rites involve unmistakable
erotic overtones:

> They put into his hand a reed, they mock: Saying: Behold
> The King of Canaan whose are seven hundred chariots of iron!
> They take off his vesture whole with their Knives of flint:
> But they cut asunder his inner garments: searching with
> Their cruel fingers for his heart, & there they enter in pomp
>
> (3. 66. 24–28)

As before in *Jerusalem*, the passion and crucifixion of Jesus is
grotesquely invoked, this time as a perverted sexual rite. Victim and victimizer work in concert, deriving a curious form of
pleasure from the infliction of bodily pain. Blake suggests that
in the fallen world eros and aggression are conflated: a people
committed to purity constantly will need to purge themselves,
and that purgation will become a sort of pleasure. The harried
men of Chapter 3 cry out, "I am drunk with unsatiated love / I
must rush again to War: for the Virgin has frownd & refusd" (3.
68. 62–63). War becomes the erotic release of the fallen; the
"true Man" or human form divine is not loved, but repeatedly
self-murdered in never-ending painful pleasure. Blake sees the
fundamental forms of fallen society as sadomasochistic—as

self-confounding mixtures. Where the Mary of *Jerusalem* had urged Joseph to experience his mixed emotions of anger and love in order to achieve an insightful inclusiveness that could recreate feeling, Blake's fallen people mix their emotions in a self-destructive, sanctimonious parody of poetic redemption.

In Chapter 4 of *Jerusalem* Blake rehabilitates the notion of sacrifice by showing what it would mean in the relational world of Los rather than the separatist world of Albion. It is Jesus' love for others rather than the pain of his crucifixion that matters from the relational perspective. And so when Albion awakes from his delusions Jesus appears before him in the similitude of Los, and offers to die for Albion; for "unless I die thou canst not live/ But if I die I shall arise again & thou with me / This is Friendship and Brotherhood" (4. 96. 14–16). Brought out of himself by wonder at Jesus' generosity Albion stands "lost in the contemplation of faith / And wonder at the Divine Mercy" and sacrifices himself in Jesus' place. His act of selflessness brings life rather than death; for as Albion throws himself "into the Furnaces of affliction . . . the Furnaces became / Fountains of Living Waters flowing from the Humanity Divine" (4. 96. 35–37).

This self-annihilating generosity of "Friendship and Brotherhood" becomes the model for the apocalypse that ends *Jerusalem*. Here Blake renders his ultimate version of the ideal of open expressiveness which we have seen generated in his tracts on religion and dramatized in *Songs of Innocence*. But the Fourfold Man Albion, the redeemed society that enacts the relations of identity in difference, cannot resemble the innocent, open, naturalistic speakers of *Innocence*—for he literally must embody everything human, and his surface must make his depths clear. This is a sight not yet revealed in human history, one that we must rely upon poetic vision to unfurl. As Blake portrays it, the Man takes up his bow, which "is a Male & Female & the Quiver of the Arrows of Love, / Are the Children of this Bow" (4. 97. 12–13), and shoots the flaming "Arrows of Intellect" (4. 98. 7) in a glorious transformation of the energies of corporeal war into what Los has called the "severe contentions of friendship & the burning fire of thought" (4. 91. 17). The Man, who is one and many, transparently "conversed together in Visionary forms dramatic . . . Creating Space, Creating Time according to the wonders Divine / Of Human Imagination . . . & they walked / To & fro in Eternity as One Man reflecting each in each & clearly seen / And seeing" (4. 98.

28–40). At the apocalypse of his development Blake's Man becomes completely inclusive, a socialized individual and an individuated society that incorporates male and female, family, childhood, adulthood, the loving emotions and the redeemed energies of aggression. Furthermore, his apocalypse is a process not a product; he walks and speaks, continually enacting cosmos. When human energies are entirely redeemed and liberated, the result is a brotherhood that is intellectual, imaginative, and conversational.

But admirable and sublime as Blake's vision of Everything is, nevertheless it may not be quite inclusive enough. For the erotic elements that lead to Albion's fall and determine the sacrificial and warlike nature of his world are not so much transformed in the apocalypse as dismissed. In *Jerusalem* Los too struggles with his erotic nature; his Spectre is male, but its complimentary form of self-alienation, the Emanation, is Enitharmon, who emerges from Los's breast as a globe of blood, as she does in *The Book of Urizen*. There he at once pursues her sexually, but in *Jerusalem* he protects her and her children from his Spectre and resists the Spectre's attempts to call her a "Sin" (1. 10. 43). Nevertheless, in Chapter 4 she tries to dominate him, declaring "This is Womans World, nor need she any / Spectre to defend her from Man. I will Create secret places. . . . A triple Female Tabernacle for Moral Law I weave" (4. 88. 16–19). Los is compelled to resist this Female Will which recapitulates the secrecy, hypocritical religiosity, and manipulativeness of Albion's daughters; and before the apocalypse can come Los must allow Enitharmon to disappear. As he tells her, "Sexes must vanish & cease / To be, when Albion arises," with "all their Crimes, their Punishments their Accusations of Sin: / All their Jealousies Revenges. Murders. hidings of Cruelty in Deceit" (4. 92. 13–16). Sexual conflict is not recreated in a state of sexual relationship; instead, the erotic aspect of human experience is cast out of Blake's apocalypse as the vision unveils a transcendental state of brotherhood. Friendship and conversation, not erotic love and sexual acts, become Blake's preferred expressions of apocalypse. Corporeal war is redeemed in imaginative friendship as spiritual warfare, but the erotic body does not undergo an equivalent transformation—Blake continues to view it as an unredeemable form of aggression. In *Jerusalem* the symbolic principle of identity in difference that organizes Blake's major poetry perhaps at last is slighted: sexual difference is eliminated in order to affirm the universal Brotherhood of Man.[10]

But if Blake excluded sexuality from his apocalypse of open expressiveness, at least his poem does show why Albion must assume the transparent, conversational form he exhibits at the conclusion of *Jerusalem*. Blake's concern is to change humanity's destructive powers into creative ones, to redeem rather than to dismiss: and so his great poem depicts the formation of a New Man—a deep self capable of imaginatively embracing and transforming the dark forces that lurk in its own depths. Out of obscurity emerges a profound, ecstatic translucency, "One Man reflecting each in each & clearly seen / And seeing."

3

WORDSWORTH
The Meditating Self

The first of Wordsworth's "Essays Upon Epitaphs" meditates on how we derive the intuition of infinity from our encounters with limits. As an example, Wordsworth imagines a young child standing "by the side of a running stream, pondering within himself what power was the feeder of the perpetual current, from what never-wearied sources the body of water was supplied" and "inevitably propelled to follow this question by another: 'Towards what abyss is it in progress?'" This stream raises the question of origins and destinations for the child, and suggests on the one hand that the notion of beginning and ending may impose life constraints. Perhaps we once were not, and when we die we will be no longer. But if the "abyss" toward which the stream flows is nothingness, and if death ends our existence, then "such a hollowness would pervade the whole system of things, such a want of correspondence and consistency, a disproportion so astounding betwixt means and ends, that there could be no repose, no joy." Consequently, the child is moved to picture the stream's destination as everythingness rather than nothingness. He imagines that these waters flow into a sea that is "a receptacle without bounds or dimensions, nothing less than infinity."[1]

Wordsworth's child is impelled to choose between alternative grounding intuitions about the nature of existence: either our lives are finite and hollow, or they are infinite. These competing intuitions resemble the opposed visions invoked by Blake in *There is No Natural Religion*. There the choice was offered between the strictly local and limited bodily existence of Lockean man or the poetic access to infinity opened by the creation of the "true Man," the relational human form divine. Just as Blake suggests that we opt for infinity because we desire it, and no basis for choice can be shown to be superior to our feelings, so Wordsworth's child chooses infinity because the imagination of fullness can create a meaningful life, one superior to a hollow existence resulting from a sense of cosmic nothingness.

Wordsworth's fascination with epitaphs involves a conversion similar to the one his child has made: faced with death, the maker of epitaphs composes a statement that changes the individual's end into a poetic evocation of endlessness. The deceased must be specifically recalled with a "distinct and clear conception . . . of the individual, whose death is deplored and whose memory is to be preserved," but at the same time, a good epitaph must "speak, in a tone which shall sink into the heart, the general language of humanity as connected with the subject of death" (p. 57). Just as Blake's "true Man" is himself and the cosmos, a symbolic interrelation of identity and difference, so Wordsworth's epitaph is both particular and general, an evocation of the individual life and an assertion of its relationship to the human community. For paradoxically, it is our individual life limits that connect us to the general experience of humankind. "To be born and to die are the two points in which all men feel themselves to be in absolute coincidence" (p. 57).

But where Blake's "true Man" is constituted in the living body as it becomes the human form divine, Wordsworth's infinity is embodied as the inscription on a gravestone. The "Essays Upon Epitaphs" make it clear that the memorial statement is not merely a verbal affair, but the appropriate association of word and place. Man's infinite embodiment is in nature, "in the church-yard . . . open to the day; the sun looks down upon the stone, and the rains of heaven beat against it" (p. 59). Only when we have ended can we truly begin—for then our lives become a totality and our bodies come home to the boundlessness of nature. The completed life is the life opened to infinity.[2]

Given these assumptions, it becomes clear how for Wordsworth the writing of epitaphs is related to the writing of autobiography. He is a poet of retrospection—for it is retrospective vision that creates wholeness. Just as the true poet in the "Preface to the Lyrical Ballads" adopts "The very language of men" (I, 130), so the good epitaph "should speak, in a tone which shall sink into the heart, the general language of humanity" (p. 57). The grave then becomes "a tranquillising object" (p. 104) as is the mind of the contemplative mourner: "Every

thing that is of importance is at peace with itself; all is stillness, sweetness, and stable grandeur" (p. 121). Similarly, in the
"Preface," the poetic "spontaneous overflow of powerful feelings . . . takes its origin from emotion recollected in tranquillity" (I, 148). Just as recollection is Wordsworth's poetic
stance, tranquillity is his poetic mood—for tranquillity is the
retrospective summation of all emotions, the attitude of wholeness, which allows for resurrection of every emotion one ever
has experienced. This is why Wordsworth's poetry begins with
tranquil recollection of emotion which "is contemplated till,
by a species of re-action, the tranquillity gradually disappears,
and an emotion, kindred to that which was before the subject
of contemplation, is gradually produced, and does itself actually exist in the mind" (148).

It is the very pastness of Wordsworth's experience which
allows for the poetic attitude that can bring life back in its
infinite aspect. For the epitaph maker, one must die in order to
become eternally alive; and for the autobiographical poet,
one's experience must be over before it can be grasped in its
completeness.

"Tintern Abbey" is a clear demonstration of Wordsworth's
poetic process, a kind of epitaph for his lost childhood which
suggests that only when the spontaneous bodily activity of
youth has ceased can we build the spiritual resonance which
grounds poetic spontaneous overflow of feelings. This poem
exchanges the exercise of body for the exercise of spirit, which
is Wordsworth's particular version of the Romantic turn from
surface to depth as constituting the poetic personality. The boy
of "Tintern Abbey" was an unreflective child, a pure body or
surface who unlike Blake's innocents did not speak out his
entire self but instead acted it out, in spontaneous, rapturous
physical expressions, "when like a roe / I bounded o'er the
mountains"[3] and the forms of nature "were . . . to me / An
appetite; a feeling and a love, / That had no need of a remoter
charm, / By thought supplied" (67–68; 79–82). In place of this
ecstatic unmediated childhood activity the adult poet sub-
stitutes a distanced contemplation of the Wye valley that leads
to a mood of organic serenity. His tranquillity is first registered
in the body as "sensations sweet, / Felt in the blood, and felt
along the heart; / And passing even into my purer mind, / With
tranquil restoration" (27–30). In dramatic contrast to the
child, the adult's physical attitude is nearly complete stillness—a stillness which so tranquillizes him that he is "laid
asleep / In body, and become[s] a living soul" (45–46).

Only when surface is inactivated or entranced can depth come alive—body must be exchanged for spirit, physical action must be sacrificed for poetic inspiration. The adult poet becomes pure depth because he meditates on what his life *means* rather than living it. His activity is spiritual, not physical. But like the maker of epitaphs, the poet surrenders physical life only to find it restored in its infinite aspect: for where the child merely existed for the moment, the adult sees "into the life of things" (49) and senses the deep "spirit, that impels / All thinking things, all objects of all thought, / And rolls through all things" (100–102). Because he sees into the world so profoundly that he senses infinity, he can serenely contemplate his own death, advising his sister to return to this place when he is gone to remember "me, / And these my exhortations!" (145–46). When he is no longer living the poet's present words will become an epitaph recollected by his sister, and her act of memory will bring him back to life, binding the community of the living and the dead in a timeless interchange of speech and listening.

Of course "Tintern Abbey" is not only a poem about death and bodily suppression but also a meditation on the process of growing up, of maturing by becoming a person of depth and insight. Certainly Wordsworth himself emphasizes the aspect of growth and I would not wish to deny this function of the poem. My point merely is that Wordsworth's meditations feature an interrelation of limits and boundlessness, the end and infinity. As such they tend to link death and growth. As an autobiographical poet Wordsworth finds it possible to interpret his development only when it is connected, openly or implicitly, to the fact of his death. In this light Blake's radicalism almost appears mild—for he merely advocates expressive openness as the pathway to infinity. Wordsworth not only dwells on death, but in much of his poetry of the 1790s he chooses to write tales of human suffering—stories of murderers, alienated wanderers, deserted women, impoverished people, and broken families. In particular his early drama *The Borderers* merits attention as a meditation on suffering.

This play centers on Rivers, a man who has broken the bond of human community by abandoning a man to die on a desert island. His act has isolated him as an individual, and to reestablish relationship with the human world he deliberately betrays his chieftain Mortimer into committing an act of abandonment similar to his own. In this way the outcast will regain community—he will be part of a select society of two, men who are extraordinary because they are capable of acts beyond the moral courage of common people. In short, the bad eminence to which Rivers and Mortimer are elevated is a perverse version of infinity. As Rivers explains,

> Action is transitory, a step, a blow—
> The motion of a muscle—this way or that—
> 'Tis done—and in the after vacancy
> We wonder at ourselves like men betray'd.
> Suffering is permanent, obscure and dark,
> And has the nature of infinity.[4]

Rivers has discovered that suffering can ground the deep self. If one commits a sin, the physical act is merely a superficial prelude that opens an endless world of interior pain, a hell which at least is infinite, and is one's own. Although the life of the villain may be agonizing, at least he is in touch with depths unknown to ordinary humanity and therefore he becomes a man of distinction.

Wordsworth did not write often about this kind of egotism, but he did retain his interest in suffering as a method of developing personal depth. His "Essay Supplementary to the Preface of 1815" offers a good explanation of how suffering can build interior resonance in readers of poetry. He begins by disparaging the eighteenth-century notion of taste as a basis for response to literature, because it assumes "the mind is *passive*, and is affected painfully or pleasurably as by an instinct." To replace taste Wordsworth advances a notion of *"power"* (III, p. 81). As he says, "Is it to be supposed that the reader can make progress . . . like an Indian Prince or General—stretched on his palaquin, and borne by his slaves? No, he is invigorated and inspirited by his leader, in order that he may exert himself; for he cannot proceed in quiescence, he cannot be carried like a dead weight. Therefore to create taste is to call forth and bestow power" (p. 82). Power is conveyed through passion, and "Passion, it must be observed, is derived from a word which signifies *suffering* . . . the connection which suffering has with effort, with exertion, and *action*, is immediate and inseparable" (p. 81). That connection is as follows: "To be moved . . . by a passion, is to be excited, often to external, and always to internal, effort; whether for the continuance and strengthening of the passion, or for its suppression, accordingly as the course which it takes may be painful or pleasurable" (pp. 81–82). The painful passions, then, arouse our power as a resisting force: we are moved to "suppression." It seems clear that for Wordsworth suffering compares to recollection in tranquillity, in that both represent a turn away from action on the surface to the world of spiritual depth. A royal road to infinity is suffering—because the suppression of suffering is accomplished by spiritual exercise. Suffering is an unmoved mover, a conservative force that at once creates and compounds spiritual depth.[5]

"The Ruined Cottage," which was written in the same period as *The Borderers*, demonstrates this view of suffering as the source of creative spiritual exercise. Where Rivers aspires to infinity in the form of villainous personal greatness, Margaret's tale is a story of common humanity, a life career so unexceptional as almost to evade notice. Her family faces the hardships commonly endured by the English rural poor in the 1790s.[6] They live on the land and eke out subsistence there, but when the harvests fail for two years running, their home begins to break up. Deprived of his weaver's labor Margaret's husband becomes restless and irritable, and finally deserts the family he no longer can support. In the following five years Margaret's son must be apprenticed, her youngest child perishes, and she herself finally dies.

The pedlar, who tells this story to the narrator of Wordsworth's poem, suggests that Margaret's fate is the fate of us all: "we die, my Friend, / Nor we alone, but that which each man loved / And prized in his peculiar nook of earth / Dies with him or is changed, and very soon / Even of the good is no memorial left."[7] But the death of Margaret must not pass unmemorialized. If it does, "a bond of brotherhood is broken" (85), the human community is destroyed. So the pedlar makes his poem Margaret's epitaph. And the place of her suffering, this "peculiar nook of earth" (70), becomes equivalent to Margaret's grave: although her body does not rest here, the ruined cottage is pervaded by her finished life. This shattered life must be redeemed by being resurrected in recollective depth.

In 1799 Wordsworth added a conclusion to the pedlar's tale which shows his narrator reacting to Margaret's story with an "impotence of grief" (500) that makes him turn aside "in weakness, nor had power / To thank him for the tale which he had told" (495–96). The narrator's distress suggests that when suffering is brought to the surface it may be expressed as weakness or impotence. Only when suffering remains in the depths—when it is poetically suppressed—can it ground a powerful personality. The pedlar teaches the narrator this by showing him how to see the weeds in Margaret's overgrown cottage garden:

> those very plumes,
> Those weeds, and the high spear grass on that wall,
> By mist and silent rain-drops silver'd o'er,
> As once I passed did to my heart convey
> So still an image of tranquillity,
> So calm and still, and looked so beautiful
> Amid the uneasy thoughts which filled my mind,
> That what we feel of sorrow and despair
> From ruin and from change, and all the grief
> That passing shews of being leave behind,
> Appeared an idle dream that could not live
> Where meditation was. I turned away
> And walked along my road in happiness.
>
> (513–25)

These weeds testify to suffering by reminding the pedlar that Margaret's garden once was cared for and filled with flowers, but now is altogether changed. They become an "image" which witnesses to Margaret's tragedy and also is a beautiful natural form. It is "so still an image of tranquillity, so calm and still and looked so beautiful" that it transforms the "uneasy thoughts which filled my mind." The image of the overgrown garden releases a transaction between beauty and tragedy, tranquillity and suffering. Margaret's story is bound to nature, and the "wretched spot" where she lived is redeemed in the poetic eye of the beholder. Her garden becomes a memorial, a place where human history and nature can be linked in meditation. Like Wordsworth's epitaphs, the garden reminds the pedlar of Margaret's bodily death only to renew his meditation on spiritual immortality.

Apparently the capacity for suffering and the capacity for experiencing beauty are related, and act to reinforce each other. The eye that can see the humble weed's beauty is also the eye that can perceive "a common tale . . . A tale of silent suffering, hardly clothed / In bodily form, and to the grosser sense / But ill adapted, scarcely palpable / To him who does not think" (231–36). Because he sees into the life of these things the pedlar is Wordsworth's common man as poet who in referring to humble forms and people speaks of the suffering, the beauty, that as human beings we all know. This common place, these common weeds, the unremarkable story of Margaret, have been rescued from the surface life by the pedlar's poetic eye, which can see into their spiritual depths.

The pedlar's power stems not simply from his ability to perceive suffering—for the narrator also was touched by Margaret's tale, but expressed his sorrow in a display of tears. Such superficial expressions strike Wordsworth as weakness, not as poetry. In contrast, the pedlar has built habits of poetic suppression that function not to deny emotion but to transform it by converting the image of Margaret's overgrown garden into a deep spiritual resolve. His "uneasy thought"—the restlessness, the *motion* of suffering—is changed into the "still" of tranquillity, and this converted energy enables the pedlar to walk onward in happiness. The pedlar's tranquillity is not static or relaxed; it is an ongoing spiritual exercise—a quiet that suppresses motion, a calm strength that suppresses pain, a sameness that suppresses changeability. His poetry has created the capacity for profound endurance. It gives him the power to proceed with his life, even in the face of tragedy.[8] The rock-firm pedlar of "The Ruined Cottage" is echoed in many other Wordsworthian poems of tranquillity and suffering, such as "The Old Cumberland Beggar," "Animal Tranquillity and Decay," and "Resolution and Independence." These poems indeed do make a case that the deepest human activity is soul-making, and that the suppression of suffering can produce human resonance.

When Wordsworth turns to the writing of his autobiography in *The Prelude*, he personally affirms the same stance of poetic tranquillity that is the pedlar's in "The Ruined Cottage." As he says of himself:

> There is a dark
> Invisible workmanship that reconciles
> Discordant elements, and makes them move
> In one society. Ah me, that all
> The terrors, all the early miseries,
> Regrets, vexations, lassitudes, that all
> The thoughts and feelings which have been infused
> Into my mind, should ever have made up
> The calm existence that is mine when I
> Am worthy of myself.[9]

Just as the uneasy thoughts that troubled the pedlar's mind were converted to the firm stillness of tranquillity, so Wordsworth suggests that the frightening, vexing, or difficult experiences of his childhood have value because they provide occasions for poetic suppression—experiences of conflict teach him how to be calm, how to endure. When he is "worthy of myself" he is a deeply tranquil man. The experience of being lost on the moor described in Book Eleventh makes this character-building function of suppression especially clear.

Before he tells his tale Wordsworth suggests its significance by explaining it is a prime example of those "spots of time, / Which with distinct preeminence retain / A renovating virtue" (257–59) when we are depressed, or worn down by the triviality of daily routine. At such times these memories have the power to refresh us as we are reminded "that the mind / Is lord and master, and that outward sense / Is but the obedient servant of her will" (270–72). The story that follows is a narrative of visionary endurance—a tale of tranquillity won against great pressures. Wordsworth's childhood memory of depression and endurance thus has the depth and intensity of poetry, whereas the adult depressions that are relieved by memory of the "spots of time" are in comparison superficial and banal. By returning to the visionary depression once experienced in childhood, Wordsworth is able to redeem his contemporary state by reconceiving his own deep selfhood. Such acts of poetic retrospection convert surface to depth by reinterpreting the quotidian present self as the heir of a profoundly significant past.

As a child, Wordsworth had been on a trip with his father's servant but somehow was parted from him, and wandered on the moor until he came to a place where a murderer had been hung in chains. At the time he did not know this; what he saw was not the gibbet-mast where the criminal had been suspended, or the man's bones,

> but on the turf
> Hard by, soon after that fell deed was wrought,
> Some unknown hand had carved the murderer's name.
> The monumental writing was engraven
> In times long past, and still from year to year
> By superstition of the neighbourhood
> The grass is cleared away; and to this hour
> The letters are fresh and visible.
>
> (291–98)

These letters cut in the grass are a kind of dark poetry, an epitaph placed not in the sacred churchyard of "Essays Upon

Epitaphs" and witnessing to the infinity of human community, but a testament to the endurance of crime and tragedy, to the infinity of human suffering. This spontaneous but lasting epitaph made by the country people is related to the world of *The Borderers*, to the hellish infinity Rivers established by his criminal act. The boy is terrified by the sight, for although he does not understand what he is seeing, the superstitious poetry of the countrymen has pervaded this place and he senses it. It immensely intensifies his predicament: very deeply he feels that he has lost his way. Fleeing the scene he sees

> A naked pool that lay beneath the hills,
> The beacon on the summit, and more near,
> A girl who bore a pitcher on her head
> And seemed with difficult steps to force her way
> Against the blowing wind.
>
> (303–7)

As Wordsworth remarks of these images of difficulty and endurance, "It was, in truth, / An ordinary sight, but I should need / Colours and words that are unknown to man / To paint the visionary dreariness" (307–10).

Just as the image of the common weeds in Margaret's garden weds beauty and tragedy into the deep tranquillity that sustains the pedlar, so these "ordinary" images of difficulty endured, perceived by the child in a moment of intense personal stress, are recollected when the youthful Wordsworth visits this spot with his beloved. The result is "radiance more divine" (323), an augmenting of love's pleasures. "So feeling comes in aid / Of feeling, and diversity of strength / Attends us, if but once we have been strong" (325–27). In turn, when the adult poet is depressed by the superficiality of his daily existence he can remember the child's poetic experience of dreariness, which will have power to redeem the ordinariness of his own present by infusing it with the intensity and depth of the recollected past. Like the pedlar of "The Ruined Cottage," the poet of *The Prelude* then can proceed upon his way sustained by a profound tranquillity that has been generated by his repeated, inclusive meditations. Thus, continually revised autobiography has the power to nurture the deep self.

This spot of time suggests that the tranquillity Wordsworth celebrates in *The Prelude* is his master emotion because it promises to unite all the conflicting feelings he ever has experienced in a structure of suppression that rightly grounds poetic expression. Where the child was terrified and the youth was radiantly in love, the tranquil narrator of this spot of time gives a resonantly mature recollection of his experiences. Unlike the narrator of "The Ruined Cottage," who was overcome by Margaret's tale because he immediately expressed his emotion rather than suppressing it so that it could return transformed from his depths as a poetic expression, the narrator of *The Prelude* aspires to become the deep self that is the evolving subject of his own story—that self who could speak in the tranquil, all-inclusive voice of maturity. The mixture of emotion Wordsworth has experienced in this place—fear, and later, love—is blended into the higher unity of the ever-growing deep self which masters its experience by continually meditating upon it.

For the Wordsworth of *The Prelude*, poetic expression is rooted in this ideal depth-stance of meditative maturity. Although he celebrates poetic "spontaneous overflow of powerful feelings" in the "Preface to the Lyrical Ballads," such overflows are not superficial, because they originate in "emotion recollected in tranquillity" (I, 148) and the product is poems embodying "a worthy *purpose*. Not that I mean to say, that I always begin to write with a distinct purpose formally conceived; but I believe that my habits of meditation have so formed my feelings, as that my descriptions of such objects as strongly excite those feelings, will be found to carry along with them a *purpose* (I, 124–26). Unlike the terrified child on the moors who lost his way, the adult poet believes he can confidently release himself in the freedom of spontaneity, because his life of continual poetic meditation has built a deep self that profoundly orients his purposes just as it blends his emotions. Meditative tranquillity therefore becomes a depth state featuring both emotional breadth and significant focus—and its resultant poetic speech ought to be inclusive yet unified.

Wordsworth's aims—to mix conflicting emotions in a poetic meditation that will yield a higher unity—resemble Blake's aims in *Jerusalem*. Just as Blake wishes to acknowledge all feelings, to cast nothing out but instead work through the spirit's entire experience in order to achieve an inclusive and redeemed New Man, so Wordsworth in "The Ruined Cottage" mixes beauty and tragedy, and in the spots of time episodes of *The Prelude* the "Discordant elements" of his experience, to work toward a comprehensively deep self. Although Blake speaks prophetically and through the use of myth, his ends, like those of Wordsworthian autobiography, are lyrical—the imaginative creation of a self so resonant and inclusive that it would be capable of encompassing the world. To this end Blake imagines apocalypse, and Wordsworth envisions an all-inclusive meditative state based in tranquil maturity.[10]

But if this is the transcendental goal of *The Prelude*, the poem itself suggests that Wordsworth's actual experience could not completely live up to his aspirations. *The Prelude* opens with an extended account of writer's block, the story of Wordsworth's return home to Grasmere as a grown-up poet intending to write his masterwork, who discovers himself unvisited by spontaneous overflow and unable even to decide on a subject for his poem. As he later explained in a Preface to *The Excursion*, the poem he really wanted to write but could not was *The Recluse*, "a philosophical poem, containing views of Man, Nature, and Society." Like Blake, Wordsworth wanted to be all-inclusive, to write the Poem of Everything. Blocked in his desire he instead "undertook to record, in verse, the origin and progress of his own powers" as a "preparatory poem." *The Prelude*, then, is a form of poetic therapy, an unblocking essay that "conducts the history of the Author's mind to the point where he was emboldened to hope that his faculties were sufficiently mature for entering upon the arduous labor which he had proposed to himself; and the two Works have the same kind of relation to each other, if he may so express himself, as the ante-chapel has to the body of a gothic church" (III, 5).

Where we delight in *The Prelude* for itself, Wordsworth could not be comfortable about his own poem because he did not see autobiography as entirely self-justifying. In the last Book of *The Prelude* he feels compelled to apologize for his poem, to hope that he will produce an enduring work of poetry "Sufficient to excuse me in men's sight / For having given this record of myself" (XIII, 388–89). Clearly he is anxious about his ability to deliver; as he says to Coleridge, the Friend who is the audience of *The Prelude*, the span of their lifetimes will be but brief: "O, yet a few short years of useful life, / And all will be complete—thy race be run, / Thy monument of glory will be raised" (XIII, 428–30). Unable to write *The Recluse*, Wordsworth refrained from publishing *The Prelude*, his "ante-chapel to the body of a gothic church" during his lifetime, but prepared the printer's copy just before his death. Thus, *The Prelude* did in fact become Wordsworth's epitaph, the "monument of glory" that perforce had to stand in place of the gothic church of poetry which he had envisioned.[11]

But possibly *The Prelude* was an epitaph as well as a "preparatory poem" from the very beginning; for in electing to write his autobiography from the idealized depth-stance of poetic maturity, Wordsworth tended not only to evolve the deep self but also to imply that perhaps his poetic development already should have been achieved. By committing himself to the standard of mature meditative tranquillity as the hallmark of the deep self, he tends to assume what he needs to build. Taking a stand upon his own construction he moves around a hermeneutical circle which continually deepens the self but cannot offer the final, all inclusive transcendental meditative resolution. The Wordsworthian self continually works toward maturity but never quite can reach it. Sometimes this opens vistas of incessant development, of something evermore about to be—but at other times the mortal poet must feel blocked when he compares his actual state with his ideal aspiration. Thus, the standard of meditative maturity creates a dual potential: it can release spontaneous overflow of powerful feelings, or alternatively, it can block expression.[12]

At any rate, Wordsworth's tendency to link growth and death, origins and destinations, is evident in the composition history of *The Prelude*. The first version of the poem (1799) is a breathtaking compendium of the childhood spots of time—virtually an unbroken outpouring of the best-known parts of *The Prelude*. This work is introduced by a desperate question, "Was it for this / That one, the fairest of all rivers, loved / To blend his murmurs with my nurse's song."[13] The question remains suspended in a void, without an antecedent—making the beginning of the ur-*Prelude* a puzzling fragment rather than the serene speech of totality. Perhaps Wordsworth's question could be rephrased as follows: was it for this unproductive life that I was given my marvellous boyhood? Does my blocked and meaningless adulthood do justice to the glimpses of infinity I knew as a child? Going back from the deathliness of adulthood to the sources of his vision in early life then truly might free him by once again opening infinity—thus releasing the Poem of Everything.

In this light, Wordsworth's childhood spots of time, the "hiding-places of my power" (XI, 335), merit special attention. When we survey them we encounter an energetic, physically active boy who forever is testing his limits and trying to prove his powers by such deeds as skating, plundering bird nests, ravaging groves, and robbing others' bird snares. In general, these spots of time begin with the child imposing his activity on nature but then experiencing a sudden reversal, in which nature becomes the active agent and the boy is acted upon. This scenario allows Wordsworth to show how his childhood physical exploits are converted to meditation—how body or surface gives way to depth, as the boy is compelled to think about the meaning of his acts.

The boat-stealing episode in Book First provides a good example. Here the boy takes a neighbor's boat for an evening excursion, but since he has not asked to borrow it his pleasure in rowing alone is mixed with guilty thoughts—"It was an act of stealth / And troubled pleasure" (388–89). Like the pedlar of "The Ruined Cottage," the child has a troubled mind. But where the pedlar stills the motion of his thoughts by meditating on the poetic image of Margaret's overgrown garden, the boy fixes his attention on a mountain ridge so that he can row to reach a chosen point. His concentration is associated with his physical exploit, for by fixing on the mountain he will be able to guide the boat in the path he desires. Totally absorbed in his effort, the boy suddenly sees rising behind his chosen ridge "a huge cliff," which "As if with voluntary power instinct / Upreared its head" (406–8).

At this moment the boy's power and activity has been transferred to nature—the cliff uprears its head and moves in upon him. In his fright the child "struck, and struck again" (408) with his oars, but the movement of his boat only serves to make the mountain follow him all the faster. Of course the actual motion is entirely the boy's, for as he rows across the lake his horizon changes and the black cliff, which at first was out of view, appears and then rises faster as he rows faster. He does not think of it in this way though, because he has been concentrating so intensely on guiding the boat that the appearance of the cliff comes as a shock—no longer is he setting his own course; he has lost his way, and lost his powers. But if his fright stems superficially from a mistake in perception—erroniously attributing his own motion to the mountain—in a deeper sense he fears because he is guilty. He has stolen the boat and ignored his troubled emotions, but now guilt arises as a feeling of being followed. For days afterward the boy meditates on this experience, imagining "huge and mighty forms that do not live / Like living men" which "moved slowly through my mind / By day, and were the trouble of my dreams" (424–26). For this child eyesight has given way to insight, surface has been replaced by depth—the mountain has become a poetic image. Remembering this process, the mature poet thanks the "Wisdom and Spirit of the universe, / Thou soul that art the eternity of thought, / That giv'st to forms and images a breath / And everlasting motion" (428–31).

But the aliveness of nature has been secured through an emotional suppression. This spot of time works to discipline the boy's physical adventurousness and ambition by imaging his guilt in a tremendous natural form, a process that the mature poet sees as a poetic purification of feeling. Nature intertwines his passions

> Not with the mean and vulgar works of man,
> But with high objects, with enduring things,
> With life and Nature, purifying thus
> The elements of feeling and of thought,
> And sanctifying by such discipline
> Both pain and fear, until we recognise
> A grandeur in the beatings of the heart.
>
> (435–41)

Guilt has been removed from the "mean and vulgar" compass of man and associated "with high objects, with enduring things"—so that the aliveness and motion of the mountain leads to a transcendental stillness, just as the emotional turmoil of the child leads to the all-embracing tranquil vision of the mature poet. The boy's guilty thoughts have been converted to sublime intimations. In short, Wordsworth's childhood action has been elevated from human scope to the range of infinity.

Comparing this transformation to the conversion wrought by Rivers in *The Borderers* is very much to the point—for Rivers' villainous action and the child's boat-stealing exploit both become pathways to infinity. Of course Rivers enters into an eternity of suffering whereas the boy grows up toward serene and all-embracing maturity, but the actions that initiate these developments clearly resemble each other. Both Rivers and the boy perform forbidden deeds to found their own personal distinction. It is easy to sympathize with this urge when it occurs in a child, who understandably is concerned with moving out into the world to establish his own power and autonomy. Nevertheless, the connection between growing up and villainy can be made—and was made by Wordsworth himself.

This becomes clear in *Home at Grasmere*, an auto-biographical poem which, like *The Prelude*, is concerned with unblocking the sources of poetry. Here Wordsworth settles into Grasmere as his final and perfect home, just as in *The Prelude* he tries to grow into an adulthood of productive meditative maturity. Looking back on his childhood, the poet makes remarks so revealing that they are worthy of extended quotation:

> While yet an innocent little-one, a heart
> That doubtless wanted not its tender moods,
> I breathed (for this I better recollect)
> Among wild appetites and blind desires,
> Motions of savage instinct, my delight
> And exaltation. Nothing at that time
> So welcome, no temptation half so dear
> As that which [urged] me to a daring feat.
> Deep pools, tall trees, black chasms, and dizzy crags—
> I loved to look in them, to stand and read
> Their looks forbidding, read and disobey,
> Sometimes in act, and evermore in thought.
> With impulses which only were by these
> Surpassed in strength, I heard of danger met
> Or sought with courage, enterprize forlorn,
> By one, sole keeper of his own intent.
> Or by a resolute few, who for the sake
> Of glory fronted multitudes in arms.
> Yea, to this day I swell with like desire;
> I cannot at this moment read a tale
> Of two brave Vessels matched in deadly fight
> And fighting to the death, but I am pleased
> More than a wise Man ought to be; I wish,
> I burn, I struggle, and in soul am there.
> But me hath Nature tamed and bade me seek
> For other agitations or be calm . . .
>   Her deliberate Voice
> Hath said, "Be mild and love all gentle things;
> Thy glory and thy happiness be there."[14]

Wordsworth describes the growth of the poet's mind as a transformation from childhood physical action to adult tranquillity, a progress also made amply clear in *The Prelude*. What is different here is the explicit tone of that transformation: from aggression to mildness, from "wild appetites and blind desires" to the love of "all gentle things." Indeed, this conversion looks more like an uneasy repression than Wordsworth's wished-for poetic suppressions; there is a fear of worldly action, a dismay at the poet's own desires, a necessity for replacing impulse with deliberation, that resonates with the egoistic evils of Rivers' activity. The repressions of this passage exist as much to check danger as to deepen personality, and so they point toward the restraint rather than the growth of the poet's mind.[15]

When Wordsworth contemplates his poetic mission in *Home at Grasmere* one can sense his lack of ease. His protected vale becomes "A termination and a last retreat, / A Centre, come from wheresoe'er you will, / A Whole without dependence or defect, / . . . Perfect Contentment, Unity entire" (166–70). However, to submit completely to such unity would be to be borne on "in pleasing rest . . . / Without desire in full complacency, / Contemplating perfection absolute / And entertained as in a placid sleep" (394–97). Absolute integration becomes spiritual flaccidity, a lack of exercise and aspiration that could convert the vale into a fool's paradise. Wordsworth tries to avoid this by creating a symbol for the poem that reconciles rest and motion, in the state of tranquillity. His image is of a flock of birds which ceaselessly circle the lake, forever on the move yet going nowhere.

> Behold them, how they shape,
> Orb after orb, their course, still round and round,
> Above the area of the Lake, their own
> Adopted region, girding it about
> In wanton repetition, yet therewith—
> With that large circle evermore renewed—
> Hundreds of curves and circlets, high and low,
> Backwards and forwards, progress intricate,
> As if one spirit was in all and swayed
> Their indefatigable flight.
>
> (292–301)

These circling birds are engaged in a "repetition" from which is at the same time a renewal, a "progress intricate" that proceeds not in a straight line but by building a formation, an elaborate circling, that enacts spiritual unity and endless energy. Later in the poem he sees the birds at rest on the lake splashing and bobbing, "And in all about that playful band, / Incapable although they be of rest . . . / There is a stillness, and they seem to make / Calm revelry in that their calm abode" (798–802).

Perhaps meditative stillness can be an activity, as Wordsworth suggests in his image of the birds at home in Grasmere; but if *The Prelude* affirms this value through its advocacy of poetic tranquillity as the definitively mature human state, one of Wordsworth's most impressive spots of time raises the question of something more than this. Almost all of his spots occur in childhood, "the hiding-places of my power," but two of Wordsworth's most notable experiences are from his adulthood—and they both involve mountain climbing. The crossing the Alps spot of time rather than the ascent of Snowden is of particular interest here. It converts physical action into meditative activity when Wordsworth, who has lost the path, enquires where the pass is only to be informed that he already has gone over it. This precipitates a deep insight—that it was spiritual rather than physical challenge he had desired all along, and that such spiritual challenges constantly sought and constantly struggled with are the very lifeblood of the deep self:

> Our destiny, our nature, and our home,
> Is with infinitude—and only there;
> With hope it is, hope that can never die,
> Effort, and expectation, and desire,
> And something evermore about to be.
>
> (538–42)

As in the childhood spots of time the poet has lost his way only to find it again in a deeper sense. In a characteristically Wordsworthian resolution especially reminiscent of "Tintern Abbey," physical action gives way to spiritual work as the poet shifts from having his experience to meditating on its meaning, an activity involving "Effort, and expectation, and desire, / And something evermore about to be." The Alps spot of time suggests that meditation can open an endlessly challenging spiritual life.

But attention needs to be returned to the physical activity Wordsworth sacrifices here, and also in his other notable adult spot of time, the ascent of Snowden. These mountain climbing efforts both involve the challenge of achieving a difficult goal, and as such they are activities that confer distinction. There is a continuity here with the childhood spots of time which also involve physical challenge—the boat-stealing, nest-robbing, and so forth. But the adult mountain climbing is different from these childhood experiences in one significant respect: this

activity is disinterested, a pure competition with oneself rather
than the violation of someone or something else. Such disinterest purges the sporting challenge, makes it a struggle for
distinction that is not polluted by Rivers's kind of villainous
motivations or the needs for domination and mastery experienced by the child, which also carry the overtones of a Rivers.

As Rivers himself pointed out, "Action is transitory, a step, a
blow"—worldly activity, as opposed to meditation, endures
but a moment and then passes beyond the realm of anticipa-
tion into the eternity of recollection. "Suffering is permanent,
obscure and dark, / And has the nature of infinity." Perhaps,
then, the recollective poet meditates on his past experience not
only to elicit its completeness and integration but also as a
method of protecting that very wholeness. At any rate, the two
preeminent adult spots of time in *The Prelude* involve a purified, disinterested form of activity in the world; and in the
main, the other type of adult activity enacted by the poem's
speaker is meditative. This raises the possibility that meditation not only fosters the poet's spiritual growth but also provides him with a form of activity which protects him from the
possibly disastrous consequences of action in the world. If he
engages in worldly activity he need not be a Rivers to suddenly
be plunged into an eternity of suffering—for we can sin unin-
tentionally as well as intentionally, and after the fatal act our
meditations must realize infinity in the form of endless suffering rather than ever-renewed integration and growth. The poet
who elevated his childhood theft of a boat to a sublime vision
of guilt must have been a man highly sensitive to remorse, and
perhaps he was prepared to sacrifice a great deal to protect
himself from it.[16]

Comparing Wordsworth's and Blake's efforts to create the
Poem of Everything reveals both marked relationships and
strong contrasts. Both poets struggle with the need to create a
deep self—a resonant interior being profound enough to see
into the heart of the world, and strong enough to resist the dark
impulses they feel they share with other human beings. Blake's
solution is to make the depths transparent, to see and acknowledge everything and to work through his unredeemed feelings,
such as anger, to convert negative energies to positive ones. His
later prophecies strive to transform corporeal into intellectual
warfare, in order to preserve his lifelong ideal of open expressiveness. Wordsworth takes the contrary path of poetic
suppression: for him infinity remains to a significant extent

obscure and mysterious, and there are sublime depths in the self that can receive our surface emotions and return them converted into profound and purified poetic expressions.

Like Blake, Wordsworth aims for absolute inclusiveness: the deep self's lyrical vision must encompass the world. But where the Blakean New Man is translucent and openly expressive, the meditative speaker of *The Prelude* articulates spontaneous overflow, a surface speech informed with the obscure sublimities of the depths. Wordsworth hopes that this spontaneous overflow is the true voice of poetry, the voice that will return humanity's unredeemed emotions to the surface in purified and purposeful forms. But for Wordsworth the release of spontaneous overflow is countered by the blockage of poetic expression, and these polarized states seem to share a deep connection. Poetic suppression can slide easily into repression; consequently, the poet's voice can shift from the speech that embodies infinity to one that imposes protective limitations. Sometimes poetic speech transforms dark impulses, but at others the darkness must be held in check. Since poetic suppression and repression are both depth processes that operate in obscurity, the Wordsworthian stance of meditative maturity can become radically ambiguous: is tranquil meditation an all-embracing state capable of reproducing every emotion in poetically redeemed form and opening developmental vistas of something evermore about to be, or is it an assumed posture—a protection against the poet's fears that his worldly activities could result in wickedness or folly? Growth and defense become profoundly, obscurely intertwined in the Wordsworthian deep self.

4

COLERIDGE
The Possessed Bard

Whereas Wordsworth was an active child, forever invading nature and testing himself through physical exploits, Coleridge was a dreamer. Coleridge's letters about his early life written to Thomas Poole show the poet's older brother Frank to have been the Wordsworthian activist of the family. It was Frank, not Coleridge, who "loved climbing, fighting, playing, and robbing orchards to distraction."[1] Coleridge himself was the youngest child and his mother's favorite, occupying a pampered position that opened him to hostility from others. In particular, "Frank hated me. . . . So I became fretful, & timorous, & a tell-tale—& the School-boys drove me from play, and were always tormenting me." Threatened, Coleridge withdrew from the field of physical action. He "took no pleasure in boyish sports—but read incessantly."[2] This tendency to stimulate the mind and ignore the body, to live in an inner world and avoid the outside, established Coleridge's character:

> So I became a *dreamer*—and acquired an indisposition to all bodily activity—and I was fretful, and inordinately passionate, and as I could not play at any thing, and was slothful, I was despised & hated by the boys; and because I could read & spell, & had, I may truly say, a memory & understanding forced into almost an unnatural ripeness, I was flattered & wondered at by all the old women—& so I became very vain, and despised most of the boys, that were at all near my own age—and before I was eight years old, I was a *character*—sensibility, imagination, vanity, sloth, & feelings of deep & bitter contempt for almost all who traversed the orbit of my understanding, were even then prominent & manifest.[3]

The hallmarks of the adult Coleridge already are present in the boy—simultaneous stirrings of superiority and inferiority, strength and weakness, inordinate passion and slothfulness. In the area of mind he is supreme, active, intense, and inclined toward feelings of "deep & bitter contempt for almost all who traversed the orbit of my understanding." But it seems likely that this hostility stems from his sense of exclusion—for it is these less intelligent others who claim the field of physical action, the area of his weakness and humiliation.[4]

Whereas the child of *The Prelude* and "Tintern Abbey" rejoices in exuberant physical activity, the boy Coleridge is an inner being who lives only through imaginative experience.[5] What nature was to Wordsworth's childhood, books were to Coleridge's. As he remarks to Poole, "I never regarded *my senses* in any way as the criteria of my belief. I regulated all my creeds by my conceptions not by my *sight*." It follows that children should read "Romances" and other works of imagination; for stories which suggest a sense of vastness and wholeness provide for Coleridge the childhood acquaintance with infinity that physical activity produces in Wordsworth. He says, "I know no other way of giving the mind a love of 'the Great,' & 'the Whole.'—Those who have been led to the same truths step by step thro' the constant testimony of their senses, seem to me to want a sense which I possess—They contemplate nothing but *parts*—and all *parts* are necessarily little—and the Universe to them is but a mass of *little things*."[6]

At the same time he was writing his autobiographical letters to Poole, he wrote to John Thelwall that "It is but seldom that I raise & spiritualize my intellect . . . at other times I adopt the Brahman Creed, & say—It is beter to sit than to stand, it is better to lie than to sit, it is better to sleep than to wake—but Death is the best of all!—I should much wish, like the Indian Vishna [Vishnu] to float about along an infinite ocean cradled in the flower of the Lotos, & wake once in a million years for a few minutes—just to know that I was going to sleep a million years more."[7] Although Coleridge lives in the mind and values the brilliance that distinguishes him from other, less acute men, nevertheless he is tempted to sloth. This is because mental relaxation, like its opposite, mental activation, offers a possible route to infinity. When Wordsworth meditates on death he understands it as the life limit that provokes us to the imaginative resistance which creates our vision of infinity. The activism of Wordsworth's assumptions is missing in Coleridge's understanding of death, for the "Death" he courts here is that slumber of the conscious self which opens the profoundest depths in ourselves—the unconscious, primordial depths.

Sometimes Coleridge is attracted to the notion of surrendering himself to this infinite flow, but he would want to "wake once in a million years for a few minutes—just to know that I was going to sleep a million years more."

This utterly relaxed, unconscious state—so different from the Wordsworthian depth state which generates the poetic voice via its profound activity of suppression—becomes Coleridge's version of the deep self. But of course, one hardly can speak of a 'self' here: the whole point is to open infinity by escaping the bounds of personality. When Coleridge writes nightmare poetry in "The Ancient Mariner," "Kubla Khan," and "Christabel," he draws on this un-selfed preconscious depth. But he also writes another kind of poetry, the so-called conversation poems, which I shall turn to first. Here his relaxation is much less profound, for it appears as a paradoxical form of activation by which play or dissipation is revealed as a form of work.

Where Wordsworthian play is identified with the unreflective boyhood physical exploits of *The Prelude*, Coleridgean play is completely interior and appears as the undirected musings of the conversation poetry's speaker. This person always is discovered in a condition of retirement—in solitude and without immediate occupation, set apart from the world in circumstances that allow his thoughts free play. "The Eolian Harp" is a typical example: the speaker finds himself reclined and daydreaming on a hill, "And tranquil muse upon tranquillity."[8]

This tranquil attitude evokes not Wordsworthian suppression, but "Full many a thought uncall'd and undetain'd, / And many idle flitting phantasies, / Traverse my indolent and passive brain" (39–41). Stillness prompts its opposite, free expression, and the abandonment of purpose leads to the playful arabesques of fantasy. The words of Coleridge's poem become analogous to the delicate notes produced by the wind harp he imagines hanging in his cottage window, which can command the hearer's attention only when the environment is still. With "the world *so* hush'd! / The stilly murmur of the distant Sea / Tells us of silence" (10–12), so that in this poem silence and sound become reconcilable opposites. Just as the sea's murmur and the harp's notes are a heard form of silence, the poet hopes that his idle fantasies, his uncontrolled and purposeless dreams, will result in a poem manifesting order—a speech that points toward transcendental silence. For if in this poem stillness leads to movement, there is also a hope that movement will lead back to a Greater Stillness.

This profound order underlying the apparently random movements of life is mirrored in the poet's identity, for the superficial playfulness of his speculations becomes grounded in an underlying deep purpose. On the surface, movement; in the depths, steadiness—paradoxically, play has become work. Or so the poet hopes. In "The Eolian Harp" he does not press this unorthodox conclusion, preferring to fall back on his wife's admonitions to orthodox faith as a means of supporting the poem's religious implications.

"Frost at Midnight," the most powerful of the conversation poems, does not require such superimposed control to sustain its order. It persuasively suggests that stillness can be a form of movement, and inactivity a form of action. As in "The Eolian Harp," the speculative movement of the poet's thought is prompted by his retirement and the stillness of the midnight world, a quiet "so calm, that it disturbs / And vexes meditation with its strange / And extreme silentness" (8–10). This absolute calm provokes its opposite, the free movement of thought. The musing poet now identifies with the only other moving thing in his still nocturnal world—the trembling wood ash in the firegrate, which commonly was termed a "stranger." Thus "the idling Spirit / By its own moods interprets, every where / Echo or mirror seeking of itself, / And makes a toy of Thought" (20–23). But if such play did not persuasively lead to synthesis in "The Eolian Harp," it does here. For it evokes the poet's recollections of his unhappy school years, when he also mused over ashes in the firegrate and desperately hoped they were a sign that a stranger would come to take him home. The recollection of this terrible loneliness momentarily arrests the flow of meditation, and in the lapse he hears the breathing of his child, which, "heard in this deep calm, / Fill[s] up the interspersed vacancies / And momentary pauses of the thought" (45–47). For indeed, except for the poet the only actually living thing in this room is not the ash film but the baby. The movements and arrests of his thought have created a reversal that brings him into rhythm with his child, into a realization that the love he longed for as a boy has been given to him through his own son. So his past is redeemed in his present. He can look confidently toward the future, when the baby will grow into an active Wordsworthian boyhood in nature that will give him a sense of participation in the universal order lacking in the poet's own isolated, outcast childhood. This participation denied to the poet in his boyhood now is conferred in his adulthood, as he discovers a father's power to love and bless.

The speculative fluctuation of his thought, playfully moving into connections and arrested at vacancies, now is completed through his reversal of vision: he perceives a profound order in his life that binds his days together, unites him with those he loves, and suggests the sacramental relationship of every thing to everything else. The poet's surface inactivity really has been deep action; his play has done work. The speech of his meditation becomes a paradoxical form of sacred silence, for it shadows forth the world's secret design, just as the "secret ministry of frost" silently has hung icicles from the poet's cottage roof while he has made his poem. As the energies of nature show their potency through their very secrecy and silence, so the power of the poet shows itself through his capacity to bring integration out of randomness, to indulge in a meditation that superficially seems speculative but actually becomes the tracing of a profound order.

In "Frost at Midnight" relaxation produces activation, play becomes work, and retirement in a sheltered place fosters a sense of the world's unity. These poetic paradoxes must have been deeply appealing to the man revealed in the autobiographical letters to Poole—for the stance of "Frost" allows the poet to remain isolated from the world and yet profoundly participate in its activity. The conversation poetry suggests that physical action is trivial compared to the deep activity of the spirit, a comforting view for someone committed to the life of the mind and loth to mingle with the world. One of the achievements of the conversation poetry is to purify Coleridge's penchant for meditative isolation, to portray it in a plausibly sacramental light, which the letters to Poole certainly do not. So if the conversation poems can be read as successful essays in social reconciliation—a reading I have given here—another kind of reading that foregrounds antisocial implications also is possible. For these "conversations" are really monologues, not true dialogues. The speaker's wife in "The Eolian Harp" is only an implied presence, and the infant in "Frost at Midnight" is too young to know language. Coleridge's narrators appear to be considering someone else, but he has made sure that their respondents cannot possibly reply—a strategy that leaves his speakers free to shape everything. From this perspective, what looks like conversation actually is ventriloquism, an inauthentic portrayal of social involvement.[9]

The latent ambivalence of the conversation poetry is reinforced by Coleridge's open need to also write a poetry of political activism. In the years 1795 to 1798 his poetry thus betrays contradictory impulses—the need to retire from the world, and the obligation to reform society. As he urges in a sonnet to his friend Charles Lloyd, "O abject! if, to sickly dreams resign'd, / All effortless thou leave Life's commonweal / A prey to Tyrants, Murderers of Mankind."

"Reflections on Having Left a Place of Retirement" most clearly reveals Coleridge's misgivings about external action; its title originally was "Reflections on entering into active life. A Poem which affects not to be Poetry." Once again the scene is his sheltered cottage with its twining roses and its quiet, invaded only by the faint murmur of the distant sea. Into this "Valley of Seclusion" comes a traveller, "A wealthy son of Commerce . . . Bristowa's citizen." His appearance prompts the poet to reflect on the evils of commerce, the harm done by a "thirst of idle gold" (9–13), which galvanizes people such as this passerby into meaningless motion, a restless urge to be forever on the move in search of material profit. The poet himself moves by being still; in his retired vale he hears the "viewless sky-lark's note," another of those delicate Coleridgean sounds that command attention only in silence, a melody "only heard / When the Soul seeks to hear; when all is hush'd, / And the Heart listens!" (19–26). By remaining in retirement, by suspending himself in attentive thought, he opens the path to his soul's growth. Such enrichment never will be experienced by the busy merchant from Bristol.

But just as the poem moves toward this resolution, it reverses to announce that Coleridge himself soon must leave his sheltered cottage to "join head, heart, and hand, / Active and firm, to fight the bloodless fight / Of Science, Freedom, and the Truth in Christ" (60–62). For although retirement indeed fosters spiritual depth in the poet, this isolated personal integration may be an unwarranted luxury in the British social world of the poem's narrative present, 1795, which is plagued by widespread poverty and inequality. As he moves into active political life the poet will revisit his cottage in dreams, but will not earn the right actually to return there until social justice is achieved. The poem ends with the prayer, "Speed it, O Father! Let thy Kingdom come!" (71).

The most interesting element in "Reflections" is Coleridge's worry about the pursuit of personal spiritual growth. Not only may this be inappropriate in a socially troubled world, he fears it also could be positively irrelevant. For the delicate feelings, the personal discrimination and fineness, built by meditation in retirement may unfit the individual for active life. He wonders if it was right "That I should dream away the entrusted hours / On rose-leaf beds, pampering the coward heart / With feelings all too delicate for use" (46–48). Apparently, the life of the spirit cannot always be regarded as the equivalent of action. In fact, at times it appears to be decadent, a self-indulgent relaxation that atrophies humane capacities. The tone here is reminiscent of the autobiographical letters to Poole, where Coleridge sees himself as an ineffectual dreamer, a coward driven from the field of boyhood sports. Once again the man of mind seems to be a weakling, and imaginative activity appears to be no fit substitute for action in the world.[10]

Coleridge's drama *Osorio* dwells on this fear that a highly developed mind may produce an ineffectual character. The play was written at about the same time as Wordsworth's *The Borderers*, and like Wordsworth's drama, it is concerned with the impact of the individual's activity in the world. In Rivers Wordsworth demonstrated how the betrayal of another human being can found a world of inwardness as infinite suffering, creating a personality that achieves greatness through its villainy and isolation. But where Wordsworth can regard the villain as a man of worldly power, Coleridge sees his villain Osorio as ineffective in the world, a threat only to himself. Osorio's sole capacity is for self-destruction.

At one point in the play he tells his life story, which suggests that he is great because he always has been a man of mind who walks apart from others. As he says of himself, "He was a man different from other men, / And he despised them, yet revered himself . . . All men seem'd mad to him, / Their actions noisome folly . . . Nature had made him for some other planet."[11] But if this alienation proves Osorio's greatness to himself, Coleridge demurs. In a manuscript note referring to this speech he comments, "Under the mask of the third person Osorio relates to his own story, as in the delusion of self-justification and pride it appeared to himself—at least as he wished it to appear to himself." Indeed, Osorio's self-esteem and contempt for others echo Coleridge's feelings about himself as a child, as expressed in the Poole letters—which were written at the same time as this play. He said to Poole that "before I was eight years old, I was a character—sensibility, imagination, vanity, sloth, & feelings of deep & bitter contempt for almost all who traversed the orbit of my understanding, were even then prominent & manifest."

The way in which such self-deluded characters behave is suggested by Osorio's description of his own villainy, his employment of an assassin to murder his virtuous brother Alfred. He speaks of himself in the third person, as though he were another; and his narration intensifies this self-distancing by implying that what he did was not at all what he willed to do:

> He walk'd alone,
> And phantasies, unsought for, troubled him.
> Something within would still be shadowing out
> All possibilities, and with these shadows
> His mind held dalliance. Once, as so it happen'd,
> A fancy cross'd him wilder than the rest:
> To this in moody murmur, and low voice,
> He yielded utterance as some talk in sleep.
> The man who heard him . . .
>   With his human hand
> He gave a being and reality
> To that wild fancy of a possible thing.
> Well it was done.
>
>   (IV, 92–108)

The arabesque of fantasy, the free range of imaginative play that leads to the discovery of deep world order in the conversation poetry, is present in Osorio's inner life. But here, such dalliance leads to intuitions of evil that Osorio fears merely need to be spoken aloud in order to be carried out. His utterance becomes a dream-poem that to his surprise is enacted in the outer world, a result alienated from its inner origins. Or so he claims. Coleridge makes it clear that Osorio's description of his involuntary actions is a sham, the self-justification of a man who desires worldly power but is too weak to accept responsibility for what he does to achieve it. If meditation creates integration in the conversation poetry, in *Osorio* it does just the opposite. Osorio's fantasies lead not to order and power, but to a divided and self-alienated self.

The attempted assassination of his brother miscarries, and Albert then unmasks Osorio's sham Gothic villainy, his fantasy of power. He derides Osorio's "faith in universal villainy, / Thy shallow sophisms, thy pretended scorn / For all thy human bretheren" (V, 188–90). These have been attitudes, postures— not real capacities. And the proof of this lies in Osorio's malicious feelings, which act not against the world but against himself: "Have they given thee peace? / Cured thee of starting in thy sleep? or made / The darkness pleasant, when thou wakest at midnight?" (V, 191–93). Osorio certainly is evil, but he also is virtually impotent. He is his own victim, a man who seems able to realize his aspirations to power only through self-destruction.[13]

But if Coleridge undermines Osorio's villainy by showing it as the overcompensation of a weakling and the power fantasy of a man who finds external action difficult, nevertheless he does not reject the notion of the superior man who walks apart. At a lull in the play's action Albert's nurse tells the story of such a man—a story that later was excerpted to become "The Foster-mother's Tale" in the *Lyrical Ballads*. It involves a baby who was found in the forest and brought to Osorio's ancestral home, growing up "A pretty boy, but most unteachable— / And never learnt a prayer, nor told a bead, / But knew the names of birds . . . / And whistled, as he were a bird himself" (VI, 182– 85). Like the child Coleridge, this mysterious natural boy "read, and read, and read, / Till his brain turn'd—and ere his twentieth year, / He had unlawful thoughts of many things" (IV, 195–97). But if his meditation does go beyond the bounds of lawfulness, nevertheless he is curiously innocent of evil. A natural poet, "his speech, it was . . . soft and sweet" (V, 200), and the lord of the manor loves to talk with him. One day as they speak together the earth heaves beneath their feet, and considering this a judgement against wickedness, the lord commits the young man to the dungeon. There he sings "a doleful song about green fields, / How sweet it were . . . / To hunt for food, and be a naked man, / And wander up and down at liberty" (V, 214–17). Later he escapes and takes a ship to the new world, finally disappearing alone into an unknown land, where the nurse presumes that "He liv'd and died among the savage men" (V, 234).

This curious narrative of evil and innocence, power and gentleness, converts the retirement motif of the conversation poetry into a mysterious retreat into nature. The youth must walk apart from men because he really is different from them. Those unlawful thoughts that could compromise others emerge harmlessly in his speech, redeemed as poetry—a poetry that notwithstanding his deep reading, is a natural expression, a voice as innocent as birdsong. Such a being cannot live in the world of men and women; he must vanish into nature, and his song must be taken up into silence. So he melts into a stillness more mysterious than that suggested by the conversation poetry, because it is demonic as well as sacred. Like Osorio's fantasies, the young man's lead to unlawful thoughts—but where Osorio speaks aloud with the unconscious desire that his words be carried into action, the youth speaks disinterestedly, as a poet. This is why he can innocently entertain evil.

Osorio suggests that Coleridge's characteristic release into fantasy, into the reverie of the relaxed mind, has been limited in the conversation poetry to areas that are socially acceptable. But total relaxation also seems to open out the realm of the unlawful. "The Rime of the Ancient Mariner," which was written soon after *Osorio*, develops this awareness of the unlawful in ways that relate to Coleridge's drama. Osorio was a villian whereas the young poet was a naturally pure being, but both were variants of the Coleridgean isolate—figures who did not act in the world. But where his inactivity was the proof of Osorio's weak character, a similar inactivity became the hallmark of the young poet's innocence. Could there be a poet not only innocent but wise, a resonant figure who plumbs the depths of experience and knows the unlawful as well as the lawful, yet is not corrupted or made ineffectual by that knowledge? And could such a poet then be capable of action? Coleridge aspires to a deep self strong enough to face everything in the infinite unconscious—an inclusive personality capable of returning from its profound interior voyage to act capably yet benignly in the world. The poem that embodies this hope is "The Ancient Mariner."

Like the conversation poetry, "The Ancient Mariner" courts the arabesques of fantasy, but its way of relaxing into the play of imagination is quite different from the retreat methodology of the conversation poetry. There the poet finds himself at leisure in still surroundings, which evoke a liberated movement of thought. The relaxation of "The Ancient Mariner" has nothing of this gradualness and calm about it. It comes so suddenly that relaxation is hardly a proper name for the phenomenon—instead, it might better be termed collapse. This suddenness appears in all the major features of the poem: the abruptness of the ballad beginning, the Mariner's summary halting of the Wedding-Guest and commencement of his story, the unmotivated precipitancy of the poem's two central actions, the shooting of the Albatross and the blessing of the water-snakes, the ship's repeated sudden transition from stillness to powerful movement, and at the end of the poem, the returned Mariner's abrupt wrench of agony, which precipitates the telling of his tale to the Hermit. These shocking disjunctive features of "The Ancient Mariner" distinguish it from the tranquil meditative continuities of the conversation poetry.

In his theater criticism Coleridge made remarks that suggest why disjunctiveness becomes a prominent feature of "The Ancient Mariner." While discussing *The Tempest* he pauses to reflect on the nature of dramatic illusion, observing the French critics suppose "that a perfect delusion is to be aimed at" whereas Dr. Johnson takes the opposite view, believing "the auditors throughout as in the full, and positive knowledge of the contrary." Coleridge himself proposes an "intermediate state, which we distinguish by the term illusion." He adds, "In what this consists I cannot better explain than by referring you to the highest degree of it; namely, dreaming." For Coleridge the dream state is radically disjunctive, because "in sleep we pass at once by a sudden collapse into . . . suspension of will and the comparative power." The dreaming self becomes a disinterested observer, an unselfed self divested of "will and the comparative power," the audience of a dream theater. Sleep "consists in a suspension of the voluntary and, therefore, of the comparative power. The fact is that we pass no judgement either way: we simply do not judge them [dreams] to be unreal, in consequence of which the images act on our minds, as far as they act at all, by their own force as images."[14]

The poet who wrote in a letter to Thelwall that he sometimes wished "like the Indian Vishna [Vishnu] to float about along an infinite ocean cradled in the flower of the Lotos" has found his most powerful poetic voice through a collapse of the conscious self that releases a nightmare world. In this dream theater the observer remains passive, neither willing nor judging, while the dream images assume the active role—a role which transcends the morality of waking life through sheer power. These images "act on our minds, as far as they act at all, by their own force as images." Coleridge's nightmare poetry makes Osorio's wistful fantasy come true: "A fancy cross'd him wilder than the rest: / To this in moody murmur, and low voice, / He yielded utterance as some talk in sleep" only to discover that the imagined action somehow has been carried out in the world.

But where in *Osorio* the protagonist was a weakling and the amoral but disinterested young poet survived by living apart from the world, in Coleridge's nightmare poetry the bard becomes possessed by the force of his imagery and utters an irresistibly powerful poem.

Whereas Coleridge's sacramental conversation poetry purifies the isolationist posture of genius anatomized in the letters to Poole, his profane nightmare poetry liberates the isolate's rage for power by transcending the boundaries of the conscious self and society. The freedom of such poetry is distinctly antisocial, as is suggested by the Mariner's audience relations with the Wedding-Guest. The Guest is forcibly detained by the power of the Mariner's "glittering eye," but this effect is made possible only by the Mariner's own possessed state. When he is a poet he is not his normal self, and only in that extraordinary condition is he powerful. During his voyage he is passive, like the Wedding-Guest, reacting to the forceful imagery of his nightmare journey; but when he returns and speaks as a man possessed he becomes a power in the world.

Apparently then, the price paid for power is annihilation of the conscious self. Wordsworth too assumed that the depth state involved stresses—for him, the stresses of suppression—but his stance is far less extreme than Coleridge's, which involves a form of self-murder. Power and coherence become incompatible in Coleridge's nightmare poetry, which implies that the understood self is a superficial self whereas the deep self transcends all explanation and law. Interpret the self's meaning, and one achieves only the delicate unworldly resonances of the conversation poetry; shatter integration, and a tremendous energy is born. Whereas Wordsworth holds to the meditative posture, shunning action in the world lest he inadvertently fall into villainy and become one of the damned, such as his character Rivers in *The Borderers*, Coleridge in the persona of his Mariner elects to enter the world and act as a possessed and hence powerful bard. The Mariner gains the potency for action by losing his conscious self, a new and more extreme route to the evasion of responsibility marked in the character of Osorio. Osorio was merely a weak and contemptible self-deceiver, but the Mariner is truly sublime—a man overwhelmed by the infinite power of his nightmare world.[15]

The radical separations in Coleridge's nightmare poetry indicate that he reconceives Wordsworthian mixing as a form of polarization. In *The Prelude* Wordsworth affirms that "There is a dark / Invisible workmanship that reconciles / Discordant elements," a unifying power that mixes clashing moods and experiences in the growing unity of the deepening soul, "The calm existence that is mine when / I am worthy of myself" (I, 352–61). Like Blake, who struggles to acknowledge all feelings and cast nothing out, thereby recreating the redeemed Albion as an inclusive mixture capable of indefinitely prolonged growth, Wordsworth envisions a self whose mixtures produce deep harmonies that resonate with the world's. Coleridge inverts Wordsworth's and Blake's patternings to conceive of the world and the self as animated by disjunction, not mixture. His nightmare visions certainly partake of the Wordsworthian "Discordant elements," but not under the aspect of randomness or chaos. Whereas reconciliation of opposites is the Coleridgean formula for mixing in the conversation poetry, polarization of opposites becomes the organizing principle of his nightmares. Bipolar opposition becomes a perverse form of soul-making, because it creates the deep self as a series of powerful self-alienations. Accordingly, the Coleridgean alternative to Wordsworth's meditative tranquillity—that all-inclusive mood which harmoniously mixes "Discordant elements"—is shock.

In "The Ancient Mariner" the repeated, shocking force of disjunction of opposites stuns consciousness in order to liberate power. Alienation, repulsion, inexplicability, become the poem's principle of energy production, the force that drives action on through a mysterious dreamworld of jarring opposites, dead stillness and violent mobility. The Mariner's ship alternately is embalmed in a stupefying calm or precipitated into terrific, unnatural motion; the world is either frozen or torrid; the Mariner either thirsts or is deluged; the crew dies, comes alive, and then dies again. At the heart of this hyperbolic opposition is the Mariner's activity, which is polarized—he slays the Albatross and blesses the water-snakes. Both actions are unconscious, for just as he kills on impulse, he also "blessed them unaware" (285).

His first, destructive action—the unmotivated killing of the Albatross—inverts the positive impulse of the conversation poetry. For where in "Frost at Midnight" the poet identifies himself with the moving ash in the firegrate because it seems to him the only companionate living thing in his still, midnight world, the Mariner reverses this social impulse by attacking the only living thing besides himself in the land of ice and snow. In killing the Albatross the Mariner acts perversely, acts against himself as well as the bird—for he rejects the bond of community. His power surfaces as a sudden inexplicable impulse toward destruction, a reaction that both divides his self and isolates him from the rest of the world. If he kills the Albatross, in a sense he also murders himself.

On the other hand, later he reverses this destruction by impulsively blessing the water-snakes. The Mariner commits one unlawful act and one sacred act in this poem; in their absolute equality the opposite actions repel each other, cancel each other out. To credit him for his blessing would be as misguided as blaming him for his murder; either he is responsible for both actions, or for neither. But if we decide he is responsible, there is a feeling of injustice—for surely he is not accountable for what he did not intend? On the other hand, to maintain his detachment, his absolute alienation from his action, also seems unconvincing. The poem's texture of opposites both encourages comparison and synthesis, and deflects it. We seek, and yet we are unable to achieve a coherent version.

And in an extreme form, this may echo the plight of Coleridge himself. Although the harmonizing Coleridge of the *Biographia Literaria* confidently could say that the primary imagination functions as the "prime Agent of all human Perception, and as a repetition in the finite mind of the eternal act of creation in the infinite I AM," his creation, the Mariner, is drawn not by the assertion that I AM but the agonizing question, "What manner of man art thou?" (577). The polarizing force of opposition, which deflects explanation, also repeatedly goads the Mariner to attempt it—to attain a reconciled sense of self that might grant him peace. But although he tells and retells his story, he can achieve only temporary relief, not resolution. His very incoherence becomes the source of his immense and indefinitely continuing poetic power.[16]

"The Ancient Mariner" capitalizes on the Mariner's inability to explain himself as a means of perpetuating the mysterious unconscious flow of poetic energy. So an unresolved sense of self produces a forceful poem—or more accurately, a representative rendition of a poem that recycles indefinitely. Because he cannot answer the question of his identity, the Mariner has power to repeat that question as long as he lives. The unity of "The Ancient Mariner" becomes a function of its obsessive repetitiveness—its power to suggest the eternal recurrence of the unanswered question.

For the Wordsworth of *The Prelude*, the deep self grows ever more profound through its self-reflexive meditations, in poetic acts of interpretation. But for the Coleridge of the nightmare poetry, the only possible form of discourse becomes repetition. The Coleridgean deep self becomes a polarized combination of blockage and precipitate expression—a self intermittently poetic but forever incapable of understanding itself; and it is this very uninterpretibility which becomes the sign of its truly authentic depth. Coleridgean poetry harbors the profound but obscure suggestiveness of dreams, not the evolving revelation of Wordsworthian meditation. Therefore, unlike the Wordsworthian overflow which begins in spontaniety but leads to purposeful poetry, Coleridgean spontaneous overflow is experienced as a brutal onslaught that swamps the conscious self in the urgencies of the depths. The Mariner passes "like night, from land to land" waiting for the "uncertain hour" when his "agony returns" and he is compelled to speak. Coleridge envisions an intermittent infinity, an irresistible flow of speech that bursts from its host and drains him into exhausted tranquillity, only to return again and again, always unpredictably.

Granted, the Mariner pays duty to integration by ending his story with a passionate appeal for community, a plea that the Wedding-Guest love "All things both great and small" (615). But this harmonious conclusion is not wholly continuous with his story, which undercuts as well as reinforces community. For certainly the Mariner himself has gained the power of eloquence by forever estranging himself from human society, becoming the alienated wanderer who can go everywhere because he belongs nowhere. As with the poet of "Kubla Khan," the Mariner holds his audience only because he is a man apart, a compelling yet mysteriously menacing figure. The demonic Coleridgean bard is a man of power who charms others, who threatens to possess them even as he himself is possessed.

These anti-social overtones indicate that Coleridge has achieved a vision of power in "The Ancient Mariner" but at the cost of showing the poet as potentially dangerous to society. Indeed, the poem overcomes the kind of personal ineffectuality evident in Osorio by the annihilation of personality through liberation of a dreamworld. But a consequence of this collapse of consciousness is the Mariner, a symbolic persona suffused with profoundly ambiguous power but lacking personal identity. If the success of "The Ancient Mariner" is that it opens the infinite depths of unconsciousness by liberating poetry from the bounds of the conscious self, this is also its threat. It could be that the Mariner is not responsible for his acts because his identity was overpowered by his spontaneous impulse, but in this case poetic inspiration becomes a mysterious force that invades and pollutes the self. Power is divorced from human agency, and in this uncontrolled form becomes alien and even monstrous. "The Ancient Mariner" suggests that to escape one's identity may be even worse than being imprisoned by it; or rather, that this escape itself is a terrible kind of bondage.

In the Mariner Coleridge created a man of power, a bard whose words become his deeds as he moves into the world to possess his audience through compelling poetry. Certainly the Mariner is a more appealing figure than the impotent Osorio, who mutters his bad desires and then denies them when they are carried out in the world. But where Osorio is a weak, despicable villain the Mariner becomes a sympathetic pro-tagonist who disturbs us, even as he is disturbed by himself, because the deep unconscious sources of his power transcend human knowledge and control. In his next great dream poem, "Christabel," Coleridge struggles to cope with the troubling ambiguities raised by the case of the Mariner. In the figure of Christabel Coleridge imagines the possibility of a sacramen-tally purged identity—a persona who unlike the Mariner, can experience fully the visitation of unconscious power without being compromised by it. Christabel becomes the Mariner's very opposite: where he threatens aggression, she embodies submission.

That Coleridge indeed did see submission as the opposite of aggression is suggested by a notebook entry of 1830, which speculates, "The first lesson, that innocent Childhood affords me, is—that it is an instinct of my Nature to pass out of myself, and to exist in the form of others. The second is—not to suffer any one form to pass into *me* and to become a usurping *Self* in the disguise of what the German Pathologists call a *fixed idea*."[17] Here the alternatives are activation or relaxation, pos-session or submission. And "Christabel" dramatizes the pos-sibility of submission in its most radical form, martyrdom. This is clear from Coleridge's remarks on Crashaw's poem to St. Theresa: "These verses were ever present to my mind whilst writing the second part of Christabel; if, indeed by some subtle process of the mind they did not suggest the first thought of the whole poem."[18]

In "Christabel" Coleridge renders his most extreme vision of the collapse of consciousness—a displacement that perhaps may lead to sanctified rather than demonic power. Submission will become a spiritual exercise that transforms humility into the holy triumph of the martyr. If this conversion can be managed, Christabel might achieve the reconciliation denied to the Mariner. Where the Mariner has the power to endlessly retell his story but cannot achieve explanation or expiation, these accomplishments might be possible for Christabel. For unlike the Mariner and Osorio she does not commit evil, she merely must become open to it. In "Christabel" Coleridge's superior man of mind who walks apart becomes a woman of superior spirituality who totally submits.[19]

Like the Mariner, Christabel is involved in episodes of blessing and violation—the two fundamental impulses of Coleridge's dream world. But in "Christabel" the order of these acts is reversed from their occurrence in "The Ancient Mariner," and their quality is altered. Blessing comes first, and Christabel's offer of hospitality to the homeless wanderer Geraldine seems much more deliberate than the Mariner's "unaware" blessing of the water-snakes; mysterious violation follows that night, as they sleep together in Christabel's bed, and this stems not from Christabel but from the manipulations of Geraldine. In blessing Christabel acts, but in violation she is acted upon. So her character has a determinacy, an integrity, forever denied to the Mariner's. She truly is good.

Unlike Christabel, Geraldine does not possess a determinate character. She shares with the Mariner an aura of ambiguity stemming from the unresolved mystery of her identity. Her story that she is the abducted daughter of Sir Roland de Vaux of Tryermaine strikes the reader of "Christabel" as dubious, and when she prepares to sleep with Christabel she shows a reluctance to do so that conflicts with her determination to carry out the act:

> Deep from within she seems half-way
> To lift some weight with sick assay,
> And eyes the maid and seeks delay;
> Then suddenly, as one defied,
> Collects herself in scorn and pride,
> And lay down by the Maiden's side!

> (257–62)

This mood of self-division is inscribed in her body; when she disrobes, "Behold! her bosom and half her side— / A sight to dream of not to tell!" (252–53). In part Geraldine seems human and in part she suggests the totally alien and monstrous. Mysterious dreadfulness is a property of her power, which like the Mariner's is marked by the poetic glittering eye—"Her fair large eyes 'gan glitter bright" (221).[20]

But if the Mariner's poetry is rendered dubious by his possessed state, it also is authenticated by it. For his drivenness ensures his sincerity: we may not know what to make of his tale, but we are sure he is telling the truth insofar as he knows it. The impression left by Geraldine is quite different. As a homeless wanderer she is weary, powerless, and unsure of herself, but after she has possessed Christabel she herself becomes quite self-possessed. The next morning she successfully misleads Christabel's father Sir Roland, convincing him that she herself is innocent and good and that Christabel is guilty of inhospitality. Where the Mariner's poetic performance is always a spontaneous overflow, Geraldine's is made possible by self-control. The Mariner tells the truth in spite of himself, but Geraldine evilly manipulates her audience. Power and self-control are united in Geraldine, but the result is not a personal identity that in any sense is reassuring. In place of the integrated speaker of the conversation poetry, whose playful surface discourse becomes an ostensible freedom that eventually traces out deep order, Geraldine's calculated control of her surface united with the deep threat of her malign powers make her into the most disturbing type of the Coleridgean isolate—the evil genius.

Geraldine's glib speech is counterpointed by Christabel's strangled silence, which can be seen as an inversion of spontaneous overflow. After the night with Geraldine she sporadically and dimly realizes the truth of her experience, but when she tries to bring it out she feels a constriction in her breast, "And drew in her breath with a hissing sound" (459). The only speech she can manage is a request to her father "That thou this woman send away!" (617). He immediately misinterprets this plea as a violation of hospitality. Not only is Christabel unclear to herself, she is unable to make herself known to others. She speaks the truth, but as a fragment that easily can be misrepresented. If sincere speech is equated with the eloquence of spontaneous overflow in "The Ancient Mariner," in "Christabel" the mark of sincerity is its speechless impotence, its utter defenselessness.

The reason for this impotence is a partial loss of identity in

Christabel. Although she has done no evil and remains the truly good person she was before, nevertheless she has submitted to Geraldine. But instead of sanctifying Christabel, this act of submission has shattered her wholeness. The mysterious relation between the women carries both erotic and maternal overtones, and in a manuscript note on plants and insects Coleridge also speaks of submission in terms that associate these kinds of relationships with martyrdom:

> All offering that is truly sacrificial, i.e. hallowing, sanctifying, proceeds from and is preceded by and the act of a *Yearning* . . . what will not the Mother sacrifice when her bowels are yearning for her children. And this constitutes the diversity of Yearning and desire . . . Yearning offers up, resigns itself—passes wholly into another. Desire [catches *crossed out*] seizes hold of, draws to itself, devours, ravishes—and in its fiercest form (*ex. gr.* See a hornet devouring a peach thro' a magnifying glass) *ravages.*[21]

The way of the martyr is "Yearning," which "offers up, resigns itself—passes wholly into another." This is the endpoint of Christabel's hospitality, the fullness of her relaxation and opening to Geraldine. In contrast, "Desire siezes hold of, draws to itself, devours, ravishes—and in its fiercest form . . . *ravages.*" Like the hornet of this manuscript note, Geraldine draws power from what she desires by consuming it, appropriating its substance, and leaving her victim an empty shell. But she could not perform this act without Christabel's yearning submission. In "Christabel" the instinctive identification with life, the movement of community, which is a sacred impulse in the conversation poetry and in "The Ancient Mariner," becomes so extreme as to be tinged with its opposite. In her absolute hospitality Christabel so relaxes, so submits herself, as to permit the theft of her identity. In its most exaggerated form, the collapse of consciousness becomes suicidal.

Christabel's mysterious opening to Geraldine becomes the central feature of this poem, because it involves the only submission that both can leave her virtue pure and yet also compromise it. She submits so completely that her consciousness is overwhelmed, leaving her to endure but not to know. When the collapsed ego returns to awareness it does not realize what has happened, although Christabel's instinct surely is that some powerful event has occurred. Where Osorio knowingly glories in his unlawful fantasies but is unable to carry them out, Christabel unknowingly entertains the unlawful and then awakes to vague and intensely disturbing dreams. Her misgivings turn her into a kind of anti-poet, a self-divided person deprived of the power to speak and act.

Christabel's alienation from her own activity is far more extreme than that of the Ancient Mariner; she registers only dreams and "sins unknown" (390), whereas the Mariner knows perfectly well that he shot the Albatross, even if he cannot say why. Where the Mariner's response to his situation must be poetic speech, the recurrent spontaneous overflows that forever retell his tale and renew his attempt at self-explanation, Christabel is so out of touch with her own activity that the only possible response is incessant mute prayer. This implies submission to God, denial of one's own wishes through resignation to His will.

Christabel unconsciously moves into the prayerful attitude after Geraldine's entrancement passes; in her sleep she smiles, weeps, and resembles "A youthful hermitess . . . Who praying always, prays in sleep" (320–22). For her, prayer and purity are natural, instinctive. But in "The Pains of Sleep," which Coleridge published with "Christabel," prayer becomes a deliberate effort of the conscious will:

> Ere on my bed my limbs I lay,
> It hath not been my use to pray
> With moving lips or bended knees;
> But silently, by slow degrees,
> My spirit I to Love compose,
> In humble trust mine eye-lids close,
> With reverential resignation,
> No wish conceived, no thought exprest,
> Only a sense of supplication
>
> (1–9)

Here the submission that comes instinctively to Christabel is deliberately built by a patterned sequence which purges the ego and composes the mind to prayerful resignation. In this poem, prayer becomes a conscious act. Coleridge confirms this notion in a manuscript note: "Prayer is an intellectual act. It is the whole man that prays. . . . *Pray always*, says the Apostle;— that is, have the habit of prayer, turning your thoughts into acts by connecting them with the idea of the redeeming God, and even so reconverting your actions into thoughts."[22] It seems likely that the resolution of "Christabel" was to involve this idea of prayer as act: for although Christabel's power of speech is interdicted, her unconscious submission to God is like a spontaneous prayer offered up continuously. She is one "Who, praying always, prays in sleep" (322), and that attitude stemming from her depths might have become an act overcoming the nightmare powers of Geraldine.

But if this was Coleridge's plan, he did not carry it out. "Christabel" remains unfinished, and perhaps this is because prayer could not accomplish what Coleridge wished for in the poem. In the note on insects and plants Coleridge said of Yearning that it "offers itself up, resigns itself, passes wholly into another"; but if this explains Christabel's submission to Geraldine it also explains Christabel's submission to God. Both her submissions are unconscious: they are action purged of volition, experience purged of knowledge. In short, Christabel's two submissions, like the Mariner's two actions, become precisely equivalent and therefore radically indeterminate. Submission emerges as an ambiguous attitude in "Christabel"— and this dooms the poem, which had attempted to purge submission of indeterminacy and portray it as holy. The sacred and the profane are linked inextricably in "The Ancient Mariner," and this ambivalence provides the interpretive indeterminacy that compels the poem to repeat itself forever. The sacred and the profane also are linked inextricably in "Christabel," but unfortunately, this ambivalence creates the dilemma that blocks the poem, bringing it to a halt because its ambiguities cannot be resolved. Just as Christabel ends in a baffled muteness that unfortunately cannot be regarded as a version of transcendental stillness, so Coleridge's poem falls silent.

"Christabel" is the endpoint of Coleridge's explorations of the collapse of consciousness. The child Coleridge described to Poole, the dreamy creature who both feared and envied boyhood physical action, grew up to be a poet who could conceive of integrity of mind only in a condition of isolation. But when he looks beyond the inner integrity achieved in the conversation poetry to seek the kind of worldly power he longed for in childhood, Coleridge gains it only by transcending personality through the dream poem. In his potent nightmare world Coleridge's imagination immediately is drawn to problems of aggression and submission, manipulation and victimization. "The Ancient Mariner" represents his closest approach to reconciling these conflicts: here power surfaces as an obsessive spontaneous overflow that creates a magnificently compelling work. But in "Christabel" Coleridge tries to purge power by showing that it can arise from saintly submission. The result is Christabel's muteness and the unfinished state of the poem. The depersonalized depths that Coleridge touched in his nightmare poetry freed his most powerful poetic voice but at the same time raised the terror of absolute alienation—of a threatening force utterly divorced from the human order. Like Blake and Wordsworth, Coleridge attempted to write a poetry of inclusiveness. But he at last discovered that the murder of self-consciousness could not open infinity in terms acceptable to him; for instead of forming a deep self, his nightmare visions intimated monstrosity. After "Christabel" Coleridge turned aside from poetry to devote his major efforts to prose. Perhaps if he was to live as a social being he felt that he must do so not as a bard but as a sage. For the poet has been proven a threat both to himself and his audience; but the critic of culture can be a thinker, a teacher, a constructive member of society.[23]

5

KEATS
The Invisible Poet

As the sonnet to Leigh Hunt, which prefaces Keats's 1817 *Poems*, proclaims, "Glory and loveliness have passed away," leaving the modern world in a drab, diminished state. So Keats saturates this first book of his poetry with Greek mythology and Spenserian romance in an attempt to force the bloom of a poetic world through the poet's intense enthusiasm and activity.[1] "Sleep and Poetry," the central work of the 1817 volume, presents an ambitious plan for Keats's next ten years of poetry. He will immerse himself in sensuous and erotic experience, but also rise to "the agonies, the strife / Of human hearts."[2] What these explorations have in common is Keats's insistence that everything should enhance actuality, that there should be a seriousness and an exalted sensuousness which transcend the "sense of real things" that "like a muddy stream, would bear along / My soul to nothingness" (157–59). The poet will rescue life from banality, making poetry a heroic action.[3]

But just as the Coleridge of the conversation poetry can imagine activity only in a state of retirement from the world, so the Keats of the 1817 volume can rise to heroism only when he escapes his daily routine. These poems were written by a student of surgery, a young man long in city pent, who travels to the country and reclines in the grass. There, in poem after poem, he depicts himself glutting on nature or reading inspiring literature or imagining remote realms of romance. The energy that Keats lavishly expends is all inner; the enhanced world he pursues is fictive. Like Coleridge, he lives the life of the isolated imagination, an elite and exciting inner existence that is the very antithesis of his drab workaday life. And just as Coleridge struggled to justify his isolate stance by suggesting ways in which the poet in retirement indirectly might become a power in the world, so Keats also explores imaginative routes for rendering the interior exterior. He is aware that failure to bring his imagination into the world will doom his poetic aspirations, turning him from a hero of poetry into an ineffectual dreamer, an escapist.[4]

From the start, then, the problem of Keats's fictions is crucially related to the problem of his personal identity. He wants to write a poetry of heroism, not escapism—but this can be done only by a poet who himself is a hero, not an escapist. The need to see himself as heroic, to see the life of the imagination as a form of action rather than of retirement, must have sparked his great interest in Hazlitt's *Essay on the Principles of Human Action*, which he discovered in the fall of 1817.[5] Hazlitt's philosophy of imaginative action provided a possible foundation for Keats's sense of personal identity. Here was a theory that portrayed the inner life as the source of external life, the imagination as the originator of action.

Hazlitt argues that "The good which any being pursues is always at a distance from him. His wishes, his exertions are always excited by 'an airy, notional good,' by the idea of good, not the reality. But for this there could be no desire, no pursuit of any thing. We cannot strive to obtain what we already possess."[6] For Hazlitt, all significant action is the pursuit of what is imagined. This view provides a justification of Keats's natural poetic ebullience, his lavish imaginative energies. According to Hazlitt, it is precisely such inner energies that activate the whole human being. The self launches forward in pursuit of what it desires, and the pursuit becomes an activity of self-development which in turn expands imaginative capacity, perpetuating the individual's forward movement. Imaginative power thus becomes an actualizing force, which explains why Hazlitt continually praises enthusiasm in his literary criticism. From "On Gusto" Keats learned that "Gusto in art is power or passion defining any object" (IV, p. 77); and from "On Poetry in General," the introductory lecture to Hazlitt's series on the English poets, he discovered that "Impassioned poetry is an emanation of the moral and intellectual part of our nature, as well as of the sensitive—of the desire to know, the will to act, and the power to feel" (V, p. 6).

In Hazlitt's view the imagination grounds meaningful action, and furthermore, such action always turns out to be disinterested. The *Essay on the Principles of Human Action* reaches this conclusion by arguing that self-interested activity is based in the body's needs and sensations, and is aimed toward preserving the existing physical self. In contrast, the imagination is engaged with the future and the unactualized, and since the self has not yet lived this condition, what it anticipates can have no personal physical basis. Therefore, when we project imaginative desire, we necessarily project not merely for ourselves but for everyone. Our imaginative willing must be categorical, not individual. "The imagination, by means of which alone I can anticipate future objects, or be interested in them, must carry me out of myself into the feelings of others by one and the same process by which I am thrown forward . . . into my future being. . . . I could not love myself, if I were not capable of loving others" (I, pp. 1–2). Hazlitt equates egotism with the conservative desire to protect one's existing self, possessions, and perogatives. Imagination becomes the counterforce to this self-interest, because it acts to alter identity, to create a renewed self through the categorical action of realizing a renewed world. The highly imaginative person also becomes a highly selfless person, a being dwelling in a metamorphic ambiance of generous energy, of flowing, transforming reality.

Hazlitt's impact is evident in the letters Keats wrote during the five months following his first acquaintance with the *Essay on the Principles of Human Action*. The glorification of pursuit, the hope that sheer imaginative energy could generate the power to transform reality, is clearly present in the November 1817 remarks on Adam's dream: "What the imagination siezes as Beauty must be truth—whether it existed before or not—for I have the same Idea of all our Passions as of Love they are all in their sublime, creative of essential Beauty. . . . The Imagination may be compared to Adam's dream—he awoke and found it truth."[7] Keats returns to this theme in March 1818, suggesting that "probably every mental pursuit takes its reality and worth from the ardour of the pursuer." Consequently, the most unreal, nebulous objects of desire are "Nothings which are made Great and dignified by an ardent pursuit—Which by the by stamps the burgundy mark on the bottles of our Minds, insomuch as they are able to *'consecrate whate'er they look upon'* " (I, no. 67).

Not only does Keats follow Hazlitt in idealizing pursuit, he also echoes Hazlitt's insistence that true pursuit is disinterested, that the most ardent emotional power is projected by selfless beings. The Adam's dream letter distinguishes between "Men of Power," who "have a proper self," and "Men of Genius," who "are great as certain etherial Chemicals operating on the Mass of neutral intellect—but they have not any individuality, any determined Character" (I, no. 43). Apparently men of power attempt to conserve their force but genius disperses itself, enters into everything in the world and like "ethereal Chemicals" works marvellous tranformations. It surrenders self, only to gain treasure through its creative participation in the world. Self-conscious power therefore seems finite, whereas selfless power is unlimited, infinite. So Keats concludes that he must free himself from self-consciousness, for only when the sense of self is eclipsed can the boundless energy of genius arise. He exclaims, "O for a Life of Sensations rather than of Thoughts" and he also condemns "consequitive reasoning," in the Adam's dream letter and several times afterward.

Thinking becomes the antithesis to feeling, self-consciousness becomes the antithesis to power. Consequently, Keats's idea of Negative Capability turns less on the poet's actively suspended judgement than on his emphatic faith that feeling can overpower doubts. For "with a great poet the sense of Beauty overcomes every other consideration, or rather all consideration" (I, no. 45). His irritation with poetry that consciously proclaims itself as poetry is marked in letters of this period: offended by Wordsworth's philosophizing, he claims, "We hate poetry that has a palpable design upon us—and if we do not agree, seems to put its hand in its breeches pocket. Poetry should be great & unobtrusive, a thing which enters into one's soul, and does not startle or amaze it with itself but with its subject" (I, no. 59). Several days later he claims, "Poetry should surprise by a fine excess and not by Singularity—it should strike the Reader as a wording of his own highest thoughts." So also for the poet, for "if Poetry comes not as naturally as the Leaves to the tree it had better not come at all" (I, no. 65). A few months later he calls himself a "camelion Poet," a being "not itself—it has no self—it is every thing and nothing—It has no character"; and he adds, "A Poet is the most unpoetical of any thing in existence: because he has no Identity" (I, no. 118). The ideal poet becomes unseen, becomes a hidden and changeable source of power invading nature and transforming it without his readers becoming aware of the effort. In the best poetry the poet's identity altogether disappears.

These letters suggest that the esteem for disinterest which Keats picked up from Hazlitt has been carried to an extreme—

for Keats aspires to be not merely a selfless poet, but an invisible one. And this will become the paradoxical form of his identity: himself vanishing, nature then will bloom. The Keatsian poet will become an unacknowledged hero by sacrificing his inwardness to give rise to a transformed outer world, in the form of inspiring poetic works—selfless, natural poems that will redeem the banality of his audience's daily lives. The Poet's personal depth shall be transformed into a public surface that has the power to renew the audience's life force, to turn them into Hazlitt's imaginative activists.

In effect, Keats's invisible poet achieves infinity by giving up his self in order to gain nature. Like Coleridge's Mariner, who becomes an effective poet in the world only when he has lost his conscious self, Keats proposes to sacrifice personality in order to achieve potency. The figures of the Coleridgean possessed poet and the Keatsian invisible poet both involve rejections of the deep self—rejections based on the assumption that power and selfhood are incompatible. But ultimately Coleridge found it intolerable to abandon personality; and as we shall see, Keats also discovered that he could not endure being perpetually selfless.

Keats's first major attempt to enact his notion of the invisible poet is *Endymion*, a poem that tries to show how love can become the self-annihilation that renews the world. Here Keats works out his heroic aspirations in the genre of romance; the poet becomes a lover, a heroic lover who withholds nothing in his quest for the beloved. Keats means Endymion to give his all for love, and through that unstinted giving to gain a poetically transformed nature. In the poem's most famous passage Endymion explains how this self-sacrifice is performed. For him, love paradoxically is both active and passive, an "ardent listlessness" (I, 825)—the highest form of attraction which "becks / Our ready minds to fellowship divine, / A fellowship with essence; till we shine, / Full alchemiz'd, and free of space" (I, 777–80). The full intensity of love disembodies lovers and divests them of personality, "till in the end, / Melting into its radiance, we blend, Mingle, and so become a part of it . . . when we combine therewith, / Life's self is nourish'd by its proper pith, / And we are nurtured like a pelican brood" (I, 809–15). Endymion speculates that the immense energies produced by this dissolving union "might bless / The world with benefits unknowingly . . . who, of men, can tell / That flowers would bloom, or that green fruit would swell . . . If human souls did never kiss and greet?" (I, 825–26; 835–42). As the lovers disappear, hidden within the flame of their ultimate intensity, a blooming world appears in their place.[8]

However, this process is not enacted in Keats's poem. Instead of demonstrating a selfless activity that intensifies until it annihilates itself in passivity and is reborn as an enhanced world, Keats offers a busy plot. Endymion interminably pursues his goddess through the earth, the underworld, the seas, and the skies—and in the end Cynthia vaguely explains it was all necessary because of her "foolish fear . . . and then decrees of fate: / And then 'twas fit that from this mortal state / Thou shouldst, my love, by some unlook'd for change / Be spiritualized" (IV, 989–93). Keats aspires to heroic self-sacrifice in *Endymion*, but what he produces is a nervous, superficial hyperactivity that thinly disguises the work's nebulousness. This poem, which Keats wrote deliberately in order to make himself into a poet, represents a forcing of energies that do not bloom into life.

He was well aware that the exaggerated activity of *Endymion* was a symptom of impotence. As he remarked in a letter of 23 January 1818, during the writing of *Hyperion*, "The nature of *Hyperion* will lead me to treat it in a more naked and grecian Manner [than *Endymion*]—and the march of passion and endeavour will be undeviating—and one great contrast between them will be—that the Hero of the written tale being mortal is led on, like Buonaparte, by circumstance; whereas the Apollo in Hyperion being a fore-seeing God will shape his actions like one" (I, no. 53). Keats sees that the hyperactivity of *Endymion* actually is a form of passivity, for instead of shaping his own actions Endymion is "led on, like Buonaparte, by circumstance." Perhaps then, heroism must be shown through the epic rather than the romance. The projected *Hyperion* will display an undeviating "march of passion and endeavour," will get down to direct action and demonstrate what power can be.

But Keats found that he could not fulfill his activist ambitions for *Hyperion*. What we have in the fragment he abandoned is not heroic power, but an impression of agonizing ineffectuality. In this tale the old order of Saturn has been overthrown, and the fallen gods inhabit a world stripped of beauty and power—a world very much like the banal world which the 1817 volume of poems continually strives to transform. In this devitalized atmosphere the dethroned sun god

Hyperion strains and glitters in his wrath, creating a huge display but failing to generate real energy. Both Endymion's hyperactivity and Hyperion's spectacular anger betray impotence. However, *Hyperion* offers the promise of true heroism in Apollo, Hyperion's successor who in the last passages of the poem awakes to an awareness of his immortal powers. But Keats no sooner introduces Apollo than *Hyperion* breaks off. Apparently, he cannot imagine what the new god will do.

The failure of *Endymion* and *Hyperion* signals a crisis in Keats's career. He has experimented with fictive forms that might help define his poetic identity, but neither the heroic self-sacrifice of romance nor the straightforward heroism of the epic provides a valid grounding for this poet. Both of Keats's poems produce hyperactivity, not confident action. So when he writes "The Eve of St. Agnes" he indeed does return to romance, but not in the mode of *Endymion*. As he himself saw, Endymion is "led on, like Buonaparte, by circumstance," and in Porphyro he does not repeat Endymion's mistake. This new hero will be the poet who creates the plot of the poem he is living. But the heroism thus evoked is hardly epic, for it notably lacks straightforwardness. Put bluntly, Porphyro is a manipulator.

At every turn in the poem Porphyro himself creates the circumstances that will permit him effective activity. Where Hyperion merely rages ineffectually, Porphyro steals into his enemy's castle, convinces his beloved's nursemaid to let him enter her bedchamber, conceals himself there, and then sets the stage for and sings the song that leads to her seduction. She responds to his call in the belief that she is dreaming, and he uses her belief in the old wives' tale that virgins will see their future lovers in St. Agnes' Eve dreams to have his own way with her. Stating the case in this way darkens Porphyro's motives excessively, for he obviously is a true lover—another Endymion who by the ardor of his pursuit hopes to win his Madeline and bring her into a new world worthy of their passion. But stating the case in this way does foreground the unavoidable manipulative element present in "The Eve of St. Agnes."[9]

In this poem, Keats's desire for poetic invisibility has taken a surprising turn. He discovers that the effective invisible poet is not Hazlitt's disinterested man, and does not sacrifice himself in the manner of Endymion. Quite the contrary: to become invisible is to manage the action of the poem one is living, without others becoming aware of this activity. Hidden in the depths, the skilled invisible poet manipulates the appearances of the surface in order to encourage others to do his bidding. In *Songs of Experience* Blake wrote a poetry of manipulation, but implicitly to reject manipulation as a poetic strategy. He passionately advocates open expressiveness, translucency—but in contrast, Keats can see some virtues in manipulative activity. After all, if Porphyro had not adroitly managed the appearances, his love for Madeline never could have been fulfilled.

For Madeline loves Porphyro, but finds it impossible to state her love openly because of her family's opposition and her own fears. After Porphyro as invisible poet has set his stage and sung his song—has had the art to invade her dream without Madeline's noticing his actual presence—she calls aloud to him, and it is this declaration of a previously unspoken love that gives him the courage to proceed with her, to actualize the physical love they both wish for. So Porphyro's invasion of Madeline's privacy happily leads to a shared privacy, making their dreams into reality as their inwardness is converted to external action.

But when Madeline at last realizes she has really acted she is dismayed, and quite understandably so. For where dream events are imaginary and without consequences in the world, her embrace of Porphyro precipitates a host of actual dangers. She awakes to find herself committed to and dependent upon her lover, in a castle inhabited by his enemies. Her days of safety and peace are over. The loss of Madeline's virginity necessitates her entry into adulthood, into a world where real action is taken and real consequences must be faced. Either she must deny Porphyro, or summon the courage to follow him. As a sleeper she was "Blissfully haven'd both from joy and pain . . . Blinded alike from sunshine and from rain, / As though a rose should shut, and be a bud again" (240–43). Dreams allow the unrestrained indulgence of the imagination, but actuality involves burdens as well as satisfactions. Having once acted, Madeline finds herself in a situation which compels further activity. As the poem closes, Madeline and Porphyro leave the castle and vanish into the storm outside. Keats portrays their resolve clearly, but leaves their fate unspecified. They face a cold and hostile world, something far worse than the merely banal reality implied by the 1817 *Poems,* and their safety is far from assured. But the only alternative to their active love and courage is the sterile prudence of Madeline's nurse and the old beadsman. Real life is purchased at the price of risk.

So the escapist self-containment of dreams is sacrificed by their actualization. Fictive plenitude and security gives way to immersion in a contingent world of potential gratifications and hazards. And if the dream's wholeness is shattered by enactment, "The Eve of St. Agnes" clearly suggests that the dreamer's personal integrity is similarly compromised. This is especially true of Porphyro. Although he has acted out of love, he has acted effectively because of his manipulative skill. Keats's previous notion of the invisible poet now can be seen as a fantasy of limitlessness, a naive wish that the integrity of the self could be preserved through a self-effacement that somehow would benevolently actualize a poetic world. But in "The Eve of St. Agnes" Keats suggests that in order to be effective, a poet must sacrifice his imaginary wholeness and accept an actually flawed identity. Porphyro makes his imagination effective through manipulation, a procedure that brings love close to betrayal, communion close to domination. The discovery of this poem is that when the imagination initiates real action, its purity is sacrificed. Where the Endymions of the world remain forever innocent but also ineffectual, the Porphyros combine their idealism with pragmatism and purchase the power to act at the expense of inevitably mixed motives. By now, Keats absolutely must part company with Hazlitt on the question of imaginative disinterestedness—the poet cannot sacrifice himself, for he has personal desires and passionately wishes them to be fulfilled.

But Hazlitt himself had modified his earlier views in his "Letter to Gifford," which Keats quoted at length in his own letter of 14 February–3 May to his brother and siter-in-law.[10] Keats's selection from Hazlitt is of great interest:

I affirm, Sir, that Poetry, that the imagination, generally speaking, delights in power, in strong excitement, as well as in truth, in good, in right, whereas pure reason and the moral sense approve only of the true and good. I proceed to show that this general love or tendency to immediate excitement or theatrical effect, no matter how produced, gives a Bias to the imagination often inconsistent with the greatest good, that in Poetry triumphs over Principle, and bribes the passions to make a sacrifice of common humanity. You say that it does not, that there is no such original Sin in Poetry, that it makes no such sacrifice or unworthy compromise between poetical effect and the still small voice of reason. . . . "Do we read with more pleasure of the ravages of a beast of prey than of the Shepherds pipe upon the Mountain?" No but we do read with pleasure of the ravages of a beast of prey, and we do so on the principle I have stated, namely from the sense of power abstracted from the sense of good . . .[11]

In these remarks Hazlitt's gusto, his love of imaginative energy, overrides his theory of disinterestedness. For him the "Original Sin" of poetry is to sometimes obliterate reason and morality through sheer emotional power. The language he uses to describe this—"immediate excitement or theatrical effect, no matter how produced"—implies an element of manipulation. The poetry of power becomes sheer energy abetted by sheer showmanship, and its headlong effect drowns out the "still small voice of reason" and of morality. In November 1817 Keats could exclaim, "O for a life of Sensations rather than of Thoughts!" in the belief that such a life promised deliverance from self-consciousness and egotism. Now it appears to him that quite the opposite may be true—that exercise of power may be one of the great selfish pleasures.

In this same letter Keats himself reflects on disinterestedness, arguing that "Very few men have ever arrived at a complete disinterestedness of Mind: very few have been influenced by a pure desire of the benefit of others." He adds that

I perceive how far I am from any humble standard of disinterestedness—Yet this feeling ought to be carried to its highest pitch, as there is no fear of its ever injuring society—which it would do I fear pushed to an extremity—For in wild nature the Hawk would loose his Breakfast of Robins and the Robin his of Worms The Lion must starve as well as the swallow—The greater part of Men make their way with the same instinctiveness, the same unwandering eye from their purposes, the same animal eagerness as the Hawk—The Hawk wants a mate, so does the Man—look at them both they set about it and procure on[e] in the same manner—they get their food in the same manner—The noble animal Man for his amusement smokes his pipe—the Hawk balances about the Clouds—that is the only difference of their leisures. This it is that makes the Amusement of Life—to a speculative Mind. I go among the Fields and catch a glimpse of a stoat or a fieldmouse peeping out of the withered grass—the creature hath a purpose and its eyes are bright with it—I go amongst the buildings of a city and I see Man hurry-

ing along—to what? The Creature has a purpose and his eyes are
bright with it. (II, no. 159)

Keats links energy with self-interest, and suggests that men
like animals are moved less by thought than by instinct. Apparently, the pure energy that he had hoped to realize through the
figure of the invisible poet issues not as a disinterested redemption of nature, but as the drive for self-preservation, which
involves incessant aggressiveness. Just as the "Hawk" forever
must pursue the "Robins" and in turn the "Robin must hunt
the "Worms," so people continually must assert their own
interests at the expense of others. In a stroke, Hazlitt's
idealistic vision has been inverted—true pursuit becomes the
hunt, a thing very different from the imagination's selfless
enactment of a beautiful and benevolent world. Keats tries to
soften this threatening view by suggesting that perhaps the
beauty of energetic attitudes and actions may compensate for
their moral ambiguity: "may I not in this be free of sin? May
there not be superior beings amused with any graceful, though
instinctive attitude my mind may fall into as I am entertained
with the alertness of a Stoat or the anxiety of a Deer? Though a
quarrel in the streets is a thing to be hated, the energies displayed in it are fine." Like Hazlitt, Keats feels that the attraction of power can override moral considerations. He attempts
to reconcile this conflict through an aesthetic attitude, which
becomes a new version of disinterestedness. Perhaps like some
"superior being" the poet can lift himself above the selfish ends
pursued by the characters he creates, and appreciate their
activity purely as an exercise of energy. But the appeal of this
disinterested aesthetic posture cannot really rival the lure of
manipulation for Keats; for like Madeline's dreaming, aesthet-
icism purchases its imperturbable integrity only by remaining
unengaged with actuality.

And so in "Lamia" Keats explores the problem glossed over
in "The Eve of St. Agnes": the moral dilemma of truly effective
poetic identity. This poem suggests that to be effective is to be
flawed, to act is to operate from mixed motives, to be a poet in
the world is to sacrifice personal integrity and wholeness.
These disintegrations are focused in the figure of Lamia, who
like Porphyro, tries to create the plot of the poem she is living.
The manipulative theatricality of "The Eve of St. Agnes"—
Porphyro's stage setting and his performance—are exaggerated in the figure of Lamia. Hazlitt had remarked that the

"immediate excitement or theatrical effect" of the imagination, "no matter how produced," might overpower reason and the moral sense, and this observation exactly describes Lamia's attempt to deceive Lycius. Although she truly loves him, her identity is flawed: as snake-woman she is the mistress of appearances, a creature of gaudy coloring and complex contortions who can do anything with Lycius, tell him anything, except the truth. Her powers of illusion become a function of her hidden weakness, for she needs all the rich resources of fictiveness to conceal her secret identity. She is flamboyant on the surface, flawed in her depths.

Thus Lamia's situation is quite different from Porphyro's in "The Eve of St. Agnes." At the right moment his truth can come out, because by then he has nothing to hide. The difference between Porphyro's and Lamia's circumstances suggests that Keats is reassessing the problems involved in nature's enhancement. His early view of a banal world requiring redemption through poetic heroism now is modified by his attention to the poet's own character. For it is Lamia's imperfection that makes her powers necessary; she must project her dream as theater because she herself is an inadequate being. And just as her character is mixed, so our reaction to her devices also is ambivalent. We see the inextricable mixture of love and force, of true feeling and dazzling performance. The simple integrity of early Keatsian heroism has given way to the complexities of theater.[12]

Keats intensifies his case by also making Lycius a mixed creature. And here he achieves a resonance, a plausibility of character that naturalizes the mixed condition symbolized by Lamia's half-serpent identity. Though Lycius gladly is entranced by his mistress, after awhile the charm wears thin. He begins to be bored. For although Lamia possesses unlimited powers of illusion and uses them with the full devotion of her love, Lycius does not have equivalent powers of attention. If Lamia is the actress in the dream, Lycius is the audience—and he could only match her tremendous performance by total absorption. Since they are involved in the realization of a perfect love, anything less than absolute commitment from either party will be insufficient. So when Lycius's attention strays for just one minute Lamia has reason to be alarmed, knowing well "That but a moment's thought is passion's passing bell." He asks her, "Why do you sigh, fair creature?" but she responds "Why do you think?" (II, 39–41). The question ironically echoes Keats's cry, "O for a Life of Sensations rather than of Thoughts!" A life of sensations rather than of thoughts is exactly what Lamia has given Lycius, and it has not been enough.

Through Lycius Keats investigates the problems involved in his own youthful aspiration to become the invisible poet involved in everlasting pursuit and the infinite play of imaginative energy. The life of sensations rather than of thoughts indeed does annihilate selfhood, but not by one's absorption in incessant action, as Keats initially has supposed. For in fact Lycius is passive rather than active—he is the audience, not the performer. To preserve their love he requires an ability to remain passive as prodigious as Lamia's power of dramatic manipulation. But he simply cannot hold self in abeyance forever. He too wants the actor's role, and at last he seizes it.

Where Lamia had hidden herself within the power of her illusions Lycius must emerge openly as himself—for he is reacting against his history of suppression as audience. If he has been dominated, he in turn will become the master. He argues, "What mortal hath a prize, that other men / May be confounded and abash'd withal, / But lets it sometimes pace abroad majestical, / And triumph" (II, 57–60). He puts his dream on exhibition to show off his power, and this crude forcing kills it. Now love is changed to cruelty, desire is changed to lust. Raw power becomes the central value of the poem. Lycius finds that "Against his better self, he took delight / Luxurious in her sorrows," and Lamia discovers that "She burnt, she lov'd the tyranny" (II, 73–74; 81). At last Lamia and Lycius find a perverted pleasure in the roles of victim and violator. Apparently it had been Lamia's invisible poetry which protected the purity of their relations; for the moment that Lycius publicly reveals their dream its latently aggressive implications become manifest. As a highly visible poet, Lycius unfortunately succeeds in unmasking the sadomasochistic element inherent in love.

Lycius's tutor Apollonius practices an even more potent form of public vision than does Lycius. He comes to the wedding and brazenly stares at Lamia until his "eye, / Like a sharp spear, went through her utterly, / Keen, cruel, perceant, stinging" (II, 299–301). By showing the powers of analytic insight to be more penetrating than the visions of poetry Apollonius destroys love's dream, converting it into a mere illusion. Truly the public eye has emerged supreme in *Lamia*, and the poem ends

with Lamia's disappearance and Lycius' death. Apollonius remains as the ultimate victor, the man of power whose science
is less concerned with the revelation of truth than with the
assertion of his own dominance.

"Lamia" points up the dilemmas of manipulation. In its
least objectionable form it is practiced by Lamia, the imaginative activist, to bring the dream of love into actuality. But if
we sympathize with her aims and appreciate her performance
nevertheless we cannot fail to notice that her subtle creation is
a triumph of power, an imposition of her will and her dream on
another person. Like the knight of "La Belle Dame Sans
Merci," Lycius simultaneously is embowered in beauty and
deprived of his freedom. In this sense, Lamia's love latently is a
species of aggression. The strategies of visible power pursued
by Lycius and Apollonius reveal the element of aggression
much more clearly, but in fact it is an unavoidable implication
of all types of manipulation in the poem. In "Lamia," all
mortal motivation becomes fatally mixed. For if people take
action at all, if they work in the world to further their visions
and beliefs, they can do so only at some expense to others. Love
becomes mixed with aggression, heroism becomes mixed with
villainy, creation becomes mixed with destruction. Action
must be purchased at a terrible price—the flawing, the fatal
compromise, of character.

The poem's prologue suggests that perhaps this is not so with
the gods. This interpolated story of divine conflict and manipulation, in which Lamia figures, ends harmoniously. Lamia
conceals a nymph who has been pursued by satyrs in order to
protect her, but when Hermes desires this creature and offers
to change Lamia into a woman if she will let him see the
nymph, Lamia betrays her charge. In making the nymph visible Lamia exerts the same kind of public power that Lycius
will use on her later in the poem. But in this case the outcome
is fortunate: Hermes mutes his force and quiets the nymph's
fear, and they vanish together in the forest to an embowered
life of eternal concord. "Real are the dreams of Gods" (I, 127),
for the bliss they enjoy is unpoisoned by those acts of manipulation that purchase it. In her happiness the nymph simply
forgets she has been coerced, and Hermes prepares to enjoy her
as a god should, free of guilt and secure within his divine
rights.

The gods intrigue Keats because they command unlimited
power—they can do anything they wish and yet never suffer

the consequences. They represent a version of unboundedness, of the infinite play of energy that exists only in the pure imagination's escape from reality. But if the prospect of power without guilt certainly is appealing, Keats does not consider it a serious possibility for human beings. While he is writing "Lamia" he is also at work on *The Fall of Hyperion*, a poem that meditates on the responsibilities of power. If he did not succeed in completing recasting of the earlier, heroic *Hyperion*, at least his intentions seem fairly clear.

The first *Hyperion* was to have been a display of heroic energy, of straightforward, god-like action. But by now he is ready to renounce this youthful fantasy. So he attempts to humanize his story by having it told by a mortal, a poet who has his vision of the gods only at the cost of great suffering. This poet finds himself before the goddess Moneta, tortured by her accusation that his life is worthless. Are you not a weak dreamer, she asks, one who poisons his own life with unfulfilled fantasies but cannot help mankind? He responds by distinguishing between dreamers and poets: "sure a poet is a sage; / A humanist, physician to all men" (I, 189–90). Had Keats been able to finish this poem presumably he would have shown that poets indeed can be physicians—figures of capable imagination who renew the world's life.

Certainly throughout his career Keats was concerned that his poetry might become escapist—that as a poet he might turn out to be an ineffectual dreamer. But if *The Fall of Hyperion* expresses this apprehension, "Lamia" suggests that perhaps his worst fears were not of the dreamer's impotence but of the poet's excessive power. Keats realizes that the engaged imagination has tremendous manipulative abilities, powers that easily can wreak destruction; and in *The Fall of Hyperion* he offers penance for the imagination's sin. Perhaps through humanization, through taking on mortal limitation and accepting suffering, the imagination could be shrieved of its guilt.

These poems Keats produced in the latter part of 1819 dwell on the dilemma of the imagination—on the one hand, its tendency toward ineffectual dreaming, and on the other, its drive to power—its love of manipulation and appetite for domination. His preoccupation with such problems throws retrospective light on the Odes, which he began writing the previous spring. Unlike Keats's romances and epics the Odes are first-person lyrics enacting brief imaginative episodes. Cast in this form, problems posited by the Keatsian imagination become much less severe—for the speaker of the Odes becomes a world unto himself, enacting the drama of his imagination as meditative theater. His objects of thought are not other people, but symbolic presences—an urn, a nightingale, personified Melancholy—so that although he has the opportunity for interaction he is dealing with symbolic aspects of himself, not with a social world. If he manipulates, if he escapes, he can harm only himself—not others.

The isolate self of the Odes becomes a world in which Keatsian imaginative mixtures can be safely deployed. In the social worlds of "The Eve of St. Agnes" and "Lamia," mixed desires and motives had created a problem for Keats—for his protagonists Porphyro and Lamia found they could act effectively only by sacrificing the purity of their characters. The Keatsian invisible poet longs to be everything and have everything, but this infinitely inclusive vision turns out to be an escapist one, maintainable only through disengagement. Keats needs to find a way of constructing a capable deep self which can include every conceivable mixture without being flawed by this very inclusiveness. His deep self must be founded on the redemption of mixture, a necessity which aligns him with Blake, Wordsworth, and Coleridge. Blake's prophecies struggle to create a deep self as a redemptive working-through of mixed emotions, the Wordsworth of *The Prelude* aspires to mix conflicting moods and experiences within the unfolding harmonies of the growing deep self, and Coleridge unsuccessfully seeks to mix power and identity, the monstrous forces of unconsciousness and the lucidity of self-knowledge, in a deep self that need not walk apart from the world. Paradoxically, the isolationist posture of Keats's Odes becomes the only possible stance from which he can command radical inclusiveness. He must draw apart in order to redeem his own dark powers, to socialize himself—but on the face of it this very project seems contradictory. And so the problem of mixture becomes the most significant issue threading through the Odes.

The world of the Odes has special affinities with the world of "The Ancient Mariner" in its theatrical aspect: both are cases of the self dreaming itself as an imaginary world, and splitting its functions so that it can act all the requisite parts and also be the audience. But where Coleridge suggests that this kind of imaginative reflexivity liberates power but destroys coherence, making the dream of the imagination a nightmare, Keats discovers a way of using mixture creatively through the resources of imaginative theater. For if the tendency to escape is treated as the mixed desire to escape from oneself, then escapism can be theraputic—for it launches the self forward in pursuit of its desires, and as in Hazlitt's *Essay on the Principles of Human Action*, such imaginative exertion can lead to the activity of self-development, the expansion of the individual's capacities. By the same token, if manipulation is taken as mixture, as the efforts of one part of the self to control other parts, the attempt to achieve domination and the effort to resist it can contribute to the self's acuity and agility, providing still another avenue of personal growth. The desires to manipulate, to dominate, to be victimized, all can be reflexively deployed in the drama of self-development.

The "Ode to Psyche," which was the first written of these poems, is the most obvious example of their theatrical reflexivity: here we plainly can see the self turning itself into an imaginary world. "Psyche" repeats the call of the 1817 *Poems* for an enhanced nature offering escape from banality, but here that enhanced world is a protected bower created within the poet himself—it is a refining of his human nature. In a world of unbelief he will make himself the habitation of the goddess, restoring ceremony and beauty to life. Psyche's proper world is within the poet; he both creates and beholds it, brings it into being and himself enjoys it. He takes on the roles of both poet and audience, creating a luxurious inner theater in which Psyche and her lover forever embrace at the borderline of wakefulness and sleep, active lovemaking and unconscious presence. The poet suggests that this suspended state is the perfection and immortality of being, without mentioning his own role in creating the condition. Like Lamia, he has made his dream and embowered his beloved within it. But the dark implications of the manipulative impulse surely are subordinated in the "Ode to Psyche," because the sin of manipulating Psyche is minimized by its reflexive context: she becomes an imagined aspect of the poet himself. Unlike Lycius, who brutalizes and destroys his dream by displaying it publicly, the poet of Psyche has the courtly discretion to conceal his dream deep within himself—so that if Psyche is immobilized, as the victims of love are in "Lamia," she also is protected. The cherishing rather than the victimizing aspects of love are emphasized in "Ode to Psyche." This poem anticipates the love story of "Lamia," but avoids the inevitable disaster of that poem by rendering the dream of love as self-reflexive theater.

The fairly obvious manipulations of "Psyche" are not repeated in the later, greater Odes. These poems conceal their
own technique, and the resulting naturalism of the poetry
becomes a surface successfully screening deep, artful operations. The two greatest Odes, "Ode to a Nightingale" and "Ode
on a Grecian Urn," begin, like "Psyche," with the speaker's
desire to escape his present circumstances. In both poems this
speaker, all brooding depth, is drawn to his opposite—the
superficial shows of the singing bird and the active people
painted on the urn. These are pure outwardness; they display
eternal energy because they are unencumbered by inner being.
Bird and urn perfectly fulfill Keats's earlier desire, "O for a Life
of sensations rather than of Thoughts!" The bird embodies
song without words, and the urn depicts action freed of the
mixed motives and consequences that bedevil human behavior.

And because the urn and bird are pure surface, they immediately invite invasion by the speaker's mind. Like Porphyro,
who first invaded Madeline's bedchamber and then her dream,
the poet is inspired to pursue these eternal but empty appearances and fill them with his imaginings. Where this urge has its
sinister aspect in "The Eve of St. Agnes," it seems perfectly
innocent in the Odes. For bird and urn are nonhuman, and
therefore absolutely superficial. Harboring no soul and belonging to no one, they invite the poet to fill them with his own
inwardness. The manipulative shadow which compromises
Porphyro's motives in "The Eve of St. Agnes" and poisons the
pursuit of dreams in "Lamia" is purified by the reflexive poem.
Since it contains only one person, this poetry eliminates the
possibility of dominating others. The poet of the Odes is free to
release his energies, to pursue his dreams and heroically force
nature's bloom. But to grasp the bird's song and the urn's
action requires more than human energy. These avatars of
immortality, these superficial presences, are able eternally to
radiate energy without depleting themselves. How is the mortal poet to match their powers?

He must contend with infinity in what seems an impossible
pursuit—but his victory comes in an instant. This happens,
because if he needs eternity, it is also true that eternity needs
him. For without the poet's habitation the urn and nightingale
cannot know what they are. They require the poet to complete
them: it takes the love and longing of a mortal being to realize
eternity's value, to make it worth striving for. Eternity needs

an audience, and this is what the enraptured poet becomes. At once spectator and manipulator, the poet is energized to play all the roles that humanize eternity. Now the appearances of infinity can resonate with inner life and awareness, and the invisible depths of the poet are given an outward form, a performance. In this moment nature blooms.

But it cannot last. Qua manipulator of infinity this poet acts with great skill; qua audience he experiences a fatal break in attention—just as Lycius does in "Lamia." Lamia knows that if she loses her audience even for a second her dream theater will be destroyed, and so she reproaches Lycius for his independent thought. In the Odes, the thinking part of the self ceases to be absorbed in the dramatic illusion for just one second, and this shatters the poet's willing suspension of disbelief. At this point he has a choice. One option would be to suppress thought and continue performance, returning to the 1817 posture of "O for a Life of Sensations rather than Thoughts!" At a similar point of decision Coleridge's dream poetry takes just this course by collapsing consciousness to generate power. But instead Keats admits the claims of thought, and destroys his own dramatic illusion.

This refusal to suppress rival powers of the soul certainly is courageous and honest, and it represents an heroic attempt at inclusiveness. But like Coleridge's suppressions, it only can lead to renewed self-division. For the poet instantly becomes aware of his mixed motivations, which create a terrible conflict within himself. He has wished for both infinity and humanity, for the invisibility of pure action and for self awareness and identity. In attempting to reconcile these ends through artistic manipulation, the poet has come so close to success that he almost was ready to manipulate himself out of existence, making himself not merely an invisible poet, but a nonexistent one. For if his dream really had come alive that would dictate the final disappearance of his inner self—himself vanishing, nature would bloom. This sentimental consummation, which Keats could wish for in *Endymion*, now must be confronted lucidly as a form of imaginative suicide. So the unavoidably self-conscious poet is left with the conflict of having created the dream that he then was compelled to destroy. Unlike Coleridge, he simply cannot collapse his consciousness to achieve power, sacrifice his self-awareness to gain the capacity for unlimited action.

At the heart of "Ode to a Nightingale" and "Ode on a Grecian

Urn" lies a penetrating critique of the entire Keatsian poetic enterprise. These poems recognize that the poet of invisibility, that paradoxical figure of absent identity and present power, is at once the imagination's desire and an actual impossibility. But if the poems unveil this contradiction, they also show it nearly being reconciled in the complex, intensive imaginative activity of the poet. His mission is to attempt what cannot be done, and the amazement of the poetry is that he almost succeeds in doing it. So his failure becomes less a defeat than a fruitful mixing of creation and destruction. These Odes recognize that the imagination perennially seeks to create that which it must itself destroy.

In one way these Odes aim at lucidity, inclusiveness, the resonant condition of wholeness—but in another, they defend illusion, self-division, the theater of the mind. For without the projection of illusions, the triumph of lucidity would be meaningless. Apollonius in "Lamia" illustrates that the completely lucid man is a shrunken and petty soul; it seems that lucidity only has value when it is counterpointed by the soul-enlarging, energizing force of dreams. Creation and destruction, illusion and lucidity, feeling and thought, must mix in the resonating soul. "Ode on a Grecian Urn" and "Ode to a Nightingale" show the escapist and realist impulses as part of a collaboration and conflict of human capacities which leads to growth. Without the urge to escape one's condition there could be no activity— but without the lucid confrontation of one's dreams there would be only unconflicted sentimental fantasies such as Madeline's St. Agnes rituals—which arrested, rather than fostered, her growth. That is why these Odes create dreams which then must end. As in "The Eve of St. Agnes," where Madeline and Porphyro enjoy their dream but later must exit into the world, the speaker of these Odes has his imaginative experience but at the poem's end must exit his dream. Paradoxically, it is the very ending of these dreams that ensures their effectuality.

These Odes use dreams rather than interminably dwelling in them. The Keatsian dream becomes not a wish-fulfillment but an instigation to developmental activity—and intensity becomes identified with the soul's mobility and penetration, the untrammeled creative mixture of its partial and competing interests. The hallmarks of the deep self evolved in the Odes are complexity and agility.

The "Ode on Melancholy" further demonstrates this Keatsian swiftness in a meditation on melancholy, a mixed mood partly pleasurable and partly painful. The poem's speaker sees melancholy as a power that descends "Sudden from heaven like a weeping cloud." This Melancholy is a manipulator, a part of the self that takes the speaker by surprise. But he will not "go . . . to Lethe" or dull his awareness in any other way to alleviate the feeling; instead, he elects to intensify his consciousness, to enter into a combat with melancholy—he will use his mood rather than being used by it. His strategy is to seek out beauty, to "glut . . . sorrow on a morning rose," or to hold his angry mistress's hand "And feed deep, deep upon her peerless eyes." By contemplating beauty in the midst of his pain he will triumph over melancholy, for it will have been used to give beauty an intensity, a poignance, that it normally lacks. Paradoxically, the melancholy man becomes the man most capable of enjoyment. By his activism this speaker has found a way of converting pain into pleasure.

But in the poem's last stanza his initial victory is reversed as he realizes melancholy is the mood that foreshadows the end of all things. If his mistress is glorious now, still "She dwells with Beauty—beauty that must die." Melancholy is recognized as the deep feeling for our human limits, and so this mortal speaker is bested—he becomes a trophy hung in the shrine of Melancholy. But the final twist of the poem is to transform this defeat into a sort of victory, as the speaker affirms his insight that "in the very temple of Delight / Veil'd Melancholy has her sovran shrine, / Though seen of none save him whose strenuous tongue / Can burst Joy's grape against his palate fine." Relentlessly strenuous and lucid, the speaker accepts his mortality and the deep meaning of the melancholy mood, yet nevertheless repeats his affirmation that the beauty won from such pain is worthwhile.

Beauty and death become inextricably mixed; and indeed, death becomes the price of the most intense realizations of beauty. It is only the connoisseur "whose strenuous tongue / Can burst Joy's grape against his palate fine" who will realize the profound value of beauty—a value that can be recognized only through beauty's very destruction.[13] The mixed motives in "The Eve of St. Agnes" and "Lamia," which rendered all the poems' actions morally ambiguous, resemble the mixed emotions that are the subject of "Ode on Melancholy." Just as in "The Eve of St. Agnes" love was inextricably mixed with aggression, so in this Ode the feeling for beauty is inextricably mixed with the feeling for death. And if Porphyro did not allow the moral ambiguities of his situation to keep him from the action that could realize his dream, in a similar fashion the speaker of the "Ode on Melancholy" does not allow the mixture of emotions to keep him from the strenuous action that can realize his pleasure. This Ode takes the extremely ambitious, activist position that profound pleasure can be experienced only by the inclusively deep self which recognizes and admits the claims of absolutely all its perceptions.

"To Autumn," the last-written of the Odes, seems at first glance to be a relaxed and reconciled poem. Indeed, it very often has been read as Keats's celebration of the natural passing of the year and his rich submission to nature's rhythms—and perhaps even to the inevitability of his own death.[14] But on closer examination, the sumptuous surface of the poem can be seen to conceal the intense manipulative activity of an invisible poet. "To Autumn" is strongly reminiscent of "The Eve of St. Agnes;" for its hidden poet arranges the year's appearances and takes us into his dream of autumn just as Porphyro arranges the appearances in Madeline's bedchamber and takes her into his dream of love.

The Ode begins by suggesting that the season itself is like a Keatsian invisible poet, for in the first stanza it is a hidden presence working to "fill all fruit with ripeness to the core; / To swell the gourd, and plump the hazel shells / With a sweet kernel." Autumn becomes a manipulator whose disguised working makes nature bloom. Beneath the surface of its fruits is a depth of action; beneath the ease of nature lurks a masterful art. The season triumphs by overpowering with a stage setting of luxurious sensuousness—in this poem nature's bloom becomes a seductive ripeness that tricks the bees into believing "warm days will never cease, / For summer has o'er-brimmed their clammy cells."

But in the second stanza the invisible season materializes as a personification, a goddess "sitting careless on a granary floor . . . Or on a half-reap'd furrow sound asleep." It is as though the poet of "Ode to a Nightingale" and "Ode on a Grecian Urn" had succumbed to his own creation, forsaking his inwardness to merge into the surface of his dream. The actress becomes a part of her own performance, and in the process loses her invisibility. Now mystery is replaced by openness, depth by surface, and action by relaxation. This personified Autumn appears in the careless attitude that Keats termed indolence.

His letter of 14 February–3 May 1819 explains that indolence involves a lack of intensity which is a pleasurable contrast for normally intense people: "In this state of effeminacy the fibres of the brain are relaxed in common with the rest of the body, and to such a happy degree that pleasure has no show of enticement and pain no unbearable frown. Neither Poetry, nor Ambition, nor Love have any alertness of countenance as they pass by me." Indolence cancels out the intense person's inclination to activity, giving him an interval of much-needed rest. Keats concludes, "This is the only happiness; and is a rare instance of advantage in the body overpowering the Mind."

In "To Autumn" the personified body of Autumn overpowers the invisible inwardness of the season; the sensuous surfaces seduce their own manipulator into coming out of hiding. She lies indolently exposed amidst her own creations in what Keats termed "the only happiness"—the illusion that activity now is unnecessary. But the poet who wrote this Ode is aware of that delusion, for he sees that the relaxed figure of Autumn is defenseless and ripe for winter's scythe. So it seems that Autumn has been a surface masking the real creator of this poem, who allows the season to reveal itself but has retained his own invisibility behind that performance. Through the indolence of personified Autumn he can show how we trick ourselves into accepting death, without himself wholly becoming a victim of the ruse. He now continues to manipulate Autumn, maintaining the illusion of easy naturalness by singing her a song which touches the aftermath of ripeness with a renewed springlike bloom. The harvested fields become "rosy," the "clouds bloom the soft-dying day," the "full-grown lambs loud bleat."

His song is a mixture of deception and truth. Evoking spring's presence in autumn cannot delay the onset of winter, yet it is a triumphant example of the same hidden manipulation that Autumn uses to "fill all fruit with ripeness to the core." Within the declining season the season of birth appears; beneath the easy surface of the song a concealed activity labors to conserve and distill beauty. The invisible poet cannot rescue Autumn and himself from death, but he can work to enhance life to the fullest extent possible.

Nature's bloom becomes subtly forced, becomes a function of incessant artistic mixtures. The naturalness of Autumn's indolent surface is created by an extreme inner intensity. Autumn herself does not have the lucidity to grasp her own self-deception, but the invisible, protectively deceiving poet maintains his self-awareness, and in the process creates a poetry of simultaneous ease and effort, naturalism and artfulness. This sophisticated Ode at last fulfills the youthful aspiration of the 1817 *Poems* for a poetic heroism that could force nature's bloom. In addition, the superb technique of "To Autumn" rounds out the Odes as a group; for it is an example of virtually invisible reflexivity, a deeper and more skillful enactment of the strategies of "Ode to Psyche." There the poet quite overtly made his mind into a world that embowered his goddess. But if in "To Autumn" he does the same thing, this time he succeeds in remaining concealed and so takes us into his dream—that it might be nature, not the human imagination, which protects and embowers the things that we love.

As a group the Odes meditate upon the mixed workings of the human imagination, showing that the creative urge has a destructive aspect—but also showing that this destruction opens new potential for growth. In these poems Keats finds a form that can cope with his need to escape and control his will to power and to manipulation, by giving these conflicting drives a vital function within the individual's process of self-development. The imaginary theater of the mind productively deploys these capacities, which in Keats's social poetry bring on destruction. The imaginative mixtures that constantly threaten to pollute Keats's social world are liberated within the sphere of the individual personality, resulting in the creation of a profoundly humane, capable deep self. But when Keats's career was interrupted by his death he was facing a problem similar to Coleridge's—he saw the isolate personality as redeemable, but he had not really found a way for this isolate being to emerge into the world without sacrificing its purity. Coleridge's conversation poems and Keats's Odes are charmed circles, havens for the individual sensibility—but they are severely threatened by the social worlds of "The Ancient Mariner" and "Lamia."

6

BYRON
The Surface Self

In 1814 Byron wrote in his journal, "When I am tired—as I generally am—out comes this, and down goes every thing. But I can't read it over;—and God knows what contradictions it may contain. If I am sincere with myself (but I fear one lies more to one's self than to any one else), every page should confute, refute, and utterly abjure its predecessor."[1] The personal inconsistency he confesses to here was frequently commented on by others. Lady Blessington, who knew Byron well during his later years in Italy, gives a particularly vivid account of it:

> Byron seems to take a peculiar pleasure in ridiculing sentiment and romantic feelings; and yet the day after will betray both, to an extent that appears impossible to be sincere, to those who had heard his previous sarcasms: that he is sincere, is evident, as his eyes fill with tears, his voice becomes tremulous, and his whole manner evinces that he feels what he says. All this appears so inconsistent, that it destroys sympathy, or if it does not quite do that, it makes one angry with oneself for giving way to it for one who is never two days of the same way of thinking, or at least expressing himself. He talks for effect, likes to excite astonishment, and certainly destroys in the minds of his auditors all confidence in his stability of character.[2]

Lady Blessington can feel no assurance of Byron's "stability of character." She suggests that his inconsistency includes not only a puzzling changeability of mood but also an unpredictable alteration of attitude from sincerity to performance, and from true belief to sarcasm or irony. Byron's personality appears to be a dazzling succession of elements that do not cohere.

This conspicuous lack of personal unity is reflected in his

poetry, which throughout his career displays a huge variety of postures and tones. Byron's incessant mobility seems to place him apart from the other Romantic poets, who value personal consistency and identity, and work to achieve a sense of wholeness in their poetry. Indeed, the difference is so marked that Byron sometimes has been considered not a Romantic poet at all.[3] But here Byron shall be approached as a Romantic, albeit a perverse one, on the grounds that he shares categorical assumptions about the deep self with his contemporaries. Like the others, Byron assumes that personal identity results from the turn toward inwardness, the creation of an interior poetic world that builds the core of selfhood. In this view real personality becomes an affair of depth, not surface; of integrity, not display. But where the other poets do succeed in finding themselves when they turn inward, Byron's explorations in depth are largely unsuccessful. This immensely mobile poet cannot discover the interior self-consistency that he deeply desires, and his very failure exacerbates his mobility—for if he cannot find himself, he can deflect his pain and puzzlement by writing a poetry of hyperbolic performance and display in an attempt at diversion.[4]

As he said of his versifying, "To withdraw *myself* from *myself* . . . has ever been my sole, my entire, my sincere motive in scribbling at all; and publishing is also the continuance of the same object, by the action it affords the mind, which else recoils upon itself."[5] But if poetry can offer the relief of self-escape, it does so at the price of increased personal fragmentation. For the more Byron evades himself, the more completely he is lost. And this becomes the penalty of any kind of activity: when the fragmented self is roused to action, the outcome must be accelerated fragmentation, in the form of increased superficiality. In *Childe Harold's Pilgrimage* Byron images this degenerative process in the form of a shattered mirror which multiplies the reflection of an originally single image, splintering the whole into a proliferating succession. It "makes / A thousand images of one that was, / The same, and still the more, the more it breaks; / And thus the heart will do which not forsakes, / Living in shattered guise."[6]

As the Byronic self becomes more various it also becomes more superficial. The image of one surface is exchanged for the reflection of untold thousands. At times Byron can live with this condition cheerfully, taking delight in the virtuosity of his poetic performances and scoffing at writers who aspire to meaningfulness and profundity. But in Canto 3 of *Childe Harold's Pilgrimage* he tries to achieve depth by writing Wordsworthian nature poetry. Of course, this attempt at profundity may be superficially motivated, for he is both mimicking another poet's style and responding to pressures from the outside—at the time Shelley was urging him to write this sort of poetry.[7] Nevertheless, for a person of Byron's temperament the poetry of depth may have held a great attraction: meditative inwardness and its literary form, the self-contained organic poem, could have provided boundaries that organized the self and stilled its incessant, confusing mobility. If he could not bear to look into himself, possibly he could achieve coherence by looking into Wordsworthian nature. Perhaps "true Wisdom's world will be / Within its own creation, or in thine, / Maternal Nature!" (3, 46).

The embodiment of these hopes becomes Lake Leman, a perfectly still, mirrorlike body of water which, like Thoreau's Walden Pond, is centered in the heart of nature. By its shores "All heaven and earth are still—though not in sleep, / But breathless, as we grow when feeling most; / And silent, as we stand in thoughts too deep:— / All heaven and earth are still." In this place of quiet fullness, mobility is suppressed to create the soul of poet and nature. "All is concentered in a life intense, / Where not a beam, nor air, nor leaf is lost, / But hath a part of being" (3, 89). The world manifests Wordsworthian tranquillity; meditative centering unveils the deep life of the spirit. "Then stirs the feeling infinite."

Byron is deeply attracted to this version of infinity, for it transcends not only the individuality of leaf, beam, and air, but also that of the poet's mind. The moment of being "purifies from self," breaks the bonds of egotism to create a transpersonal, all-uniting reality. Ironically, for Byron the achievement of depth offers an escape from self, an annihilation that converts Wordsworthian inwardness into yet another form of Byronic surface. And even if he had found it possible to center self in nature, the Lake Leman passage suggests that Byron would have experienced this tranquil profundity not as fulfilling, but as boring. Transcendental stillness permeates Lake Leman but a moment; almost immediately Byron finds it necessary to shatter the quiet by imagining a splendid storm approaching over the Alps. Wordsworthian calm has constrained his native mobility, and he must find relief through a vision of unsuppressed energy. The tempest is "wondrous strong, / Yet lovely in your strength . . . let me be / A sharer in thy fierce and far delight" (3, 92–903). But he cannot help realizing the flaw in the storm's magnificence: "But where of ye, oh tempests! is the goal?" (3, 96). The storm's drive, like the poet's own energies, is superficial motion, a splendid display without an interior purpose. And Byron reflects on his own ceaseless flow of words— "Could I embody and unbosom now / That which is most within me . . . into one word, / And that one word were Lightning, I would speak" (3, 97). The self-containment of the organic poem might center the self and allow it to utter its identity in one word—but this is an achievement impossible for Byron.

Transcendental stillness having proven unsatisfactory, Byron considers the opposite posture—heroic mobility. Canto 3 of *Childe Harold's Pilgrimage* meditates on the fate of great men, men of action who make an impact upon the world. Like the superb storm over Lake Leman, such men seem to him splendid forces of nature. Napoleon becomes Byron's prime example. A man of mobility, an inconsistent "spirit antithetically mixt" and "Extreme in all things!" (3, 36), Napoleon bestrides the world but finds that he cannot rule his self—"An empire thou couldst crush, command, rebuild, / But govern not thy pettiest passion, nor, / However deeply in men's spirits skill'd, / Look through thine own, nor curb the lust of war" (3, 38). Napoleon's energy recoils against itself because his heroic mobility makes self-knowledge impossible. The same energy that fuels his victories beomes a "fever at the core, / Fatal to him who bears," a "fire / And motion of the soul . . . once kindled, quenchless evermore" (3, 42). Unable to look into himself, Napoleon becomes a driven soul, a compulsive activist who moves on helplessly from conquest to conquest, finally turning his heroism to villainy, his creative social effort to destruction. Ironically, he becomes the victim of his own aggressive impulses. In his hands revolution degenerates into reaction; and now the vast European populations he has stirred up turn on him, reciprocating his aggressions with a popular outpouring of wrath. "He who surpasses or subdues mankind, / Must look down on the hate of those below" (3, 45). The collisions that fragment the great soul disease the social fabric and produce the mob, the "hot throng" that jostles and collides in endlessly irritating motion, causing the mind to "overboil" so that we "become the spoil / Of our infection . . . In wretched interchange of wrong for wrong / 'Midst a contentious world" (3,

69). To be a man of action is to be an infected soul, and to be in collision with others. They all "join the crushing crowd, doom'd to inflict or bear" (3, 71).

The turn toward the outside represented by Napoleon's heroic activism produces aggression and chaos. Personal mobility gives rise to social collision, demonstrating that great spirits "antithetically mixt" can destroy not only themselves, but also the world. To contain these dangers and yet preserve the option of heroic mobility, Byron contemplates the notion of poetic heroism. His example is Rousseau, a hero of the imagination who glorified "ideal beauty" (3, 78). But in confining his activism to the realm of the imaginary, Rousseau does not succeed in protecting either himself or his audience. Quite the contrary: instead of satisfying human passions, Rousseau's flights of imagination artificially inflate desire, build up a terrific longing that makes any human satisfaction impossible. Instead of liberating man from life and preserving his peace, Rousseau's poetry of eternal pursuit and eternal unfulfillment drive him mad. It exaggerates the disruptive process of ordinary living, producing a disease larger than life. Like Napoleon, Rousseau becomes a carrier of infection, a poet whose words precipitate dreadful actions—they "set the world in flame, / Nor ceased to burn till kingdoms were no more: / Did he not this for France?" (3, 81). Rousseau inspires his audience with revolutionary desires so tremendous as to be unfulfillable, and the result is a bloodbath. In spite of himself he becomes a man of action working in concert with Napoleon, and the readers of his poetry become the mob. Far from preventing aggression, the case of Rousseau suggests that poetry may fuel it.

In drawing a parallel between Napoleon and Rousseau, Byron recognizes that poetry is not always the harmless, exclusively interior activity he often wishes it to be. Nevertheless the conclusion of Canto 3 reverts to the escapist posture, suggesting that "these words" may be "a harmless wile,— . . . Which I would sieze, in passing, to beguile / My breast, or that of others, for a while" (3, 112). Perhaps, then, the perfect solution for Byron's contradictory needs is a poetry of maximum mobility and forcefulness and yet minimum effect—a poetry which appears to be powerful but actually has no impact on the world. These requirements could be met by a poetry of superficial power, a dazzling poetry that implies the existence of inwardness and depth without actually creating it.

In effect, Byron's needs dictate an approach to poetry that is the virtual opposite of Keats's. Where Keats aspires to a poetic heroism that will renew nature through the invisible and powerful participation of the poet, Byron wants to be highly visible and superficially impressive, but actually powerless. The other Romantic poets are worried about coming out into the world—not only Keats, but also Blake, Wordsworth, and Coleridge are concerned about the imagination's potential power to affect external events. They all realize that the poetic imagination has its benign aspects, but also delights in the domination and manipulation of others. To control these tendencies the other Romantics turn within, and attempt to redeem themselves by creating a deep self that could purify the imagination's darker impulses. Byron also desires purification—he does not want to be a Napoleon or a Rousseau—but his solution is the opposite of the other Romantics'. For him Rousseau illustrates the danger of their procedure: to turn within, to create depth, is merely to exaggerate normal desire, making one's imaginative aggressions even more potent than before. So Byron turns to the surface for the same reason that the other Romantics turn to the depths—to purge aggressive feeling, to render it harmless.

And thus the Byronic hero is born. This figure is repeated over and over again in the Turkish Tales, which are escapist works because they present a hero who feigns profound inwardness without actually possessing it. Like Napoleon and Rousseau, and like Byron himself, the Byronic hero is always a figure "antithetically mixt," a man of extraordinary but self-defeating energy whose personal wholeness has been shattered by some dark action in the past. He responds to fragmentation by displaying a cold, firm, silent posture toward the world. "Prometheus" conveniently summarizes this attitude: Byron sees in the Titan "A silent suffering, and intense," a "patient energy," the "endurance, and repulse / Of thine impenetrable Spirit."[8]

Byron creates a poetry of glittering surface, a heroic rigidity that exists for the purpose of being seen. He feigns interior resonance through a clenched posture, an attitude that identifies with the resolve never to change. Where the other Romantics approach the deep self as a never-ending process of mixing emotions and experiences to attain resonant inclusiveness, Byron defiantly deploys the surface self as a spectacularly self-confounding collection of elements "antithetically mixt," a

persona eternally incapable of growth—and one who grounds
his very being in this incapacity. By his highly visible suffering
the Byronic hero elevates himself above the throng, so that he
can be properly wondered at. His armored public posture isolates him, suggests his superiority, creates an outlet for the
energy of his hostilities—but it does not produce inwardness,
soul.

But if the Byronic hero is a superficial figure, at any rate he
does share one characteristic with the Romantic poetry of
depth: both Byron heroism and the organic poem establish
boundaries in order to produce identity. The self-containment
of the organic poem permits the creation of Romantic depth,
and it is this wholeness that the rigidly isolated Byronic hero
mimics. The Byronic hero exaggerates normal Romantic practices by a marked separation of inwardness from outwardness.
Where the Wordsworthian poem is bounded but nevertheless
permeable, allowing interchange between the poet's mind and
nature, Byronic inwardness in impermeable—and therefore,
conveniently inaccessible. The Byronic hero can be observed
only from the outside, and so his inner life can only be inferred.
In this figure Byron has discovered a superficial method of
feigning depth, a kind of inversion of the organic poem.

"The Prisoner of Chillon" becomes an important commentary on the Turkish Tales, for it seriously explores the effects of
absolute self-containment. This poem departs from the
glorification of Byronic heroism by turning Byron's isolated
hero into a wretched prisoner confined in a dungeon. Like the
Byronic hero or the organic poem, Bonnivard, the prisoner of
Chillon, is isolated from the world. He is imprisoned along
with his brothers, but they die one by one, at last leaving him
entirely alone. The result is not the creation of his depth and
character, as might be expected from the normal constitution
of the Byronic hero, but the very opposite: the prisoner's personality is annihilated, rendering his inwardness a void.

Bonnivard and his two brothers are lively men—for them,
imprisonment is a torture, for it blocks their expression of
energies. These men of natural mobility are forced to be still,
and Byron is outraged by the constraint. Emphatically, their
stillness does not build Wordsworthian tranquillity. Because
they are deprived of the opportunity to react to the world's
stimuli they grow weak in body, they become "rusted with a
vile repose" (6); and eventually, this lack of exercise, this decline in physical feelings, leads to the loss of feeling in the

heart. Bonnivard's energy is replaced by a coldness, a stillness of spirit, an inability to respond. He ends in a quiet that is tantamount to the death of the soul.

The prisoner's ordeal climaxes with the death of his second and last brother, the only remaining companion in his dungeon world. This "last, the sole, the dearest link . . . Which bound me to my failing race" (215–18) now becomes a part of the prison's stillness; and as Bonnivard clasps "that hand which lay so still" he realizes that "my own was full as chill; / I had not strength to stir, or strive" (221–23). The loss of all life, all motion, in Bonnivard's world leads to a corresponding vacancy in his soul—not tranquillity, but a horrifying blankness. Suddenly "came the loss of light, and air, / And then of darkness too: / I had no thought, no feeling—none— / Among the stones I stood a stone" (233–36). In this extraordinary moment of negative vision, everything disappears: "There were no stars—no earth—no time— / No check—no change—no good—no crime— / But silence, and a stirless breath / Which neither was of life nor death; / A sea of stagnant idleness, / Blind, boundless, mute and motionless!" (245–50). This annihilation becomes an inversion of the visonary organic poem—it solves the problems of mobility and variousness by expunging everything so that the world, insofar as it still can be said to exist, lies in a homogeneous state of profound calm. Here is a whole and consistent universe, but one without life.

In this crisis Byron explores the possibilities for an organic inwardness that could fill the void of Bonnivard's soul. But the forms of organic focus contemplated by the prisoner turn out to be fallacious. The first is a bird that perches in the dungeon window and begins its song. Similar circumstances stimulate Keats's speaker into poetry in "Ode to a Nightingale," and for a moment it appears that this also will happen to Bonnivard. As he listens to the melody, "by dull degrees came back / My senses to their wonted track; / I saw the dungeon walls and floor" (259–61). As he begins to perceive the world again he also begins to regain his capacity for feeling. And it seems to him that the bird links him to life, sings a "song that said a thousand things, / And seemed to say them all for me!" (269–70). Perhaps this bird even "might be / My brother's soul come down to me" (287–88). But this illusion of purpose, the impression that human feelings and natural events may be significantly related, evaporates for Bonnivard when the bird suddenly flies away. After all, the song was not meant for him.

The bird's appearance and disappearance do not manifest meaning, they merely embody the incessant mobility of nature. The bird turns out to be a creature of surface, not depth.

Next Bonnivard climbs up to his dungeon window, and for the first time since his imprisonment sees the world outside—a beautiful vista of Lake Leman and the Alps. Here is the world of nature, the landscape of Wordsworthian poetry, which perhaps may revitalize his feeling. But the view does not evoke a Wordsworthian poem. Quite the contrary: it acts ironically and disassociatively, for the life of nature brings home to Bonnivard the death of his own soul. The eternal organic forms of the mountains "were the same, / They were not changed like me in frame" (332–33). The unchanging aspect of nature, which links Wordsworth to life and leads him to intuitions of infinity, only serves to alienate Bonnivard. So nature's stillness emphasizes man's mobility and degeneration, and Bonnivard's meditative sequence reverses the normal progression of Wordsworthian nature poetry from surface event to the creation of spiritual depth.

Having failed to revitalize his soul through organic forms of focus, Bonnivard at last comes to find blankness a comfort. He avoids the view from his window, he declines activity, he protects himself from any kind of stimulation—for to bring his feelings alive would be to live in a world of pain. Th dungeon becomes his chosen home; protective isolation and voided feeling become his chosen mode of selfhood. When the prisoner eventually is freed he makes peace with his life by turning the entire world into a replication of his prison. He has "learned to love despair" (374), and so he avoids action as much as possible. Bonnivard ends as an extremely inner being, but Byron shows this to be a pathological state. The dazzling trappings of Byronic heroism recede here, to reveal absolute isolation as a pathetic rather than a heroic condition. The possibility raised by "The Prisoner of Chillon" is that effective selfhood actually may be an affair of surface, not of depth. Perhaps the poets of inwardness are incorrect in suggesting that it is the meditative activation of organic poetry that builds the self—for what Bonnivard needs is not increased inwardness, but rather, the courage to reach outside himself and become involved in the activities of life.

"The Prisoner of Chillon" suggests that a real case can be made for the surface self. Perhaps the profound innerness,

consistency, and integrity promoted by the poets of depth are
not the only possible human values. So in Canto 4 of *Childe
Harold's Pilgrimage* the poem's narrator sings a hymn to the
ocean, which suggests the values made possible by a surface
approach to life. The depths of this Byronic ocean certainly do
exist, but they are made evident only as surface effects—the
pitch and roll of the waves. Where the prisoner of Chillon
imagined his voided world as "a sea of stagnant idleness, /
Blind, boundless, mute and motionless!" this lively ocean is
"boundless, endless, and sublime—/ The image of Eternity" (4,
183). The petty ravages of man "mark the earth with ruin" (4,
179) but ocean lifts him up and dashes him to pieces, "Spurn-
ing him from thy bosom to the skies, / And send'st him, shiver-
ing in thy playful spray / And howling, to his Gods" (4, 180).
But where other men die in the depths the narrator of *Childe
Harold's Pilgrimage* loves the ocean's rolling surface and learns
to skim over it; he was "a child of thee, / And trusted to thy
billows far and near, / And laid my hand upon thy mane" (4,
184). The risk of riding the breakers creates a "pleasing fear"
(4, 180), transforms ocean's destruction into the singer's exhila-
ration. He knows life's wholeness, but he knows it as a surface;
what he experiences is not profound inwardness, but the stim-
ulus of the waves' challenge and the pleasure of his own mastery.[9]

And so the Byronic vision of infinity converts depth to surface, which in turn implies the conversion of action to reaction.
Byron finds it more congenial to adapt to events than to initiate them, for the kind of focus needed to control activity requires a purposeful deep self, a core of identity that he lacks.
The Byronic hero cannot really organize action; his firmness is
limited to the capacity for heroic resistance. But the kind of
reactive flexibility demonstrated by the rider of the sea in
Childe Harold's Pilgrimage is exploited by the Byron of *Don
Juan*. This poem abandons the heroic posture of resistance for
the comic posture of adaptation. Just as the rider learns to stay
mounted on the ocean's billows, appropriating the power of
the waves by adjusting himself to it, the narrator of *Don Juan*
adapts to his poem's flow of events and thereby masters them.
He does not originate the energy of infinity, but by becoming a
creature of surface and learning to stay afloat, he appropriates
powers that far exceed the capacity of Byronic heroism.[10]

Where the Byronic hero remains in one rigid posture, adopts
a hyperbolic consistency meant to authenticate his in-

wardness, the mobile narrator of *Don Juan* blithely announces his poem has no plan or purpose. And indeed, *Don Juan* abounds in contradictions, chance collisions, abortive episodes, incongruous juxtapositions, sudden reversals. These unreconciled mixtures, these testaments to man's inability to maintain purpose, become the motive power of the poem—the force that propels it randomly onward. Byron's Juan is tossed ahead by the surging ocean of life, and this becomes comic because he cannot sink; he is a superficial creature and he continually bobs up like a cork. Juan learns very little from his experience, which is why he can happily continue his experiencing.[11]

And so *Don Juan* becomes the great Romantic poem of surface, as *The Prelude* is the great Romantic poem of depth. *The Prelude* is the autobiography of a man who examines his past in search of an inner self that is latent there and needs to be brought into present awareness. Thought and speech are vital to Wordsworth's procedure, for he is reflecting upon himself, examining the apparently incomplete events of his past to bring out the depth of their meaning, the manner in which these incidents have contributed to the development of his mature self. In making his poem he both recounts and extends his own self-development; the inwardness initiated by his childhood experiences is continued and expanded by his ongoing poetic interpretations. But while Wordsworth's procedure creates an immense field of inner activity, it also does pose problems. He tries to see all the events of his life through the focus of his self-development, a focus that validates not only the significance of his own life but the way in which all events are purposeful, all episodes partake of infinity, all things of the world rest in God. By demonstrating the success of his own self-development he seeks to affirm the harmony of the world.

In contrast, Byron's poem of surface denies all claims to unity and focus. The author of *Don Juan* gives up the attempt to make complete sense of his experience. His is a poem of middle age, a stream of words that begins to flow when "I / Have spent my life, both interest and principal, / And deem not, what I deem'd, my soul invincible" (I, 213). He writes because he is losing the physical capacity to act, and he believes that the next best thing to sensuous experience is the imagination of it. So Byron splits his self between the mindless but cheerful physicality of the young Juan, who learns nothing from his experiences and never grows up, and the incessant verbal flow

of the poem's middle-aged narrator, who exists to escape
Wordsworthian interpretation—to avoid looking into himself
by constantly searching for new external stimuli, new diver-
sions.

Wordsworth and Byron become contraries: where Wordsworth's poem is halted by his middle age, Byron's begins there.
Wordsworth's poetry of spontaneous overflow is inhibited and
finally cut off by his immense need to have the spontaneous
reveal design, to have utterance in the present embody the
significance of the entire past life. But it is Byron who truly
practices poetry as spontaneous overflow: "I write what's up-
permost, without delay," and the words become "a straw,
borne on by human breath," a self-created but meaningless
plaything that generates the enthusiasm to produce an addi-
tional rush of words (XIV, 7–8). The openness, the inconsistency of *Don Juan* allow it to become endless. As long as
Byron's life continues, his poem also is free to proceed. As an
alternative to the focus of the organic poem, he offers the
delights of extension—the indefinitely prolonged unfurling of
new surfaces, new stimuli.[12]

So Byron manages to write an autobiographical poem that is
the polar opposite of *The Prelude:* instead of going into himself,
he turns himself inside out and becomes the world. For him
youth is the time of inwardness, the time when one believed in
one's dreams and subscribed to the proposition that the self is
its own universe. But at thirty, the poet cries, "No more—no
more—Oh! never more, my heart, / Canst thou be my sole
world, my universe!" Now "The illusion's gone forever" (I, 215)
and the poet is left "To laugh at all things—for I wish to know /
What after *all*, are *all* things—but a *Show?*" (VII, 2). Byron
himself becomes this show of life by unleashing an incessant
flow of words that cause a world to appear.

It is his most effective way of fulfilling his desire "To withdraw *myself* from *myself*," which "has ever been my sole, my
entire, my sincere motive." The poetic shows of *Don Juan*
become a form of self-escape. They lead not to the growth of the
poet's mind, but to displacement from selfhood, to entertainment. In *Childe Harold's Pilgrimage* Byron had criticized Rousseau for making his audience believe in the illusion of a poetic
idealism that created havoc in the actual world. His own poetry does not promote the willing suspension of disbelief that
can lead to this unfortunate result; he constantly deflates his
performances by his own narrative intrusions, which become

yet another kind of amusing show. We are never allowed to
forget for long that everything in this poem is surface. Given
these procedures, the compulsive force of a Rousseau simply
cannot build up. Like the poem's narrator, who fails to develop
a consistent center of self, *Don Juan* may lack a central purpose—but reading it certainly is a pleasure.[13]

But if the poem attempts to escape inwardness, its superficiality cannot be branded as merely escapist. It is the Turkish
Tales that offer true escape, for their heroes are designed to
create the illusion of power without its actual impact. In his
completely escapist moods Byron wants poetry to be "a
harmless wile," but *Don Juan*, as well as seeking pleasure, has
one item of real business—to attack the notion of the deep self
and to debunk the poetry of inwardness, on the grounds that
the imagination of profound inner selfhood is the only dangerous illusion. Where the poet of *Don Juan* brings illusion to
the surface, constantly unmasking his own performances,
those who believe in inwardness create an illusion that they
mistake for truth.

As the narrator of *Don Juan* claims, "For me, I know nought;
nothing I deny, / Admit, reject, contemn" (XIV, 3). Apparently
it is not this speaker but the people who aspire to deep selfhood
who are constantly denying, admitting, rejecting, con-
demning—using words to proclaim a truth which they then
proceed to impose on themselves and on others. But if interpretations are merely another form of appearance, then they have
no special claim to authority. They should be worth neither
more nor less than any other show. Wordsworth particularly
draws Byron's fire because of all contemporary poets he is the
strongest advocate of interpretation, of the word as a guide to
meaning, inwardness, and reality. Byron did not have the opportunity to read *The Prelude*, but an acquaintance with "Tintern Abbey" and the other *Lyrical Ballads* would have been
enough to give him a feeling for Wordsworth's methods of
building inwardness. In "Tintern Abbey" childhood action is
exchanged for the adult's poetic interpretations—the body's
activity is succeeded by the authority of the word. Wordsworth's exchange of the body for the word, of action for interpretation, creates an inwardness that Byron is moved to
discredit. What he notices is not the Wordsworthian soul, but
the willing surrender of body that has produced it. Why should
soul be valued over body, depth over surface?

Juan's first experience of love dramatizes these issues. When he begins to have feeling for Julia, it registers as thoughts "unutterable" (I, 90), an unfocussed, restless affect that creates the need for definition, outlet activity, the drive toward some kind of goal. But Juan cannot find relief in action because he does not know what troubles him. In his perplexity he becomes a naive Wordsworth, wandering in nature and hearing "a voice in all the winds" (I, 94), thinking great thoughts and pursuing "His self-communion with his own high soul." He turns "without perceiving his condition, / Like Coleridge, into a metaphysician" (I, 91). Juan interprets his restlessness through the use of words, but this is not a case of unveiling reality. On the contrary, it is the transposition of energy from one form to another—not a higher form, merely a different one. The body's urges and the mind's metaphysics both are forms of appearance; the only sure thing is that interpretation fails to soothe Juan's restlessness. His naive poetry formulates his energies, but does not terminate them. This inner focus cannot bring stillness, for it neglects to notice the original source of restlessness in the human body itself. "If *you* think it was philosophy that this did, / I can't help thinking puberty assisted" (I, 93). Finally Juan finds relief in sexual activity with Julia, but this is not a lasting answer either—it leads to an imbroglio with her husband that forces his exile from home and begins the wanderings recounted in *Don Juan*. Mobility may be channeled through various forms of appearance, but it never can be finally centered or stilled. Wordsworthian sacrifice of the body therefore strikes Byron as a form of repression, of authoritarianism. As the contrary of Wordsworth, Byron stands for the liberation of all appearances, the free play of energies through whatever forms they may take. In unbinding the life force Byron releases delight and vitality, which he feels is surely preferable to the deadliness of Wordsworth's interminable explanations. If life is purposeless, at least it might as well be enjoyed.

Although Byron rejects the claim of the word to meaning and authority, he by no means condemns verbal behavior. To do so would be to repeat Wordsworth's error in inverted form, by authorizing body over word. Words and bodies both are forms of appearance that incarnate energy, and Byron recognizes that in some situations words may do the better job. Middle age is one example; the body's decreased capacity gives way to the lightning of the mind, which produces *Don Juan*. Another example is the intrigue hatched by the Duchess of Fitz-fulke.

Her story of the ghostly Black Friar, who walks the halls outside Juan's bedroom every night, employs the conventions of
the Gothic novel to stir up Juan's interest and apprehension.
She maneuvers him into a state of mind where his supernatural frisson can be converted into an expression of sexual energies, as he finally reaches out to touch the ghostly Black Friar
but instead finds his hand upon the Duchess. In using fiction to
create the conditions that give her sexual possession of Juan,
Fitzfulke is engaging in a manipulative process that compares
to the audience manipulations incessantly attempted by the
narrator of *Don Juan*. For this speaker, manipulation is an
amusing, enlivening process.

The poets of depth cannot adopt Byron's cheerful attitude
toward manipulation because their business is to create the
illusion of inwardness, not only for their audiences but for
themselves. The creation of inwardness involves a necessary
element of self-deception, a problem salient in Julia's developing responses to her lover Juan. Juan himself first felt the
physical restlessness of love and then transposed it into Wordsworthian verbalizing, and similarly, Julia sublimates her physical feeling into the terminology of Platonic love. By adopting
the language of Platonism she seeks to create love on the spiritual plane, the realm of depth and soul. But in focussing on
Platonic visions she neglects the sexual energy they sublimate,
and allows herself to be overpowered by the force hidden
within her own expressions. In becoming Juan's lover she at
last does what she has really wanted to do all along, but her
satisfaction must be prepared for by what Byron sees as a
complicated and ridiculous process of self-deception. Those
who believe in inwardness must elaborately manipulate themselves before they are able to do anything at all. The narrator of
Don Juan himself proposes to be more direct, and more active.
He wants to be the master rather than the pawn of his own
words; they will do things for him, rather than the other way
around. By denying inwardness, by bringing everything to the
surface, he liberates words as an effective form of energy. The
rider of the sea who writes *Don Juan* also must become the
rider of the word—the poet who has the skill to use the speech
to his own advantage.

Like Blake, Byron stands for the relief of suppression, for
absolutely open expression. But where Blake's imaginative
man is a translucent deep self, a speaker whose words are
redeemed, much as are Wordsworth's, through the experiences

of growth that transform and resonate his being, Byron's speaker simply acknowledges all his impulses and having brought them out, then proceeds to manipulate them. Where the other Romantics distrust manipulation Byron is attracted to it, for it represents the only version of activism available to the surface self. If life is merely an affair of changing appearances, as Byron assumes, then the effective artist and the capable men are united in the character of the manipulator: it is he who has the skill to constantly arrange and rearrange the appearances, influencing life's events in his own favor. Byron's surface manipulations provide an outlet for his native mobility—and since they indeed are on the surface the dark implications of normal Romantic manipulation are largely dispersed. Byron is out openly to manipulate and dominate; we are made aware that we face a clever opponent, and should realize that we must be on our guard.

Since life is an affair of power not purpose, the narrator of *Don Juan* really can see no way out of manipulation. He himself undoubtedly manipulates by using words as a form of power, but then so do the interpretationists. Interpretation is simply another form of appearance, and since it is constantly rearranging its own appearances, interpretation itself must be a manipulation. Therefore, the only difference between the poet of *Don Juan* and the Lake poets must be in the gravity of their operations. The Dedication to *Don Juan* condemns these Laker interpretationists because not only are they manipulators, they are also longwinded and distinctly boring. Where Byron offers vitality and entertainment, Wordsworth writes "a rather long 'Excursion'" . . . "the vasty version / Of his new system to perplex the sages" (4). Coleridge, the "hawk encumber'd with his hood" is forever "Explaining metaphysics to the nation—I wish he would explain his Explanation" (2). Like Julia, these poets conceal their motives behind a massive smokescreen of sanctimonious words, which stuns the audience. But putting people to sleep is exactly what the British government wants its poets to do. For a slumbering populace cannot revolt. By diverting people into a dull semblance of action through writing and reading the poetry of depth, of a self-contained world, Wordsworth and his colleagues help preserve the status quo. A grateful government, relieved of the necessity to directly suppress its citizens, rewards its poets with sinecures and respectability.

Byron charges that the poetry of inwardness deadens feeling,

the sense of individuality, and the capacity for response. Far
from contributing to the growth of the mind, it suppresses and
atrophies human powers. His audience relationships will aim
at the opposite effect—to wake people up. The narrator of *Don
Juan* does this by releasing his aggressive feelings, which can
assume a positive role in the poem. His tendency to irritate, to
jolt, to collide with people, functions to startle his audience
into awareness. This adversary relationship with the audience
minimizes the morally suspect aspects of manipulation and
maximizes its possibilities for liberation, for by jarring people
the poet forces them to become alert and think for themselves.
As he says, "I wish men to be free / As much from mobs as
kings—from you as me" (IX, 25).

Before *Don Juan* Byron had maintained a speciously collaborative rather than an adversary audience relationship. He
wrote of the Byronic hero again and again not only to feign his
hero's inwardness, but also his audience's. For through reading
the Turkish Tales every man could imagine himself a hero and
every woman could experience romance. The spiritual collusion in this arrangement had as its physical analogue the exchange of cash. Byron's poetry sold well; flattery turned out to
be viable commodity. In *Don Juan* Byron casts the Lakers in
this pandering role, remarking that "You have your salary;
was't for that you wrought?" (Dedication, 6). Manipulation, it
turns out, is not practiced only by poets—audiences too can
manipulate, by paying for what they like to hear and encourag-
ing the poet to produce more of it. But this mutually manipulative relationship falsely enriches both parties at the same
time that it really demeans everyone. In *Don Juan* Byron rejects such an exchange by rudely calling attention to its suppressed basis: he hails us as his "gentle reader! and / Still
gentler purchaser!" (I, 221).[14]

We are forced to see that the relationship between poet and
reader always threatens to become mutually manipulative, an
exchange of cash for an inflated sense of self-importance. The
author of the Turkish Tales certainly knows what he is talking
about here; but as his youth gives way to middle age Byron
ceases to see any point in taking cash in exchange for poetic
flattery. He imagines his past life as an analogue of money, and
realizes that "I / Have squander'd my whole summer . . . I /
Have spent my life, both interest and principal" (I, 213). His
past is spent, and no amount of money can recover it or offer
adequate compensation for the loss of his youth. Still, "I *have*

succeeded . . . succeeded in my youth, / The only time when much success is needed: / And my success produced what I in sooth / Cared most about; it need not now be pleaded— / Whate'er it was, 'twas mine" (XII, 17). Recovery of the past is impossible, and so the only wisdom must be to live as fully as one can in the present. Byron cheerfully dispersed his energies in his youth, and he continues to do so in middle age by openly speaking his mind, squandering his credit with his audience. He is the spendthrift, but the spendthrift is the only truly wise man—he realizes he cannot save anything, and so he throws everything away, tries to use all his energies before he loses them. Generosity becomes the best adaptive posture toward the inevitable decline of life.[15]

By spending his energies Byron becomes the antithesis of Wordsworth, who tries to conserve his. *The Prelude* is written in the faith that one's past is not lost, that it can be recovered and compounded in value through the process of interpretation. Like Byron, Wordsworth practices an economy of the word. Because he believes in focus, in the possibility of the organic poem, he finds it possible to gather his life's energies and compress them into the intensity of poetic speech. The analogy between poetry and money, suppressed in Wordsworth, is brought to the surface in *Don Juan*. But where Wordsworth would have thought of himself as a prudent investor, Byron sees conservative poets as misers. Or rather, he sees the miser as "your only poet;—passion, pure / And sparkling on from heap to heap, displays / *Possess'd*, the ore" (XII, 8). Like the recollective poet, the miser turns to hoarding money when his youth is spent and he is no longer able to physically exert power in the world. He becomes a parody of the interpretive poet, a man who despises "every sensual call, / Commands— the intellectual lord of all" (XII, 9). In possessing the world the miser cannot truly enjoy it, but he certainly can exert intellectual domination by owning everyone and everything possible. In *Don Juan* money and worldly power finally buy the heroes and the lovers; the Empress Catherine purchases the victors of war for her bed, and English society turns love into a marriage market. The miser carries these tendencies to the extreme by sacrificing all sensuous enjoyment to his intellectual lust for absolute domination. He is the ultimate, the pure manipulator, and his heaps of pure gold are the analogue to the pure compression of the self-contained poem.

The analogy between money and poetry remains only an

analogy for Byron; as with the other analogies in *Don Juan* it never is granted symbolic status. For symbolism is an assertion of identity, a claim that the part indeed is the whole. Byron cannot move from part to whole symbolically, for although he does identify one great whole in life—the infinite ocean of surging energy—he also believes that the whole manifests itself only variously, appearing now as money, now as love, now as physical power, now as verbal dexterity, and so on. There is never a great moment of meaningful unity, of reality focussing all the appearances, such as is expressed by the symbol. Instead, "The eternal surge / Of time and tide rolls on, and bears afar / Our bubbles; as the old burst, new emerge, / Lash'd from the foam of ages" (XV, 99). Given this state of affairs, the fiscal conservatism of symbolic poets is misplaced. For life becomes a moving surface requiring the economics of risk and liquidity. The poet must become a speculator; he must learn to play fast and loose with the appearances.[16]

In the final cantos of *Don Juan* Byron shows English society behaving in just this way. The marriage mart in which Juan finds himself enmeshed is a "sweepstakes for substantial wives," a "lottery" in which the speculator may "draw a high prize" (XII, 37); and the women who are the prizes carefully tend their "floating balance of accomplishment" (XII, 52). In this society every relationship is in a speculative key, "For good society is but a game . . . / Where every body has some separate aim, / An end to answer, or a plan to lay" (XII, 58). The poet of analogy sees manipulation surfacing everywhere, in the financial ventures and in the games of relationship that people forever play to get the better of each other.

Once again the narrator's adaptation to life threatens to dissolve, for he knows that this English shell game of appearances is cold—it lacks heart, interior. He can cheerfully disregard his own lack of inner identity, but when he looks at English society he can see only meaningless motion and vacant quiet. In this superficial and sensation-mad society, life speeds on at a terrifying rate until "Change grows too changeable, without being new" (XI, 82), motion accelerates until it becomes a vapid stillness. At that point "Society is now one polish'd horde, / Form'd of two mighty tribes, the *Bores* and *Bored*" (XIII, 95).

But the solution cannot be to develop interior being, for the narrator feels no sense of inner existence. His only option is to take bigger risks, to play the inevitable game with even greater verve. And this, finally, is why poetry is important for him—not because it means anything, but because it is the best game of all.[17] The insular and self-contented English think their world is everything, just as the poets of inwardness believe their poems are worlds—but Lord Byron in exile looks back on "that microcosm on stilts, / Yclept the Great World" (XII, 56) and knows its insignificance. He resists it not by setting up poetry as a rival, a source of the significance society lacks; instead, poetry becomes valuable because it is the best device for keeping the poet afloat in a treacherous but boring world. To counterpoint the financial speculations of the English, the narrator floats his own kind of paper; "I'm serious—so are all men upon paper; / And why should I not form my speculation, / And hold up to the sun my little taper?" (XII, 21). The notion that poetry is a cultural resource, that poems link the generations and provide a kind of immortality, is ridiculous to him. Poetry simply cannot harbor and conserve meaning in this way. Asked why he publishes, the narrator replies, "why do you play at cards? / Why drink? Why read?—To make some hour less dreary." The fallible and perishing results of his labor "I cast upon the stream, / To swim or sink" (XIV, 11).

But if he finds no solutions, at least he is brought alive by his poetic game—for it involves risk. Where Wordsworth values spontaneous overflow because it reveals the latent meaning of his life, Byron enjoys it because it results in happy accidents, marvellous recoveries, spectacular fabrications. These bringings together of appearance are comic, not symbolic; the organic fusive power that truly mixes emotions is no part of Byron's experience. Instead, he delights in taking great risks and winning tremendous, but temporary, resolutions. He constantly threatens to drown in the sea of life, but yet once more he resurfaces. In poetry, "I think that were I *certain* of success / I hardly could compose another line. . . . In play, there are two pleasures for your choosing— / The one is winning, and the other losing" (XIV, 12).

Poetry gives him the power to adapt, the power to remain ebullient, not only when he considers English society, but when he reflects on life itself. For if the English are incessant manipulators, their devices are nothing compared to the world's. It is life's energy and not the poet that is the original manipulator of us all—for it fuels a restlessness, an unremitting mobility, which suddenly can turn love to hate, honesty to deception, good to evil. A prime example of this is the war cantos of *Don Juan*, which climax in a vision of Juan as "Love turned a Lieutenant of Artillery!" (IX, 44). We see that if it is Juan's extraordinary energy which makes him an ardent lover, it is this same energy that fuels his lust to kill. Aggression and eros are unfortunately linked, for Juan's energy surfaces in contradictory forms that suddenly can be reversed. Byron responds to this confusing situation by attempting to out-manipulate life. His poetry becomes a creative adaptation that plays fast and loose with the facts in order to avert destruction. As he says, his muse is "the most sincere that ever dealt in fiction" (XVI, 2), for by the sudden reversals of poetry the false can become true and the contradictory consistent—or the other way around. He makes this remark as prologue to the story of Fitz-fulke and Juan, which indeed does demonstrate how the manipulations of fiction can creatively rearrange the facts of life. We marvel at the Byronic mobility that can change faster than life itself, beat life at its own game. The poet of surface becomes the great trickster, the saver of appearances who preserves our capacity for laughter and keeps us afloat on the ocean of eternity. Byron's achievement is essentially manipulative. In *Don Juan* the rider of the sea converts the lack of inner identity and of consistency of purpose that had vexed his early career from tragedy into comedy, from his loss into his triumph over life.[18]

But by inverting the normal Romantic assumptions, perhaps Byron does manage in a sense to confirm their attractiveness. He repudiates the deep self, consistency of character and purpose, the organic poem—the great Romantic postulates of wholeness. To replace them *Don Juan* exfoliates an endless world of incessantly mobile surfaces that is at once an escape and an exile from the inner self. In Byron's surface world aggression is largely disarmed by being brought out into the open, where it becomes yet another aspect of life's unending mobility. Given this character it can become a spur to action—an energy that facilitates the poet's adaptiveness. Certainly this is a great advantage not enjoyed by the other Romantic poets, who must labor to curb or transform their aggressive energies. But the Byronic surface self does not really succeed in building a social world any better than does the normal Romantic deep self. Byron shares with his fellow poets the problems of the isolate. Where the others find themselves isolated because of their inwardness, ironically, Byron discovers himself isolated because of his outwardness. Byronic society perforce becomes an atomistic affair of clashing personalities and interests, a superficial and mobile world that never can be stilled. Where the other Romantics struggle to unify the self and relate it to a harmonized society, Byron renounces these values but then is compelled to struggle for equilibrium in the absence of any fundamental organizing principle. He can conceive of wholeness only as a form of anarchy—anarchy manipulated and temporarily bested by the poet's improvisational art.

7

SHELLEY
The Deep Self Surfaced

Like Byron, Shelley is a poet of incessant mobility. But where Byron's mobility stems primarily from his unstable personal moods and attitudes, Shelley's restlessness is also a consequence of his passionate idealism. As he remarks in his sketch "On Life," "man is a being of high aspirations 'looking before and after,' whose 'thoughts that wander through eternity,' disdain alliance with transience and decay, incapable of imagining to himself annihilation, existing but in the future and the past, being, not what he is, but what he has been, and shall be. Whatever may be his true and final destination, there is a spirit within him at emnity with nothingness and dissolution (change and extinction)."[1] For Shelley, the man of "high aspirations" cannot rest in "what he is' "; his identity is not an object or fixity but a process of exploration, a hearkening to the future and the past, a wandering through eternity. Personal identity resides not in resolutions but in transitions, in unremitting mobility.[2]

Alastor, the major poem of Shelley's early career, makes this point forcefully. In the Preface Shelley describes his protagonist as "led forth by an imagination inflamed and purified through familiarity with all that is excellent and majestic, to the contemplation of the universe," a pursuit of the "magnificence and beauty of the external world" that directs his desire "towards objects . . . infinite and unmeasured." For Shelley's Poet mobility and infinity are crucially related; his aspiration is directed toward the world, which in its magnificence opens outward into visions of the infinite.

The poem's initial example of this process is the Poet's visit to an ancient Egyptian temple in "Dark Aethiopia" (115) where "dead men" have hung "their mute thoughts on mute walls around" (119–20). Although apparently he understands neither the dead languages nor the characters in which they are written, he "ever gazed / And gazed, till meaning on his vacant mind / Flashed like strong inspiration, and he saw / The thrilling secrets of the birth of time" (125–27). Here rapt attention leads to a flashing inspiration, a sudden decipherment of what has seemed incomprehensible. These ancient characters are replete with mute meanings but lack an interpretive key that could unlock their speech. The Poet's passionate contemplation provides this key; absorbed wholly in the images on the walls he finds them suddenly internalized—they cease being things as they become comprehensible meanings, and the worlds of lost civilizations become a part of himself. His "vacant mind" is filled with "The thrilling secrets of the birth of time"; the world and the self are simultaneously enlarged, simultaneously opened toward infinity. The Poet's personal identity originates in his regard for what is beyond himself. And poetic mobility is revealed as a species of attention that has the power to transform things.

As long as he remains interested in the "magnificence and beauty of the external world," the exploring Poet retains his transforming powers. But when he dreams of his ideal beloved one night, his capacities are destroyed. As Shelley says in the Preface, "He images to himself the Being whom he loves," but within this one image is contained "all of wonderful, or wise, or beautiful, which the poet, the philosopher, or the lover could depicture." This vision turns the world outside in, brings everything that one could love and strive for home within the Poet himself. But once infinity is summoned inside it is immediately divided, through the generation of a self-reflexive dream theater that involuntarily images the totality of his desires in the vision of a woman who is himself but not himself—the best of the world and himself transformed into the form of one woman.[3] As Shelley describes it, "Her voice was like the voice of his own soul / Heard in the calm of thought; its music long, . . . held / His inmost sense" (153–55). His reaction to this extreme experience of symbolic displacement and focus is vigorously erotic. Taken in by his own poetic imagery, the Poet mistakes it for an actual being and "reared his shuddering limbs and quelled / His gasping breath, and spread his arms to meet / Her panting bosom" (182–84).

The outcome is not mastery, but loss. As he entwines himself in "her dissolving arms" he loses both consciousness and himself, later waking to a superficial and empty world that he emptymindedly gazes upon "as vacantly / As ocean's moon looks on the moon in heaven" (187, 201–02). His visionary experience has reversed the inspirational process which allowed him to decipher the ancient Egyptian characters. Where that interpretation began in vacancy but moved toward comprehension and the sense of an enlarged world, his dream begins with a promise of infinitely gratified desire but dwindles to utter vacancy. After his dream experience the *Alastor* Poet never regains his interest in life. The wonders of the world are nothing to him, and he waits impatiently for the death that he hopes will break through the vacant surface of life to reunite him with his dream lover, in some transcendental existence beyond the human ken. The Poet's attention is centered deeply within himself, and ironically, this focus results in the attenuation of his identity. Contemplating himself in the "liquid mirror" of a forest pool he sees the profound image of his own self-destruction; "His eyes beheld / Their own wan light through the reflected lines / Of his thin hair . . . as the human heart, / Gazing in dreams over the gloomy grave, / Sees its own treacherous likeness there" (462, 469–74). His personal powers withered, his sense of coherence lost, the Poet finally resigns himself to extinction.

Alastor traces a pathology wherein mobility is changed to fixation, and attention to the world is changed to a killing obsession with mysterious depths. Regard for existences other than himself, which hitherto had characterized Shelley's Poet, are converted to a disastrous form of inwardness—the yearning for an unattainable beloved who is a misunderstood poetic self-image. This solipsistic vision of infinity rivets the Poet's attention on one object, blocking his life and eventually destroying him. In *Alastor* Shelley describes a form of the deep self which as it becomes increasingly inner becomes increasingly obsessive, incapacitated, and incomprehensible to itself.

Whereas the other Romantic poets are impressed with the imagination's ability to create social discord through its domination or manipulation of other people, Shelley's most intense anxieties concern the imagination's isolate condition—the "self-centered seclusion" that he warns against in the Preface to *Alastor*. Most of the other poets find some comfort in retreating to inwardness, where aggressive impulses may be transformed through formation of the deep self; but Shelley is distressed by the notion of solitude and moves toward outwardness, as the authentic form of socialization. Perhaps the self could be saved from itself, through its involvement with life beyond its own restricted center.

Like Byron, Shelley is driven to a poetry of surface because he simply cannot embrace the deep self. Byron thought it an illusion, but Shelley sees it as something worse than that—a self-destroyer.[4] But if Shelley and Byron exhibit affinities in their rejection of the deep self, they are quite different in their employment of outwardness. The Byron of *Don Juan* is interested in debunking interpretation, that central activity of the deep self; he is out to show that if life is meaningless, nevertheless it can be a vital and often pleasurable affair. Shelley has no such desire to repudiate meaning—indeed, it is precisely meaningful fulfillment of his love that the *Alastor* Poet so longs for. But would it be possible to write a poetry of outwardness that embodied meaning, or must the surface inevitably remain superficial? *Epipsychidion*, a poem written six years after *Alastor*, but dealing with the same subject—the imaginative search for ideal love—demonstrates that indeed a meaningful poetry of the surface can be written.

The cardinal difference between the poems involves the attitudes they imply toward fictiveness. The *Alastor* Poet was never sure whether his vision was an illusion or a deep reality, but deciding did not really matter—for if his beloved was a superficial representation she was not actual, and if she existed within the transcendental depths of the world then she was beyond his reach. But in *Epipsychidion* the ontological status of poetic imagery is no longer the salient question. Instead of inquiring into their reality, this poem simply *uses* fictions. *Epipsychidion* was occasioned by Shelley's attraction to Emilia Viviani, an unattainable beloved who perhaps raised the same questions for him as the dream lover did for the Poet of *Alastor*.[5] How can one embrace a presence that seems unreachable? To cope with this situation the poet writes a poem which embraces the lady by using her as the figure that draws out his narrator's poetic expressions to clarify and transform his understanding of love. *Epipsychidion* thus becomes a poem of soul-making, for it functions to bring its narrator's impulses to the surface, where they can be arranged and rearranged in the attempt to render his life coherent.

Like the narrator of *Don Juan*, who brings his impulses to the surface so that he can use his own emotions rather than being used by them, the narrator of *Epipsychidion* enacts imagination as a process of self-consciousness. For both Byron and Shelley, a capable poetry must be a poetry of the surface—a poetry that masters the depths by making them available for the poet's imaginative arrangements. It is precisely this shift to the surface that was impossible for the *Alastor* Poet, who incapacitated his imagination by brooding on his depths and finally allowing his own obscurely self-destructive emotions to kill him. To approach the self as a fiction, a surface arrangement of figurations capable of incessant refiguration, rescues Shelley because it restores the mobility and outgoingness that are this poet's lifeblood.[6]

In the first hundred lines of *Epipsychidion* the poem's narrator begins on a high lyrical note, a passionate outpouring of metaphor and imagery. And the intensity of the poet's love is matched by the chaotic luxuriousness of his figuration. As the roses, birds, Moons, fountains, lutes, stars, and Spouses continue to multiply, the reader begins to suspect that this is a poetry out of control. Indeed it is, but control is not the value here—what passion produces at the outset of *Epipsychidion* is sheer poetic abundance. The generous heart spends itself freely, exhausting its energies and finally failing ("Ah, woe is me! / What have I dared? Where am I lifted? how / Shall I descend, and perish not?") (123–25). But its defeat is a kind of victory, for when the narrator temporarily retreats he leaves behind him a huge, littered landscape of poetic figuration that invites reconfiguration. The immensity of the narrator's first failure is a prerequisite for the generous dimensions of his ultimate success. He wants to bring a large array into identity, not a mere handful of fragments. His love aspires to spiritual complexity, to the resonances of infinity.

Shelley's attitude toward the fragmentary contrasts interestingly with Byron's, who in *Childe Harold's Pilgrimage* had compared his shattered heart to "a broken mirror, which the glass / In every fragment multiplies; and makes / A thousand images of one that was, / The same, and still the more, the more it breaks" (3, 33). Byron is distressed by the fragmentary because it demonstrates the tragedy of mobility—the self's never-ending, proliferating inconsistency. But Shelley takes this imagery in *Epipsychidion*, and shows how it can be transformed. He sees the Byronic mirror not as an irremediable grief, but a marvellous opportunity. For him, "Love is like understanding, that grows bright, / Gazing on many truths; 'tis like thy light, / Imagination! which from earth and sky, / And from the depths of human phantasy, / As from a thousand prisms and mirrors, fills / The Universe with glorious beams" (162–67). Here poetic multiplicity refracting "As from a thousand prisms and mirrors" fills the universe with light, generating an infinity of the surface rather than of the depths—an infinity of never-ending reflectiveness.

In short, poetic multiplicity yields a way of surface soul-making for Shelley. As an alternative to the interior deep self he offers the deep self surfaced—an attentive persona continually moving outward toward the proliferating reflections of its own meaning. The *Alastor* Poet's decipherment of the Egyptian characters provides a good illustration of how such a surfaced deep self might operate. In understanding the mysterious ancient images the Poet himself became the interpretive key; for by his rapt absorption he gave himself to the characters, which then opened to him. The flashing of his inspiration became an interrelation that simultaneously clarified himself and the world, as he suddenly experienced understanding. Such acts of decipherment make the Shelleyan soul—and it then becomes clear how Shelley differs from Byron. Both create a poetry of the surface, but where the Byron of *Don Juan* views the surface's temporary coherencies as either happy accidents or the triumphant manipulations of the poet, Shelley foregoes the Byronic emphasis on inconsistency to stress the soul- and world-evolving capacities of poetic arrangements. Both Byron's and Shelley's vision remains determinedly open and mobile; but where Byron finds his interest in exploiting the incongruities of surface Shelley focuses on the gathering shapes of meaning, the oncoming coherence of self and world which opens in promise although it never can be embraced in completion.

But if *Epipsychidion* forges a surfaced deep self through its decipherments of the speaker's proliferating imagery, its efforts to configure these figurations into a viable world is not smooth or continuous. At the end of the poem's first movement the lyricist sinks into quiescence, exhausted by his immense outburst of song. In *A Defence of Poetry* Shelley speaks of such moments of interruption. He claims that "Poetry enlarges the circumference of the imagination by replenishing it with thoughts of ever new delight, which have the power of attracting and assimilating to their nature all other thoughts." The result of this abundance is not the indefinitely prolonged enlargement of the imagination; instead, the imagination's very expansion "form[s] new intervals and interstices whose void for ever craves fresh food" (488). In *Epipsychidion* proliferation leads to breakdown; but this return of fragmentation is in itself a great opportunity, for it allows the narrator to reconfigure himself and his world in novel ways. In *Alastor* fixity was portrayed as a relentless form of inwardness that focused on one object—the Poet's beloved. *Epipsychidion* breaks through this rigidity by reaching outward to create infinity as a variety of worlds, a variety of selves.[7]

Just as Byron, that other poet of surface, found it impossible to confine his restless mobility within the organic poem, so Shelley finds it impossible to focus on only one poem, one self, or one world. In order to remain alive he must keep moving, which means that he must continue to configure worlds that approach completion but then break open into a new collection of fragments that become the materials for renewed world-making. The Shelleyan poem will pursue resolution but never quite attain it; and so the lyricist of *Epipsychidion*'s first move-ment flies high but never quite high enough to embrace his beloved—but when he sinks into exhaustion he leaves behind him an abundance of extremely useful fictions that invite re-configuration. Shelley will rewrite the organic poem not as one but as many, as a series of episodes that constantly promise closure only to break open yet again. On the one hand, he forever is closing in on identity—on the self-contained co-herence of the organic poem—but on the other, his focus con-tinually ruptures to admit a newly enlarged field of poetic fragments, an enticing variety that makes possible the creation of a transformed world. His style of poetic perception becomes the enactment of Shelley's subject matter in *Epipsychidion;* for the narrator sees his love for Emily as a unity-in-variety: "Love is like understanding, that grows bright, / Gazing on many truths. . . . Narrow / The heart that loves, the brain that con-templates, / The life that wears, the spirit that creates / One object, and one form, and builds thereby / A sepulchre for its eternity" (162–63; 169–73).

Shelley's revision of the organic poem as a multiplicity of worlds, an interplay of unity and variety, represents his at-tempt at Romantic inclusiveness. Where the poets of the deep self tend to regard infinity as the world humanized and brought within the self, a transformation that produces a reso-nant, profoundly centered character, Shelley approaches the problem of inclusiveness in just the opposite way. By repeat-

edly giving himself to the world in such openness that his
vision of things repeatedly expands beyond enduring and again
breaks apart, this poet enacts a decentered mode of ever-wid-
ening perception ethically motivated by selflessness and generosity. Through surrendering his isolate inwardness he gains
the world, not as his possession, but in the communion of love.
Epipsychidion becomes an important poem for Shelley because
it demonstrates this vital interdependence of love and imagination.

And so, the exhausted lyricist of the poem's first movement
inhabits a shattered world that must be recreated by the renewed power of loving vision. His song had been an unmediated outburst—an ungrounded, unconditioned self-bestowal.
In the second movement of *Epipsychidion* he works to repair
the "intervals and interstices" of his first poem, "whose void
. . . craves fresh food." He will establish his being by supplying
his life's story; his new work will become his autobiography.
But if this is a new poem, in another way it also remains the old
one. For he brings to it the materials of his exhausted lyrical
outburst—that expired metaphorical burden of Stars, Moons,
and Spouses. These expressions he reuses in telling the story of
his life.

In the manner of Dante, whose *Vita Nuova*, Shelley cites in
his poem's Preface as one of the models for *Epipsychidion*, this
new poem becomes a spiritual autobiography, which is to say
for Shelley, a fictive one—a life's story whose truths can be
related only through figuration. Where Dante's figurations
point toward transcendental realities and his vision is unified
by his belief in one God, Shelley's decentered figurations become the unfurling of surfaces that incessantly may be arranged and rearranged. Because his poem has formally
changed from lyric to autobiography, the relationships between his figurations now can become different. This second
poem becomes a renewed attempt at divining love's mystery
by proceeding under a new fictional hypothesis, the self-as-
history rather than the self-as-singer, which reconfigures the
fragments to produce a novel world.

Because he uses his old astronomical metaphors to refer to
the various loves of his life, speaking of one as "the Moon, the
Queen of Heaven's bright isles" (281), another as "the Planet of
that hour" (313), and Emily as "an Incarnation of the Sun"
(335), the pressures of the speaker's language progressively
configure a centering image; at last he sees that he has related

his planet-loves within a poetic solar system. He becomes the
Earth, and his women become Sun and Moon. This system
wheels forever in the dance of love, its energies coordinated
and conserved by the dynamic balance of gravitation. The
outcome of his autobiography is a cosmic vision of coherence
and constancy that reverses the exhausted shambles of his
initial lyrical outburst.

This second, autobiographical section of *Epipsychidion* becomes a fictive illustration of the Shelleyan surfaced deep self,
for it makes clear that a genre shift will alter the nature of both
the poet and the poem.[8] The autobiographer of *Epipsychidion*'s
second movement is not quite the self of the poem's first movement; he simultaneously inhabits and creates a rather different
world and, quite appropriately, enacts this shift by building
the master image of a "world of love" (346). Where the world of
the lyricist had become a chaos, the world of the autobiographer achieves a self-sustaining order. Not only does this
new configuration confer stability; in addition, it clarifies the
poet's vision of love by showing how variety and unity can be
reconciled. As imaged by the solar system, the truth of his love
is like the ubiquitous power of gravitation, which unites the
various planets in an eternally moving configuration which
nevertheless preserves their separate identities. Seen in this
way, the paradox of love's oneness-yet-manyness is better understood.

In these ways the second world-poem of *Epipsychidion* is an
advance upon the first, for it offers a stability and interpretive
clarity lacking in the lyrical outburst. But if Shelley's poem
makes progress in this respect, it makes sacrifices in another;
for the autobiographer's image of coherence—his vision of his
love-relationships as the configuration of a solar system—expresses his meaning with a certain distance and dryness. To
figure the spirit of his love in the image of a solar system
compromises the passion and immediacy of the narrator's earlier lyrical overflow. By distancing his desire he also abstracts
it; his poem threatens to become a fiction in the superficial
sense—a plaything, an object to be manipulated, a possession
of the poet. In order to remedy this spiritual dryness the poet
must return to the poem, give himself to it. He acts, however,
not to convert surface to depth but rather to transform his
detached literary vision into truly passionate expression.

So he creates another work, a Romantic nature poem. By
imagining a new world centered in an island paradise, and

bringing Emily and himself home there, he can fashion a renewed sense of social self. No longer the disembodied voice of the unmediated lyricist or the rather abstracted meditation of the spiritual autobiographer, this third expression of *Epipsychidion* locates the self in an edenic landscape and allows the poet to imagine himself as an idealized physical presence within nature. With Emily he will inhabit an ancient tower that is "a pleasure-house" where "Our simple life wants little," for "Nature, with all her children, haunts the hill" (491, 525, 528). The poet has created a place and a self-presence that allow him to give himself to his beloved, to express his devotion physically. Once again the astronomical expressions of *Epipsychidion* crop up, but this time they enact mutually rapturous sexual activity. Emily and her poet come together in "eclipse" (567), the merger of "two meteors of expanding flame" (576), the apotheosis of "Love's rare Universe" (589). This orgasmic climax leads to the absolute identity of the lovers, which the poet experiences as world decreation—"one death, / One Heaven, one Hell, one immortality, / And one annihilation." And at last the spent singer cries, "Woe is me! . . . I pant, I sink, I tremble, I expire!" (585–591).

Ironically, this conclusion recapitulates the *Alastor* Poet's vision of his beloved; and in a way, the two imaginative experiences are quite similar. Both poets have at last embodied infinity in an idealized self-image, and they both attempt a passionate embrace of their imagery, only to discover that this absolute identity leads to destruction. But where *Alastor* shows its Poet as taking these experiences literally and destroying himself through a kind of poetic naivete, *Epipsychidion* is a self-consciously literary poem capable of staging its destructions in a fictionalized way. The mobile astronomical imageries of this poem suggest that its speaker is aware he is making himself and his world—that love indeed does spread out toward infinity, through a series of transforming cosmic visions. Where Shelley portrays the *Alastor* Poet's destruction as a kind of spiritual fixity or obsession which narrows his vision, the generous and outgoing destruction of *Epipsychidion* is simultaneous with the poem's conclusion. This singer and his expressions terminate in a glorious lyrical outburst that works toward his meaning by expressing love's truth as the spiritualization of the sexual act.

In creating this consummation, the singer of *Epipsychidion* has rendered the surface meaningful—for he has endowed the

body with soul, shown the spiritual truths that can be incarnated in human sexuality. The Byron of *Don Juan* writes a
contrary type of poem when in Canto I he shows how young
Juan's Wordsworthian meditations are caused by his passion
for Julia, and can be relieved by his making love to her. Where
Byron deflates inwardness by showing that it actually is a
misunderstood form of the body's imperatives, Shelley redeems inwardness by displacing it to where it can be shown
and seen—on the surface of things. By making fictional worlds,
he works to render the spirit visible.

And indeed, the poet's sexual climax—his moment of completion and failure—markedly contrasts with the final lyrical
failure of the poem's first movement, which implied his impotence. There his "moth-like Muse has burnt its wings" (53),
unable to reach a beloved elevated to the level of a goddess, "a
mortal shape indued / With love and life and light and deity . . .
An image of some bright Eternity" (112–51). On the contrary,
the conclusion of *Epipsychidion* elevates the singer and his
beloved into a shared embodiment of love's rare universe in a
paradoxical instant of identity and extinction. This glorious
failure becomes the end of the poem's mobility—not a fixed or
obsessive ending such as the *Alastor* Poet's, but an apotheosis.

Such an ending invites comparison with the paradoxical
destructive victories of the imagination enacted in Keats's
Odes. In those poems the narrator struggled to become an
absolutely invisible poet—a spirit invading and possessing the
outerness of eternity's avatars so completely that he threatened to terminate his own existence. The Odes show the Keatsian desire for invisibility and self-awareness, eternal
performance and mortal consciousness, played out as the reversal of the imagination, its necessary return from transcendental flight to human life. In this way the Odes persuasively
chart the experience of imagination as episodic, an inclusive
but limited movement that creates the depth and complexity
of their speaker's soul. But when *Epipsychidion* reaches an
equivalent point its singer makes the choice rejected by
Keats—to press on toward eternity, to give up the soul's inwardness in generous activity, to renounce all in the attempt to
become identical with infinity. Just as Keats's Odes manage to
portray his choice as a valorization of human life, so does
Shelley's poem. Shelley's courageous singer projects his all
outward in an unrestrained act of generosity, the triumphant
death of selfhood. In *Epipsychidion* the image of sexual giving

becomes the final figuration that embodies love's rare universe. At last the poet has redeemed himself from isolation by fully giving himself to another. This is the human decipherment that parallels but immensely advances upon the *Alastor* Poet's self-giving in his decipherment of the Egyptian characters. Sexual union becomes Shelley's ultimate social image, for it enacts the utter interpenetration and transformation of knower and known.

Like Keats's Odes, *Epipsychidion* is persuasive because it holds to the complexities of human experience. Where Keats discovers that the imagination's infinite desire must suffer reversal and return to human life, Shelley finds that the imagination can embrace infinity, but only for a moment. This poet of mobility affirms eternity, but not as an object or a fixity—for him it is a momentary apotheosis that must pass away. The obsessive self-destruction of *Alastor* is redeemed in *Epipsychidion*, for the latter poem manages to reveal the creative possibilities inherent in certain kinds of destruction. This is an aspect of Keats's Odes also; both Keats and Shelley portray the acts of the imagination as inevitably mixing creation and destruction in the enterprise of soul-making. These poetic minds that feed upon infinity discover they must envision growth in necessary interrelationship with death. And *Epipsychidion* takes this insight to its extreme, by making the narrator's moment of greatest spiritual development identical with the moment of his poem's dissolution.

The glorious world and self of Shelley's triumphant conclusion to *Epipsychidion* is succeeded by an earthly epilogue showing the poet's return to his mundane life in a forsaken mood—wistfully musing that "Love's very pain is sweet, / But its reward is in the world divine / Which, if not here, it builds beyond the grave" (596–98), a thought that could have been entertained by the *Alastor* Poet himself. By suggesting that the triumphs of poetry are momentary, *Epipsychidion* acknowledges not only the imagination's transcendental drive toward identity, but also the variousness of its mobility. Like Byron, Shelley can acknowledge the inconsistency of human moods and attitudes. *Epipsychidion* does not supercede *Alastor* so much as it offers a glorious alternative to the earlier poem, a creative testament to variety and possibility.

Epipsychidion shows that Shelley's succession of poetic worlds does not always imply a movement of progress. Although the three world-making movements of the poem do enact an ever-enlarging inclusiveness, a passionate advance toward infinity, the final breaking-open of this poem leads to a new world that surely is not an improvement upon the preceding one. In an instant, the poet is precipitated from his apotheosis to a state of emptiness and depression. At some times, then, poetic vision can create an organic, progressive movement in which the materials of world-making repeatedly can be transformed into the unfurling surfaces of ever-enlarging worlds—but at other times the transition between worlds comes as a sharp break, a manifestation of inconsistency. Shelley's vision of inclusiveness must be honest enough to acknowledge the possible defeats as well as the victories of poetry.

The master image of love's solar system that climaxes the autobiographical movement of *Epipsychidion* hearkens back to the transformed world envisioned in Act IV of *Prometheus Unbound*, which Shelley had written a year and a half before. There, at the play's culmination we hear a great cosmic lyric sung by cooperating spirits who "build, in the Void's loose field, / A world for the Spirit of Wisdom to wield" (IV, 153–55); and by the Act's end a rapturous Earth and Moon wheel through the spacious heavens, revolutionizing the universe through their dance of love. This concluding figuration is Shelley's greatest expression of the surfaced deep self. Where in *Epipsychidion* lovers discover themselves as solar systems, in *Prometheus Unbound* Prometheus and his beloved Asia, the protagonists of Shelley's drama, fade away so that in the drama's last Act a transformed cosmos may unfold. In this play the personal concerns of *Epipsychidion* are expanded to social concerns, and love is politicized as Shelley shows it to be the fundamental social passion, the outward-tending emotion capable of revolutionizing the human order.

The unrestrained lyrical interchange between all spirits in the final Act of *Prometheus Unbound* suggests the Shelleyan social ideal—the hope that we all might give of ourselves unreservedly, and that this giving might result not in destruction or chaos, but in the active yet coordinated liveliness of a world. Shelley's planets rapturously wheel about each other, perpetually moving yet always maintaining their course—for their law is the law of gravitation, the mutual balancing-out of their energetic forces. But this paradisiacal condition of coordination in variety certainly does not prevail at the drama's opening. There we find Prometheus bound to a cliff in the Caucasus.

He hangs there because of his curse of Jupiter, a lyrical expression intended to thunder his defiance of tyranny but one that unfortunately incorporated the very will to power which he had hoped to denounce. This curse was a blind outpouring, an unpremeditated expression of fury—and so beside himself was Prometheus at the moment he cried out that later he cannot remember what he said. The unmediated expressiveness of this curse tellingly resembles the unmediated lyrical outburst that begins *Epipsychidion:* in both cases, we have moments of absolutely open expression that issue from depths uncomprehended by their speakers. Or rather, the spontaneous overflows of powerful feelings come from distinctly un-Wordsworthian sources, because there is no well-formed deep self within to support them. The *Epipsychidion* poet's song and Prometheus' curse simply *appear*, powerful manifestations of pure undeliberated emotion. Neither speaker has thought about what he feels, and so their emotion is strangely alienated from themselves. Just as *Epipsychidion* is a poem devoted to the speaker's progressive understanding of what he means when he says that he loves Emily absolutely, so *Prometheus Unbound* is a drama devoted to Prometheus' progressive understanding of what he meant when he cursed his foe, and why he wishes to curse no living being ever again. These poems of development show how the self is formed by integration of thought and emotion, as we learn what it means to experience our feelings. Like the Byronic self, the Shelleyan self must be made by bringing its obscure impulses to the surface—by becoming self-conscious.[9]

But at first it is precisely self-consciousness that Prometheus wants to avoid. He needs to recall his curse but does not want to hear it repeated by "aught resembling me" (1,220). So as his spokesman he summons up the Phantasm of Jupiter from the deep world "underneath the grave" (I, 197), hoping to disassociate his own words from himself by placing them in the mouth of his archenemy. But his strategy backfires, for Prometheus' companions Panthea and Ione see that Jupiter's "gestures proud and cold, / And looks of firm defiance, and calm hate" (I, 218–220) form an appropriate image to accompany Prometheus' vicious curse.

In *Prometheus Unbound* Shelley gives his most profound analysis of aggression. Here his subject is not only the imagination's capacity for poetic self-destructiveness, as in *Alastor* and *Epipsychidion*, but also, the much broader political question of social expressiveness, of revolutionary behavior. Thoughts of the French Revolution must never have been far from his mind as he wrote this poem. For like the revolutionaries, who bravely proclaimed a new world but then inadvertently destroyed it through the misunderstood aggressiveness of their own liberated feelings, Shelley's Prometheus brought civilization to the human race but then destroyed it by the unreflective barbarity of his curse.

The spectacle of his own words issuing from the mouth of the tyrant therefore images the truth: when Prometheus cursed, in effect he became Jupiter—for he made himself over in the image of tyranny. The Phantasm of Jupiter is related to the central figurations of *Alastor* and *Epipsychidion*, the Poet's dream beloved and Emily, those idealized poetic self-images that are the self but not the self, the best of the self transformed into the form of woman. Just as these figures harbor infinity, so does the Phantasm—for he is an infinitely brutal self-image, the worst of the self transformed into the one essence of oppression. But as he says of himself, he is "a frail and empty phantom" (I, 241), a pure surface, who can curse only by being filled with the voice of a living being. So it is Prometheus's inwardness which has issued from the image of Jupiter—and we see that the Shelleyan vision of variable identity implies that as we speak so shall we be seen, and become: by turns we can create ourselves as an Emily, or—unfortunately—as a Jupiter. By his curse Prometheus has perverted poetic expression, releasing a primal hatred that flows out over the surfaces of life and refigures them as a vision of tyranny. His polluting expression simultaneously has made his victimized self and the oppressive world in which he now suffers.[10]

The expression of infinity which Prometheus's curse brings to the surface is one of such absolute willfulness that it swamps self-consciousness in blind hatred. Prometheus has goaded Jupiter to "blast mankind" and to uncreate the world, letting "thy malignant spirit move / In darkness over those I love: / On me and mine I imprecate / The utmost torture of thy hate" (I, 275–79). Thus he turns himself into an inversion of the world-creating God of Genesis. In his hyperbolic hatred he sacrifices the world to his own self-assertion: his imagination must prove its powers through releasing infinite destruction, which then can be heroically countered by infinite resistance. This debased Promethean self comes into being as primal conflict, a perpetual self-struggle which unlike the soul's internal conflicts portrayed in Keats's Odes, works not toward heightened lucidity and creative soul-making but stands the self off against itself in locked stasis.[11]

The interdependence of self and world creation now becomes evident: one cannot proclaim one's own identity without also positing the sort of world appropriate to that existence—and such worlds inevitably will be social, for to be someone is to be in relationship to something outside the self. To be a torturer one requires a victim, and to be a victim one needs one's torturer. Identity therefore must be multiple: we proclaim ourselves not as a self-contained essence but as an active inter-relation of roles—an interrelation which creates not the deep isolate selfhood of *Alastor*, but the unfurling figures of a world.

To say that Prometheus has imagined a world of tyranny is by no means to imply that tyrannical behavior always is some sort of self-generated illusion. In fact, Prometheus's world presently is dominated by Jupiter, who is as ruthless a tyrant as Prometheus possibly could wish for. Nevertheless, Prometheus' self-victimization is the primal imaginative act that makes him subject to the actual tyrant. Without it, he would be free to choose some alternative response. In *Alastor* Shelley demonstrated that his worst fears were of the imagination's potential self-destructiveness, and in *Prometheus Unbound* this view is given a social application: our imaginative worlds help mould the actual social worlds in which we must live, and so the self-destructive imagination becomes the primal source of human aggressiveness, against both itself and all others. Therefore in order to cope with aggression, the first imaginative act must be the reformation of the self.

When Prometheus has heard his curse again, as it issues from the Phantasm of Jupiter, the global relations involved are driven home for him. He is appalled at his words and takes them back quite simply by saying, "It doth repent me: words are quick and vain; / Grief for awhile is blind, and so was mine. / I wish no living thing to suffer pain" (I, 303–05). Like the curse, this quiet recantation is a global statement. Prometheus has understood his own terrible meanings and now self-consciously revises his willing—he wishes "no living thing to suffer pain." These new words suggest a new world figuration in which heroism no longer is predicated as willful defiance, the egotistical resolve to distinguish oneself by enduring infinite pain. Now the hero will be the gentle man, who in loving outreach goes beyond himself to care about the condition of others. Where the cursing Prometheus had called down

Jupiter's tortures "On me and mine" this new Prometheus demonstrates his social vision, his compassion, by willing the well-being of everyone. And because his statement is global in its inclusion of all living things, perforce he wills his own protection, his own well-being also. He has renounced the victim's role, and along with it that of the torturer. Prometheus has unfurled his heroism as a new world poem—a poem of loving strength, care, and protection. No longer need the true hero remain painfully locked in an attitude of rigid defiance.

Prometheus' transformation may reflect not only Shelley's own meditations on self-destructiveness, but also his reaction to the figure of the Byronic hero. Two years before *Prometheus Unbound* Byron had written his own "Prometheus," which portrays Prometheus as enduring "A silent suffering, and intense. . . . All that the proud can feel of pain, / The agony they do not show." Here is the Byronic hero, that creature of impenetrable surface who establishes his identity by stoically refusing to reveal his pain. Shelley's Prometheus implicitly shows up the self-aggrandizing effect of this posture: the values embodied in the figure are individualistic rather than social, for the real impact of Byronic heroism is to glorify the isolate's stance rather than to serve humanity. The Byronic resolve never to change really is a form of fixedness designed to display heroism on the surface rather than to create a truly heroic soul—and in this perspective, resistance becomes aligned with showiness rather than with real feeling. Significantly, when Shelley's Prometheus changes his mind and takes his curse back, his audience is dismayed. The Earth laments, "Misery, O misery to me, / That Jove at length should vanquish thee" (I, 306–7). Although Prometheus's flexibility is mistakenly interpreted as capitulation, he shows no concern for saving the appearances—for his interest is not in looking like a hero, but in discovering what he must become to truly be one. Shelley differs from the Byron of the Turkish Tales in suggesting that the capacity to change rather than to remain implacably defiant is the necessary prerequisite for heroism. Where the hero remains the constant center of attention in Byron's poems, Shelley's socialized Prometheus now resigns center stage in order to allow other beings to play a part in remaking the world.

And so the action of Act II is carried out by Asia, a new Promethean alter ego who now replaces Jupiter as the mirroring Other than enfolds the Titan's identity. When he spoke his poem of world hatred Prometheus's appropriate figuration indeed was the "frail and empty phantom" of Jupiter (I, 241), but his poem of world love requires a reflecting agent who is not simply a superficial and passive image. Instead, as a being in her own right Asia engages the creative capacities of surface—the power of mobility, the potential to act and to change things. In *Alastor* and *Epipsychidion* the beloved women are the beau ideal, the object of their poets' quests. *Prometheus Unbound* alters this pattern to show Asia as an active agent as well as an ideal beloved. Her participation makes the play's world transformation into a collaboration between herself and Prometheus—into the loving relations that could exist between equal beings.[12]

The Act's first scene shows Asia and her companions Panthea and Ione discussing a variety of dreams they experienced during the preceding night. Like the *Alastor* Poet, they have had dream visions; and like the speaker of *Epipsychidion* in his lyric outburst, they express their feeling through a multiplicity of images—for between themselves they possess not one vision, but five. Asia and her handmaidens bring poetry to the surface by converting deep images into social discussions, by proliferating rather than fixing the significance of their private experience. Their dreams are deeply mysterious, deeply evocative—they are primal material, like Prometheus's curse. He had to bring his impulses to the surface to formulate them and understand himself, and in this respect Asia's process of soul-making is quite similar. As deep images her visions have no intrinsic significance; it is only as she brings them out and acts upon them that she really will come to understand what she means.

Panthea has dreamed of Prometheus as a sunlike being drawing her upward in desire, and Asia looks into her eyes and sees Prometheus reflected there not as a sun, but as the vanishing moon. A rough "shape" succeeds him, crying "Follow, follow!" (1, 127, 131). This vision reminds Panthea of a second dream, in which she felt driven along by a rude and windlike presence. The recollection prompts Asia's memory of her own forgotten dream of drivenness, wherein she found herself in a windswept spring world whose images also were inscribed *"Follow, O follow!"* (1, 153). As with the prolific lyrical imagery that initiates *Epipsychidion*, the multiple visions of *Prometheus Unbound* function as evocative fragments—various formulations of the truth that create not chaos but the stimulation of desire and the initiation of an expansive outward movement that begins to enlarge life. But the socialized interpretive situation of *Prometheus Unbound* produces a kind of poetry that goes beyond *Epipsychidion:* because they discuss their dreams together, the women's visionary intensity is converted to public vocalization. Their excitement mounting, the repetitions of "Follow, O follow!" grow progressively louder until the words echo back to them from the surrounding mountains. They begin to follow these enticing calls under the impression that mysterious voices from the outside beckon them into a quest— but the reader of *Prometheus Unbound* can see that these cries actually are the echoes of their own outreaching desire.

Asia's descent into Demogorgon's cave brings Shelley's poetry of the surface to its highest point of development; for it is here that Asia extends her intuitively self-externalizing activity to a new intensity of realization, as she begins to become self-conscious about what she is doing. At the deep heart of the world, the place from which oracles issue, Asia confronts a king and discovers that unlike the kingly Phantasm of Jupiter, that "frail and empty phantom" of mere surface, Demogorgon is unfigured—cryptic and invisible. She sees only a formless darkness brooding over the throne; and Demogorgon can only tell her that "a voice / Is wanting, the deep truth is imageless" (iv, 115–16). As pure depth Demogorgon comprises potential, but does not body forth meaning—for meaning is an unfolding function of surface, of the proliferation of images and interpretations.

Demogorgon's deep imagelessness calls into question the reflexive poetic processes that led to Prometheus's projection of himself as Jupiter, and Asia's pursuit of her own voice of desire. This allows Asia to become conscious of such self-reflexiveness in a way that Prometheus really was not. She realizes that whatever the world's deep truth may be she does not perceive it—she perceives the truth, the world, that is figured by herself. But this discovery leads not to the blankness and solopsist despair of the *Alastor* Poet's postvisionary state; quite the contrary, it empowers Asia by making her realize that if she generates her world then she also is capable of changing it. If she does not want a world in which evil rains down like "the immedicable plague, which while / Man looks on his own creation like a God / And sees that it is glorious, drives him on, / The wreck of his own will" (iv, 100–104), she herself must project a more creative regime. Her belief in Jupiter has ceased, and in this moment he is overthrown—for his tyrannical power depended upon the consent of his victims, their inadvertent collusion in maintaining his destructive world order of domination and submission.

Asia has learned how to use her fictions rather than be used by them, and her self-consciousness simultaneously is reconfigured as the individual's triumphant soul-making and her liberation of the world. Her poetry of surface is revealed as both sophisticated and revolutionary; for now we can see that it is the self-conscious imagination which is truly capable. Having unbound itself from the obscure menace of its own deep impulses by bringing them to the surface and refiguring them in transformed forms, this imagination is able to reach outward as a truly creative, active agent capable of changing the world for the better.

From the start Asia has been a lover, a being who reached beyond herself in imaginative desire. Now she has become a responsible agent as well, a person who self-consciously realizes that she makes what she sees. With this insight *Prometheus Unbound* politicizes the notion of love. It becomes the truly social passion which generates human society through the collaborative creative of figurative worlds—the worlds of culture that Shelley celebrates in *A Defence of Poetry*, and the redeemed poetic cosmos of the play's last Act.

As a mobile poem of worldmaking *Prometheus Unbound* invites comparison with *Don Juan*. Byron's generosity, like Shelley's, is a consequence of his incessant mobility: he knows he can save nothing and so he gives everything away, becomes a poetic speculator who uses his energies freely. His successes become the result of his rapid dexterity—the happy juxtapositions, surprising reverses, and last-minute recoveries by which he outmaneuvers life's changeableness. This generosity is exhilarating, and does perform the social function of enlivening his audience—but Byron cannot conceive of his imaginative manipulations as really formulating a world or a society. *Don Juan* demonstrates the meaninglessness of all surfaces and therefore generates the incessant mobility of the surface self as an art which rearranges the appearances but does not reveal their significance. Byron's poem, Byron's world, are truly endless because he conceives of the universe as an unstoppable succession of altering forms that never will achieve closure.

Shelley, however, envisions the gathering of meaning, the oncoming coherence of the world. His surfaced deep self simultaneously exfoliates the sense of selfhood and the significance of the cosmos. Where self-consciousness is apt to be disassociative or ironic in Byron, involving as it does a rueful recognition of humanity's dark or wayward primal impulses, self-consciousness in Shelley becomes a route to soul-making, a way to convert primal material into the unfolding surfaces of redeemed human meanings. But this Shelleyan surfaced self is perpetually in motion, so that if his vision configures human society nevertheless it cannot underwrite that society's stability. The pressures to transform will be incessant, as will our responsibility to rightly manage these transformations.

Demogorgon emphasizes this truth at the play's conclusion by announcing that the redeemed world again could fall into chaos, for it is not grounded in the depths but simply is the unfurling figurations of Prometheus's and Asia's revolutionary poetry. Just as the triumphant apotheosis of *Epipsychidion* was followed by a forsaken postvisionary epilogue, so the mobility of the poetic moods and attitudes in *Prometheus Unbound* possibly could result in the disfiguration of the world. There are no sure safeguards against the resurgence of destructiveness, the reexpression of a world-ruining curse. Demogorgon therefore counsels the only kind of fixity imaginable in a constantly mobile cosmos: the resolve to not be overcome by whatever happens. It is the constancy of patient hope, the necessity "To live, and bear; to hope, till Hope creates / From its own wreck the thing it contemplates" (573–74) that becomes the final value of *Prometheus Unbound*.

This is a brave position, and yet unavoidably also a tenuous one. Just as Byron found the deep self and its leading poetic manifestation the organic poem twin impossibilities, so Shelley cannot envision the self as deep, centered, and stable and the poem as a triumphant imaginative resolution. For Shelley the self, the poem, and human society always are in process. He strives toward a poetry of progress, a poetry in which ever-renewed world making enacts the continual expansion and advancement of humane vision; but he knows that the revolution, the point of transition between worlds, sometimes can represent a violent break rather than a poetic transformation. Unfortunately, love's world never will be secure; and so the poet's mission is to do all he can to make human mobility a creative act of the imagination rather than an enactment of destruction.[13]

8

CONCLUSION
The Dilemmas of Selfhood

The preceding chapters have displayed six minds that feed upon infinity—and that recognize themselves as infinite through the boundlessness of their desires. As Blake expressed it in *There is No Natural Religion,* "less than All cannot satisfy Man." These poets respond to their desire by forming the deep self, that human version of infinity whose hallmarks are centered meditative profundity, humane wisdom, and indefinitely continued growth. Even Byron and Shelley, who turn away from the depths to create their separate versions of the surface self, do so as a defensive reaction against the profound appeal of the deep self; for Byron reluctantly concludes that the meditative Wordsworthian personality is a self-serving illusion, and Shelley fears that his own depths threaten to destroy him.

So the persuasive voices that we hear speaking in such depth poems as Wordsworth's *The Prelude* and Keats's Odes issue not from purely humane sources but from originally infinite desire—which includes the appetite for domination as well as the aspiration to transcendence. Inevitably the Romantic imagination becomes tainted by dark impulses, and the deep self must be formed to control aggression as well as to foster development. Growth and defense become intertwined, and the result is not triumphantly autonomous poetic voices but conflicted, ambiguous ones. Their efforts to create humane self-identities indicate the poets' desire for a socialized, harmonious human order; but on the other hand, the deep self, which is to effect this end, often engenders a new and more radical state of isolation. A cardinal example is the persona of Keats's Odes, who in isolation becomes one of the most profound and attractive of all Romantic voices, but accomplishes this only by confining his meditations to the inner world of his own self— for to turn outside, to give his attention to other persons, inevitably would lead him to distressing social relations of domination and submission, manipulation and victimization.

The conflicted nature of the deep self is reflected in the difficulties these poets experience in managing it. For as we have seen in the preceding chapters, none of them can easily or permanently establish a depth identity. They are great poets not because their created personas solve the problems that inspired their poetry, but because they continue to register such difficulties, and to struggle with them. Their poems become episodes, tentative imaginative essays produced within each poet's characteristic sense of his own condition—ongoing attempts to reconcile the desire for infinity with the limitations of selfhood. Because these poetic essays are evoked by infinite desire, they are bound to fall short; for the essential Romantic aspiration is to write the Poem of Everything, a perennial goal and a continual impossibility. Blake's and Wordsworth's approaches to this Poem of Everything perhaps are paradigmatic. Blake struggles to bring the world inside his poetic Man and there to make it humane and translucent, and the Wordsworth of *The Prelude* works toward a similar end by creating a persona capable of meditating on his own life so profoundly that he becomes representative man who reflects the deep harmonies of the world. But Blake's and Wordsworth's ambitious inclusiveness cannot embrace everything: Blake's visionary insistence on unity tends to slight difference and diversity, particularly in his treatment of sexuality in *Jerusalem*, and Wordsworth's reliance on meditation potentially isolates him from action in the world.

Blake's and Wordsworth's failures of inclusiveness perhaps can be described as failures to imaginatively recreate aggression. It was Blake's prophetic ambition to convert corporeal to spiritual warfare, to retain the power of aggressive desires but change them into creative energies—but at last he is unable to transform sexual conflict into a vision of sexual relationship. Similarly, Wordsworth hoped to portray poetic meditation as a purified form of action, a mature and humane activity that transcended the possible hostilities and follies involved in worldly involvement—but he leaves us with the suspicion that his meditative stance may exist as much to protect the poet from the world as to foster his soul's growth. Both poets succeed very considerably in their attempts at imaginative transformation, but since their desire was for totality their failure to achieve it cannot be overlooked, and calls into question the imagination's self-sufficiency.

The experience of the other poets resembles Wordsworth's and Blake's, for they too find it impossible to include totality and entirely transform aggression. In his conversation poems Coleridge succeeds in creating a benevolent and universal imaginative order in the meditative mold of Wordsworth, but his nightmare poetry suggests the limitations of poetic harmony by releasing infinity as a monstrous, alienated form of power divorced from the humane agencies of the poet's conscious self. Keats aspires to world harmony by creating the persona of the invisible poet, that heroic figure who in sacrificing himself makes nature bloom; but eventually he acknowledges his own self-interested desires and in the Odes creates a deep self capable of turning within the world of himself to make his own human nature bloom, but never depicted as interacting with other persons. At a stroke Byron solves the problems posed by the deep self by simply denying its existence, but his refreshing acknowledgement of the self's and the world's frequent hostility and randomness leaves us searching for a sense of order—an order that is only tentatively provided by the ad hoc and improvisational Byronic imagination. Shelley tries to disarm his own self-destructiveness by turning the deep self inside out, converting it into the unfurling surfaces of renewed worlds; but his appetite for totality is expressed through a universal embrace which in striving to include everything tends to at last overreach itself and break down. Destruction and recreation must proceed incessantly for this poet, and as a result his vision of order, like Byron's, at best can be only provisional.

The failure to include totality, the persistence of destructiveness, the tendency of socializing visions to yield new forms of isolation—these are the poets' perennial problems, the difficulties that could not be definitively overcome through the heroic exertions of the Romantic imagination. But paradoxically, it is these very dilemmas that are the lifeblood of the deep self. For if the self is to grow incessantly it must do so by continually transcending itself; and that transcendence is a kind of self-overcoming. In other words, growth necessitates conflict.

In this volume we have observed the warring tendencies within the deep self, which must clash in search of resolution. Blake's *Jerusalem* perhaps provides the clearest illustration: his poem-as-heterocosm envisions the competing aspects of self as characters who continually strive in the severe contentions of friendship, forever attempting a resolution which will include everything, that refrains from casting out any aspect of the self. Wordsworth too tries to mix the "Discordant elements" of his experience into "one society" through the ever-expanding incorporations of his poetic meditation. Coleridge permits the murder of the conscious self in order to liberate the infinitely powerful bardic voice of the possessed poet. And for the Keats of the Odes, the drama of the soul's growth is staged through the perennial attempt of the conflicting aspects of self to manipulate or dominate each other.

In fact, the Romantic imagination's social dreaming not only sets the self off against society, but also applies this model of social conflict to the very construction of the self itself. Strife becomes a prerequisite to integration not only in social relations, but in the formation of individual personality. But if the development of a deep self finally at peace with itself is a perennial Romantic desire, at the same time it is paradoxically undesirable. For the end of discord also would mean the end of activity, and a soul that no longer grew would no longer be alive. Growth and defense, creation and destruction, are necessarily interrelated in Romantic soul-making—each member of these bipolar pairings comes into existence as a function of the other.

The literary history of the later nineteenth century increasingly reveals the problems generated by the Romantic imagination's social dreaming. Establishing social order on the foundation of the deep self, that humane sensibility which underwrites civilization, becomes more and more difficult. But as I have tried to show, at the century's beginning the Romantic poets already were experiencing significant difficulties in the formulation of the deep self. Although they appear optimistic in contrast to such writers as Tennyson or Arnold, their creations of profound selfhood are at best tentative. Their failures certainly raise the question of whether a society can be built on the basis of the humane individual's vision; but on the other hand, their openness to the question and their heroic persistence in struggling with it continue to merit our attention and our admiration.

NOTES

Chapter 1. Introduction: Routes to Infinity

1. Hyder Edward Rollins, ed., *The Letters of John Keats 1814–1821*, 2 vols. (Cambridge, Mass.: Harvard University Press, 1958), vol. 2, letter 159, p. 102.

2. Clifford Siskin, *The Historicity of Romantic Discourse* (New York: Oxford University Press, 1988), 11. For two good accounts of the deep self as continually involved in the process of growth see Stephen Prickett's *Coleridge and Wordsworth: The Poetry of Growth* (Cambridge: Cambridge University Press, 1970) and Robert Langbaum's chapter, "Wordsworth: The Self as Process," in his *The Mysteries of Identity: A Theme in Modern Literature* (New York: Oxford University Press, 1977).

3. Harold Bloom, *The Anxiety of Influence: A Theory of Poetry* (Oxford: Oxford University Press, 1973).

4. Quotations are from the 1805 version of *The Prelude*. See Jonathan Wordsworth, M. H. Abrams, and Stephen Gill, eds., *William Wordsworth: The Prelude 1799, 1805, 1850* (New York and London, W. W. Norton and Company, 1979). Book Thirteenth, lines 69–70.

5. See the section titled "Imagination and Napoleon" in Chapter 1 of Alan Liu's *Wordsworth: The Sense of History* (Stanford: Stanford University Press, 1989), pp. 23–31, for an intriguing discussion of the Napoleonic overtones in Book Sixth of *The Prelude*.

6. Charles J. Rzepka, *The Self as Mind: Vision and Identity in Wordsworth, Coleridge, and Keats* (Cambridge: Harvard University Press, 1986), p. 29.

7. Rzepka, pp. 26–27.

8. Rzepka, p. 23.

9. For a classic study of the relationship between class conflict and emerging class-consciousness in late eighteenth and early nineteenth-century England, see E. P. Thompson, *The Making of the English Working Class* (London: Victor Gollancz, 1963).

10. Some of the important decentering books include Harold Bloom et al., *Deconstruction and Criticism* (New York: Seabury Press, 1979); David Simpson, *Irony and Authority in Romantic Poetry* (Totowa, N.J.: Rowman and Littlefield, 1979); Anne K. Mellor, *English Romantic Irony* (Cambridge: Harvard University Press, 1980); and Tilottama Rajan, *Dark Interpreter: The Discourse of Romanticism* (Ithaca and London: Cornell University Press, 1980).

11. Jerome J. McGann, *The Romantic Ideology: A Critical Investigation* (Chicago and London: The University of Chicago Press, 1983), p. 134.

12. See chapter 1, "Insight and oversight: reading 'Tintern Abbey,'" in Marjorie Levinson's *Wordsworth's great period poems: Four essays* (Cambridge: Cambridge University Press, 1986).

13. Jon P. Klancher, *The Making of English Reading Audiences, 1790–1832*

(Madison: The University of Wisconsin Press, 1987). Klancher describes the creation of three new nineteenth-century audiences—middle-class, radical, and mass—which come to recognize themselves in opposition to each other.

14. Marlon B. Ross, *The Contours of Masculine Desire: Romanticism and the Rise of Women's Poetry* (New York: Oxford University Press, 1989), p. 49.

15. Ross, p. 25.

16. For a good introduction to Bakhtin's thought, see Tzvetan Todorov, *Mikhail Bakhtin: The Dialogical Principle* (Minneapolis: University of Minnesota Press, 1984).

Chapter 2. Blake: The Translucent Man

1. Quotations from Blake's poetry and prose are from *The Complete Poetry and Prose of William Blake*, ed. David V. Erdman; commentary, Harold Bloom. Newly Revised Edition (Berkeley and Los Angeles: University of California Press, 1982).

2. For good accounts of Blake's reaction to Locke, see "The Case Against Locke" in Northrop Frye's *Fearful Symmetry: A Study of William Blake* (Princeton: Princeton University Press, 1947), and "The Critique of Vision" in Peter F. Fisher's *The Valley of Vision: Blake as Prophet and Revolutionary* (Toronto: University of Toronto Press, 1961). Edward Larrissy gives a good discussion of the seventeenth and eighteenth-century backgrounds for Blake's tracts on religion in his *William Blake* (Oxford and New York: Basil Blackwell, 1985). See Chapter 4: "The Ambiguity of Bound: There is No Natural Religion (ca. 1788), Europe (1790)."

3. For two accounts of Blake's symbolism of the human body, see Thomas Frosch's *The Awakening of Albion* (Ithaca and London: Cornell University Press, 1974), and Anne K. Mellor's *Blake's Human Form Divine* (Berkeley: University of California Press, 1974). A third, and partly critical account is Leopold Damrosch Jr.'s *Symbol and Truth in Blake's Myth* (Princeton: Princeton University Press, 1980). Damrosch argues for a Blake who wishes to reconcile the particular and the universal symbolically in Jesus, who must be "a body as well as a mind" (p. 24). However, this reconciliation is frequently an uneasy one: "Blake refuses to accept the distinction between unity and diversity, declaring over and over again that the many are one in Jesus, but admitting at the same time that this unity is hoped for more than experienced. Hence the constant tension in Blake between the unity we ought to enjoy, in which subjectivity would disappear along with the gap between subject and object, and the individual perception that in fact separates us from each other" (pp. 31–33).

4. For a good discussion of Blake's imaginative vision of the senses, see Robert F. Gleckner, "Blake and the Senses," *Studies in Romanticism* 5 (1965): 1–15.

5. I regard interpretation of the *Songs* as involving a problem of balance between particular and universal considerations, between immediate human utterance and symbolic system. Critics who emphasize the systematic in Blake tend to see the presence of point of view in the individual *Songs* as the multiple appearances of essential oneness—and so the separate human dramas of the *Songs* become subordinated to the elucidation of Blake's symbol system. Perhaps the best approaches in this vein are Robert F. Gleckner's *The*

Piper and the Bard (Detroit: Wayne State University Press, 1959), and Hazard Adams's *William Blake: A Reading of the Shorter Poems* (Seattle: University of Washington Press, 1963). In "Blake's Symbolic Technique," his principal chapter on Blake's methodology, Gleckner argues that "Each of Blake's song series (or states or major symbols) is comprised of a number of smaller units (or states or symbols), so that the relationship of each unit to the series as a whole might be stated as a descending progression: from the states of innocence and experience to the *Songs of Innocence and of Experience*, to each individual song, to the symbols within each song, to the words that form the symbols. Conceivably ignorance of or indifference to one word can prohibit the imaginative perception and understanding of the whole structure. 'Every word and every letter is studied and put into its fit place,' Blake wrote in the preface to *Jerusalem*" (pp. 62–63).

6. See *Leviathan: or the Matter, Forme and Power of a Commonwealth Ecclesiastical and Civil*, part 1, chapter 13. For an excellent account of the Hobbist overtones of *Experience*, consult D. G. Gillham's chapter on "Blake's Criticism of 'Nature'" in his *Blake's Contrary States: The Songs of Innocence and of Experience as Dramatic Poems* (Cambridge: Cambridge University Press, 1966). In addition, see pages 133–38 for a compact account of Blake's disagreements with the selfist moral philosophies of the seventeenth and eighteenth centuries.

7. In *Blake's Apocalypse: A Study in Poetic Argument* (Garden City, N.Y.: Doubleday and Company, 1963), Harold Bloom suggests that the union of Los and Urizen may reflect Blake's awareness of a potential merger between aspects of himself: "Urizen is within us as he was within Blake, and there is even a self-mocking aspect of his poem, demonstrating how uncomfortable Blake was in trying to keep the compass-wielding categorizer in his place" (p. 175). Christine Gallant makes a similar point in her reading of the poem. See the chapter on "Myth and Non-Myth" in her *Blake and the Assimilation of Chaos* (Princeton: Princeton University Press, 1978). She feels that "the Lambeth Books consciously show the paradox central to Blake's situation. There is at once the satiric self-awareness in them of the basic problem of the systematic thinker, and also the determined reassociation through myth of that which seems most dissociated in actual experience. Either may lead to rigidity: in the first case, to a tired and ironic resignation to the impossibilities of the work confronting the mythmaker; in the second, to a petrifying of the imagination as the myth becomes fixed" (p. 13). See also W. J. T. Mitchell's reading of the poem, "The Human Illusion," in his *Blake's Composite Art: A Study of the Illuminated Poetry* (Princeton: Princeton University Press, 1978).

8. For a persuasive Jungian reading of Blake's career that sees him making increasingly inclusive attempts to incorporate the unconscious into his poetry, see Christine Gallant's *Blake and the Assimilation of Chaos*.

9. There are many interesting discussions of Blake's turn toward synchronicity in his prophecies. See Leslie Tannenbaum's *Biblical Tradition in Blake's Early Prophecies: The Great Code of Art* (Princeton: Princeton University Press, 1982); Hazard Adams' "Blake, *Jerusalem* and Symbolic Form," *Blake Studies* 7 (1975): 143–66; Robert F. Gleckner's "Most Holy Forms of Thought: Some Observations on Blake and Language," *ELH* 41 (1974): 555–77; Ronald L. Grimes's "Time and Space in Blake's Major Prophecies" in *Blake's Sublime Allegory*, ed. Stuart Curran and Joseph Wittreich (Madison:

University of Wisconsin Press, 1977); Stuart Curran's "The Structures of *Jerusalem*" in *Blake's Sublime Allegory;* the chapter on "Form" in Morton D. Paley's *The Continuing City: William Blake's Jerusalem* (Oxford: Clarendon Press, 1983); and W. J. T. Mitchell's chapter on *Jerusalem* in *Blake's Composite Art.*

10. For Jungian defenses of Blake's treatment of sexuality in *Jerusalem,* see Christine Gallant's chapter on the poem in her *Blake and the Assimilation of Chaos,* especially pages 170–73, and Morton D. Paley's discussion of "Spectre and Emanation" in his *The Continuing City.* For another defense of Blake see Irene Tayler's "The Woman Scaly," *Midwestern Modern Language Association Bulletin* 6 (Spring 1973): 74–87.

The Winter 1982–83 number of *Blake: An Illustrated Quarterly* is devoted to critical examination of Blake's view of women; see especially Anne K. Mellor's fine "Blake's Portrayal of Women." Other thought-provoking critiques of Blake are chapter 5 of Leopold Damrosch Jr.'s *Symbol and Truth in Blake's Myth* and Susan Fox's "The Female as Metaphor in William Blake's Poetry," *Critical Inquiry* 3 (Spring 1977): 507–20.

Chapter 3. Wordsworth: The Meditating Self

1. *The Prose Works of William Wordsworth,* ed. W. J. B. Owen and Jane Smyser 3 vols. (Oxford: The Clarendon Press, 1974), vol. 2, pp. 51–52. All further references to Wordsworth's prose refer to this edition, and appear in the text.

2. Two recent books approach Wordsworth's poetry via the "Essays on Epitaphs." The first is D. D. Devlin's *Wordsworth and the Poetry of Epitaphs* (Totowa, N.J.: Barnes & Noble Books, 1981). See especially Chapter 4, "The Poem as Epitaph." Devlin argues that "Wordsworth, especially in the *Essays upon Epitaphs,* saw . . . reconcilement of opposites as the aim and purpose of his poetry, and that the greatest virtue of the epitaph was its ability to unify things separate and to bring together discordant qualities" (pp. 109–10). Frances Ferguson offers an interesting consideration of Wordsworth's poetic language as emanating from the elegiac impulse in *Wordsworth: Language as Counter-spirit* (New Haven: Yale University Press, 1977). "Although Wordsworth might seem to offer 'language-as-incarnation' as a replacement for the eighteenth-century notion of 'language-as-dress,' both the 'Essays upon Epitaphs' and Wordsworth's poetry generally prompt a reevaluation of what linguistic 'incarnation' might be. For the 'fallings from us,' the 'vanishings' within the life of the individual, and the multiple miniature deaths which figure as part of that Wordsworthian life suggest that neither human incarnation nor linguistic incarnation is a fixed form which can be arrived at and sustained. The life of language in poetry, like the life of the individual, is radically implicated with death" (6–7). See also an earlier attempt to approach Wordsworth's poetic theory through the "Essays on Epitaphs"— Ernest Bernhardt-Kabisch's "Wordsworth: The Monumental Poet," *Philological Quarterly* 44 (1965): 503–18. Bernhardt-Kabisch argues that Wordsworth "came to find in the epitaph and the monument conceptual metaphors expressive of what he generally felt poetry should be and do. . . . Poetry to Wordsworth meant the search for permanence and universality through

simplicity, naturalness, and the fusion of motion and rest, the particular and the general, time and eternity" (p. 509).

3. The text of "Tintern Abbey" is from *The Poetical Works of Wiliam Wordsworth*, ed. Ernest de Selincourt and Helen Darbishire, second edition (Oxford: at the Clarendon Press, 1952–1959). Lines quoted are 67–68.

4. This quotation is from Wordsworth's first version of the play, written in 1797–99. There is also an 1842 version in which Rivers is renamed Oswald and Mortimer is renamed Marmaduke. See *The Borderers*, ed. Robert Osborn (Ithaca and London: Cornell University Press, 1982), p. 214.

5. For a discussion of suffering, see James H. Averill, *Wordsworth and the Poetry of Human Suffering* (Ithaca and London: Cornell University Press, 1980). Averill argues that "In blending the experience of tragedy with that of sublimity, Wordsworth follows the current of his age. As W. P. Albrecht has shown, 'the merger of the sublime and the tragic took place during the eighteenth and early nineteenth centuries, completing itself in the definitions of sublimity and tragedy offered by Hazlitt and Keats.' In Wordsworth, certainly, the merger is virtually complete, in terms of response if not theory. The pathetic, for him, is a source of psychic energy equivalent to other forms of the sublime. The 'Essay, Supplementary to the Preface' gives the pathetic and the sublime as the two major sources which the poet can tap to 'call forth and to communicate *power*' (*Prose*, 3, 82). . . . The sublime and the pathetic share a single aim, to move the reader by poetic power 'to be excited, often to external, and always to internal, effort' (3.81–82)" (pp. 114–15).

6. The poem was written in the 1790s and reflects contemporary conditions, but Wordsworth displaced the action to the 1780s. See *The Ruined Cottage and The Pedlar*, ed. James Butler (Ithaca: Cornell University Press, 1979), p. 5.

7. My reading of the poem follows m.s. D (1799) as printed in the Cornell Wordsworth. See Butler, ll. 68–71.

8. For a reading of "The Ruined Cottage" as a tragedy, see Jonathan Wordsworth, *The Music of Humanity: A Critical Study of Wordsworth's "Ruined Cottage"* (London: Thomas Nelson and Sons, 1969). See also Averill's chapter on "Suffering and Calm in the Early Poetry 1788–1798," which offers a cathartic view: "Whether he had in mind Aristotle's terminology or not, Wordsworth could find, on the beat of his own pulse and in contemporary theories of the sublime and the pathetic, ample evidence of the cathartic value of pathos. Notably, *The Ruined Cottage* is only one of several early poems where natural tranquillity follows a tale of suffering. The dynamic juxtaposition of suffering and calm forms an important habit of the poet's imagination; time and again, human misery provides the psychic energy necessary to purge life of its petty irritations and to make accessible the cathartic calm" (p. 61).

9. See *The Prelude 1799, 1805, 1850: Authoritative Texts Context and Reception Recent Critical Essays*, ed. Jonathan Wordsworth, M. H. Abrams, and Stephen Gill (New York: W. W. Norton and Company, 1979), Book First, 352–61. My quotations from *The Prelude* are from the 1805 text of this edition.

10. For a provocative analysis of mixing, see Clifford Siskin's *The Historicity of Romantic Discourse* (New York: Oxford University Press, 1988). Siskin argues that transcendence was written up in early nineteenth-century texts

by a psychologizing strategy which naturalized "the transformation of hierarchy from a structure based on inherited, unchanging distinctions to one
that posits an initial equality subject to psychological and developmental
difference." Consequently, distinctions of generic kind were collapsed into
distinctions of degree, and imagination then "becomes the ever-present link
we all share (primary), *and* a means of establishing natural hierarchy" (46). It
follows that "Within Romantic discourse, mixing is the activity by which the
self always transcends itself—it is how that self develops. As such, it is . . .
revisionary: parts and wholes, past and present, mix in a mutually interpretive process that reformulates desire as 'something evermore about to be.'
The self that mixes becomes a complex mix that is deeply in need of ongoing
interpretation" (155).

11. For a detailed account of the composition of *The Prelude* and *The
Recluse*, see Kenneth R. Johnson, *Wordsworth and The Recluse* (New Haven:
Yale University Press, 1984).

12. This dual potential of blocking and release in Wordsworth's construction of the deep self is discussed in two good essays on the speaker of *The
Prelude*. See Mark Reed's "The Speaker of *The Prelude*," in *Bicentenary Wordsworth Studies In Memory of John Alban Finch*, ed. Jonathan Wordsworth;
assistant ed., Beth Darlington (Ithaca: Cornell University Press, 1970). Reed
concludes that *"The Prelude* is not best read, as a poem, as presenting a
speaker who claims secure possession of a redemptive imaginative vision. . . . Imagination, as the 'moving soul' of the speaker's labor, reveals
itself in the work of a human poet subject to uncertainties and incapacities
and constant in his acknowledgement of them through an apparently literal
personal voice. The poet's giving of 'a substance and a life' (11, 341) to his
limitations is one of the means by which the revelation of the power of the
Imagination takes place" (pp. 291–92). See also Charles Altieri's "Wordsworth's Wavering Balance: The Thematic Rhythm of *The Prelude*," *The
Wordsworth Circle* 4 (1973): 226–40. Altieri persuasively outlines the developmental aspect of identity in *The Prelude* as a process of error correction:
Wordsworth "reconciles himself to the problematic aspects of identity by
recognizing that while each act of self-consciousness is incomplete and in a
sense self-denying, each act also creates new dimensions of consciousness
which enrich the dynamic potential of consciousness to experience itself
more deeply and more capaciously in subsequent acts" (p. 237).

13. For detailed accounts of the early versions of *The Prelude*, see Jonathan
Wordsworth and Stephen Gill, "The Two-Part *Prelude* of 1798–99," *JEGP* 72
(1973): 503–25, and Jonathan Wordsworth, "The Five-Book *Prelude* of Early
Spring 1804," *JEGP* 76 (1977): 1–25.

14. Text followed is m.s. B of the Cornell Wordsworth. *Home at Grasmere*,
ed. Beth Darlington (Ithaca: Cornell University Press, 1977).

15. For an account of Wordsworth's restraint, see Edward Bostetter's
chapter on Wordsworth in *The Romantic Ventriloquists* (Seattle and London:
University of Washington Press, 1963). Bostetter argues that "The Romantic
movement did indeed produce a body of magnificent poetry that was 'expressive of vitality, confidence, largeness of view.' But all too often these
qualities were purchased at the expense of ignoring or rationalizing crucial
areas of experience and knowledge" (p. 5). In the case of Wordsworth, what is
progressively left out of the poetry is his own disturbing passions and his
inability to respond to the needs and sufferings of others. He retreats from

human life into transcendental abstractions in order to assure his own tranquillity. In the end, "He had exorcised, along with the druids, the impending rocks and gloomy woods and wild winds; reduced the swollen cataracts to soft murmuring falls; tamed and subdued nature–and in so doing he had exorcised the passions within himself which gave life to his poetry, but which he feared as destructive and evil" (p. 81).

16. For a persuasive account of Wordsworth's difficulties in presenting himself to the world, and the ways "he seeks to alleviate his anxieties over self-representation by various forms of manipulation" (62), see "Wordsworth: Making a Place in the World," in Charles J. Rzepka's *The Self as Mind: Vision and Identity in Wordsworth, Coleridge, and Keats* (Cambridge: Harvard University Press, 1986), pp. 31–99.

Chapter 4. Coleridge: The Possessed Bard

1. *Collected Letters of Samuel Taylor Coleridge*, ed. Earl Leslie Griggs, vol. 1 1785–1800 (Oxford: the Clarendon Press, 1956), letter 208, p. 348.

2. *Letters*, vol. 1, no. 208, p. 347.

3. *Letters*, vol. 1, no. 208, pp. 347–48.

4. For an intriguing discussion of the *Biographia Literaria* that relates it to Coleridge's childhood problems, see Donald H. Reiman's "Coleridge and the Art of Equivocation," *Studies in Romanticism* 24 (1986): 324–50. Reiman suggests that "Coleridge's psychological orientation, sketched in early biographical letters and reflected in his least artful early poems, left him feeling estranged from his peers (his childhood age cohort and his adult social class); he therefore turned for protection and approval first to adults and later to those whose wealth and social or political eminence provided him with a similar sense of security. Coleridge repeatedly resorted to irony, parody, and insulting humor (but with increasingly greater subtlety) to avenge himself upon his peers and rivals, though he frequently later felt guilt for having done so" (p. 349).

5. For a comparison of Coleridge's and Wordsworth's routes to inwardness, see chapter 4, "Archimedes' Machine," of Charles Sherry's *Wordsworth's Poetry of the Imagination* (Oxford: the Clarendon Press, 1980). Sherry argues that for Wordsworth nature is the medium of discovery for the poet's mind, but "For both Shelley and Coleridge the nature which finds its place in their poetry is not a thing separate from the mind of the poet, but a being constituted by the mind and posited by it as its means of interpreting itself to itself. The interplay of mind and nature is grounded upon the play of the mind with its own images, both of itself and of nature" (p. 93).

6. *The Notebooks of Samuel Taylor Coleridge*, ed. Kathleen Coburn (New York: Pantheon Books), vol. 1 1794–1804 (1957), entry number 1771.

7. *Letters*, vol. 1, number 209, p. 350.

8. The edition of Coleridge's poetry quoted in this chapter is *The Complete Poetical Works of Samuel Taylor Coleridge*, ed. Ernest Hartley Coleridge (Oxford: the Clarendon Press, 1912), 2 vols.

9. Tilottama Rajan's reading of Coleridge makes these dubious implications of the conversation poetry admirably clear. See chapter 5, "Image and Reality in Coleridge's Lyric Poetry," in her *Dark Interpreter: The Discourse of Romanticism* (Ithaca and London: Cornell University Press, 1980), 204–59.

10. For an account of Coleridge's struggle between his impulse to retire from the world and his need for social involvement, see two articles by Max F. Schulz. The first, "Coleridge Agonistes," *JEGP* 61 (1962): 268–77, offers primarily a biographical approach. The second, and more literary treatment, is via Coleridge's texts: "Coleridge and the Enchantments of Earthly Paradise," in *Reading Coleridge: Approaches and Applications*, ed. Walter B. Crawford (Ithaca and New York: Cornell University Press, 1979). Schulz concludes that "Earthly paradise—a NEW PARADISE 'Perdita" Robinson called Xanadu in her poem to Coleridge—was not for him, he concluded in bleak self-judgement. As a son of fallen Adam he was heir to the need for work and striving. Only such activity would provide the necessary defense against the temptress Indolence and the sorceress Pleasure. The garden enclosure had for Coleridge an ambivalent meaning. He anxiously dreaded that Xanadu, removed from the regular course of life, isolated, rarefied, and exclusive, might be a fool's paradise, where a 'dream of great internal activity' might lull him into sterility of spirit and imagination and 'outward inefficience' . . . Given his pre-nineteenth-century sense of social activism and piety, and his personal guilt over his sloth, failed promise and sensual addiction to drink and drugs, there is little wonder that Coleridge uneasily feared that every flowery bower was in reality an enchanted garden, and the paradisal breadth and depth of earth and sky a barren void" (pp. 158–59).

11. 6, 83–88. Text quoted is from *The Complete Poetical Works of Samuel Taylor Coleridge*, ed. Ernest Hartley Coleridge, vol. 2: Dramatic Works and Appendices.

12. *Poetical Works*, vol. 2, p. 567, f. 1.

13. For an alternative view, see Edward Bostetter's reading of *Osorio* in *The Romantic Ventriloquists* (Seattle and London: University of Washington Press, 1963), pp. 100–104. Bostetter argues that "Through Osorio and Ferdinand [the assassin Osorio employs to murder his brother] he is exploring the helplessness of men before their own minds and the forces that made them. He is also exploring opposite aspects of himself. Osorio has been made different from and superior to other men. His phantasies come unsought, so that he is not responsible for his evil impulses; his mind has the power, in turn, of hypnotizing the weaker man into carrying out the impulses. Osorio murmurs; Ferdinand hears and executes" (p. 103).

14. Thomas Middleton Raysor, ed., *Coleridge: Shakespearean Criticism* (London: J. M. Dent and Sons Ltd., 1960), vol. 1, pp. 115–16.

15. See Charles J. Rzepka's chapter, "Coleridge: Speaking Dreams," in his *The Self as Mind: Vision and Identity in Wordsworth, Coleridge, and Keats* (Cambridge, Massachusetts: Harvard University Press, 1986). Rzepka expands upon the Ancient Mariner's "glittering eye" to derive a principle of mesmeric vision in Coleridge. This power possesses and overpowers the poet's audience: "he depicts his poet figures as overcoming the threatened expropriation of the self in the eye of another by an exertion of imaginative—or of what . . . can aptly be termed mesmeric—power over the mind of his listener. With this power the poet seeks to appropriate, literally to 'keep in mind,' the world from which others emerge to threaten him, and to establish, to his satisfaction, an empathic unity with them on the level of the volatile self as mind, the 'one Life' that permeates and shapes creation. In this way poetry itself becomes a reenactment of the primal creation of a world held in the Divine Mind. The poet's word becomes the Word- *Logos*" (p. 145). I would

add that the aggressive overtones Rzepka discovers in Coleridge's poetic vision are also self-reflexive; for they turn back toward the self as well as outward toward the audience. In the nightmare poetry the enabling act of vision is the act of self-murder, the annihilation of the conscious self, which allows a dreamworld to arise.

16. Three excellent readings of "The Ancient Mariner" emphasize the Mariner's lack of personal identity, a feature of the poem that strikes me as extremely important. They are "The Mariner's Nightmare" in Paul Magnuson's *Coleridge's Nightmare Poetry* (Charlottesville: University Press of Virginia, 1974), A. M. Buchan's "The Sad Wisdom of the Mariner," *Studies in Philology* 61 (1964): 669–88, and the "Coleridge" chapter of Edward Bostetter's *The Romantic Ventriloquists* (Seattle and London: University of Washington Press, 1963).

17. *Inquiring Spirit: A New Presentation of Coleridge from his Published and Unpublished Prose Writings*, ed. Kathleen Coburn (London: Routledge & Kegan Paul, 1951), entry 53, p. 68.

18. *Letters, Conversations and Recollections of S. T. Coleridge*, ed. Thomas Allsop, 3rd edition (1864), pp. 104–05.

19. Several critics have noted Coleridge's displacement of what perhaps are his own concerns through the creation of two female protagonists. See J. B. Twitchell's "The Female Vampire" in his *The Living Dead: A Study of the Vampire in Romantic Literature* (Durham, N.C.: Duke University Press, 1981). Twitchell says that "While the male vampire story was a tale of domination, the female version was one of seduction. . . . [We must] suppose that Christabel is a displacement or substitution of male consciousness, perhaps even a projection of the poet himself" (pp. 39–41). A Jungian version of sexual displacement is suggested by Edward Strickland in "Metamorphoses of the Muse in Romantic Poesis: Christabel," *ELH* 44 (1977): 641–58. In Strickland's reading Geraldine becomes the anima figure in a visionary poem. For other accounts of Coleridge's possible self-projection into Christabel, see Kathleen Coburn's "Coleridge and Wordsworth and 'the Supernatural,'" *University of Texas Quarterly* 25 (1955–56): 121–30, and "Coleridge" in Arthur Wormhoudt's *The Demon Lover: A Psychoanalytical Approach to Literature* (New York: Exposition Press, 1949). See also Barbara A. Schapiro, *The Romantic Mother: Narcissistic Patterns in Romantic Poetry* (Baltimore and London: The Johns Hopkins University Press, 1983). In her chapter "Coleridge: the Drama of Ambivalence" Shapiro suggests that *Christabel* may reflect the love and rage Coleridge felt for his mother.

20. Evil arises within a relation between Christabel and Geraldine, a relation that admits multiple overtones, and disturbs us because of its mysterious openness to interpretation. Such possibilities include not only those of a psychosexual type, but also of a relation with inhuman evil—vampirism, and the mysterious repertoire of Gothic literature. For a good review of these various interpretive options, see Virginia L. Radley's "Christabel: Directions Old and New," *SEL* 4 (1964): 531–41. For the best accounts of the vampire possibility see Arthur H. Nethercot's *The Road to Tryermaine: A Study of the History, Background, and Purpose of Coleridge's "Christabel"* (Chicago: University of Chicago Press, 1939), and "The Female Vampire" in James B. Twitchell's *The Living Dead*. For good discussions of the maternal interpretation see "Christabel: The Drama of Ambivalence" in Barbara Schapiro's *The Romantic Mother: Narcissistic Patterns in Romantic Poetry* (Baltimore: The

Johns Hopkins University Press, 1983), and "Coleridge" in Arthur Worm-houdt's *The Demon Lover*. For the best analysis of the sexual possibility, see "Coleridge" in Edward E. Bostetter's *The Romantic Ventriloquists*. See also "Coleridge's Christabel" in Roy P. Basler's *Sex, Symbolism, and Psychology in Literature* (New Brunswick: Rutgers University Press, 1948) and Edgar Jones' "A New Reading of *Christabel*," *The Cambridge Journal*, November 1951, p. 106.

21. Coburn, *Inquiring Spirit*, entry 185, p. 224.

22. From "Notes on the Book of Common Prayer" in *The Literary Remains of Samuel Taylor Coleridge*, ed. Henry Nelson Coleridge (London, 1838), 4 vols. vol. 3, p. 6–7. Reprint: AMS Press Inc., New York, 1967.

23. For a provocative account of Coleridge's aggressive tendencies, see "Coleridge" in Edward E. Bostetter's *The Romantic Ventriloquists*.

Chapter 5. Keats: The Invisible Poet

1. For accounts of Keats's interest in classicism see Douglas Bush's "Keats," in his *Mythology and the Romantic Tradition in English Poetry* (Cambridge: Harvard University Press, 1937) and "The Death of Poetry" in Richard Jenkyns's *The Victorians and Ancient Greece* (Oxford: Basil Blackwell, 1980).

2. Quotations from Keats's poems in this chapter are from *The Poems of John Keats*, ed. Jack Stillinger (Cambridge: the Belknap Press of Harvard University Press, 1978).

3. For mythic treatments of Keatsian heroism, see Walter H. Evert's *Aesthetic and Myth in the Poetry of Keats* (Princeton: Princeton University Press, 1965) and Dorothy Van Ghent's *Keats: The Myth of the Hero* (Princeton: Princeton University Press, 1983).

4. The strongest analysis of Keats as an escapist poet is Edward Bostetter's chapter on Keats in *The Romantic Ventriloquists* (Seattle and London: University of Washington Press, 1963). Bostetter argues that although Keats gave up his physician's training for a career in poetry, he retained a strong desire to be of use to the world. This fostered Keats's need to produce a poetry of truth, a poetry that would aid and comfort mankind. But at the same time Keats also desired a poetry of pleasure and non-commitment. Ultimately, he felt that his needs for pleasure and truth were incompatible. Bostetter views this dilemma sympathetically, as a species of tragedy: "In theory he was able to sever poetry from metaphysical and ethical responsibilities. But in practice he could not, and thus he was drawn relentlessly toward a psychological impasse in which the poetic self was in danger of being reduced to silence" (p. 179).

A vigorous alternative to Bostetter's escapist Keats is Jack Stillinger's hardy realist—a poet who begins as a dreamer but rejects fantasizing in order to live in the real world. See *The Hoodwinking of Madeline And Other Essays on Keats's Poems* (Urbana: University of Illinois Press, 1971). Leon Waldoff also argues for the adaptive Keatsian imagination in his *Keats and the Silent Work of the Imagination* (Urbana and Chicago: University of Illinois Press, 1985).

5. The most complete discussion of Keats's awareness of Hazlitt is Walter

Jackson Bate's biography, *John Keats* (Cambridge: Harvard University Press, 1963). In particular, see Bate's chapter on "Negative Capability" (pp. 233–63), which assesses Keats's reception of the Hazlitt works I am concerned with here—the *Essay on the Principles of Human Action*, the *Lectures on the English Poets*, and "On Gusto." For other views on this subject see Herschel M. Sikes, "The Poetic Theory and Practice of Keats: The Record of a Debt to Hazlitt," *Philological Quarterly* 38 (1959): 401–13, and Kenneth Muir's "Keats and Hazlitt" in *John Keats: A Reassessment*, ed. Kenneth Muir (Liverpool: Liverpool University Press, 1959).

   6. *The Complete Works of William Hazlitt in Twenty-One Volumes Centenary Edition*, ed. P. P. Howe (London and Toronto: J. M. Dent & Sons, Ltd., 1930), vol. 1, p. 12. All subsequent quotations from Hazlitt refer to this edition.

   7. *The Letters of John Keats*, ed. Hyder Edward Rollins (Cambridge: Harvard University Press, 1958), 2 vols. letter no. 43, to Benjamin Bailey, 22 November 1817, vol. 1, pp. 184–85. All citations of Keats's letters in this chapter are from the Rollins edition.

   8. This passage of *Endymion* figures prominently in Earl R. Wasserman's general view of Keats. See *The Finer Tone: Keats' Major Poems* (Baltimore and London: the Johns Hopkins Press, 1953). Wasserman argues that Keats evolved a metaphysical world view that divided existence into the realm of the "human and mutable on the one hand, and the immortal and essential on the other" (p. 14), which can be poetically related at "the knife-edge where the two meet and are indistinguishably present" through a "mystic oxymoron" (p. 15). The result is a fellowship with essence, which "raises us beyond the misery of mutability by identifying us with 'a sort of oneness,' the mysterious core of life" (p. 27).

   I prefer a less elaborate view of *Endymion* as a youthful poem of erotic pursuit and aspiration, an expression of the wish to transcend selfhood in order to become involved in ecstatic action. So I am in sympathy with two treatments of the poem that dismiss another metaphysical interpretation—that it is a neo-Platonic allegory—in order to argue that it is a poem about physical passion. See Newell F. Ford's *The Prefigurative Imagination of John Keats: A Study of the Beauty–Truth Identification and its Implications* (Stanford University Press, 1951), and E. C. Pettet's *On the Poetry of Keats* (Cambridge University Press, 1957).

   9. This manipulative element has been the focus of recent critical discussions of "The Eve of St. Agnes." An earlier critical tradition regarded the poem as a happy romance in the vein of *Endymion;* for that approach see especially Earl R. Wasserman, *The Finer Tone;* Newell F. Ford, *The Prefigurative Imagination of John Keats;* and R. A. Foakes, *The Romantic Assertion* (New Haven: Yale University Press, 1958).

Jack Stillinger's important essay on the poem in *The Hoodwinking of Madeline* first called attention to the manipulative element, but perhaps exaggerated it in comparing Porphyro to Satan. For modifications to Stillinger, see the chapter on "The Eve of St. Agnes" in Leon Waldoff's *Keats and the Silent Work of Imagination*, Stuart M. Sperry's chapter on the poem in *Keats the Poet* (Princeton: Princeton University Press, 1973), and Michael Ragussis's chapter on the poem in his *The Subterfuge of Art: Language and the Romantic Tradition* (Baltimore: the Johns Hopkins University Press, 1978). Ragussis argues that the narrator of the poem is a character being self-manipulated by his own storytelling, much as the narrators of Keats's Odes are self-manipulated by the very expressions they use to relate their imaginative experiencings.

10. See Edward Bostetter's discussion of Keats's reading of the letter to Gifford in *The Romantic Ventriloquists*, pp. 150–55. Bostetter suggests, "Now, though Keats claims for poetry a detachment that Hazlitt does not, nevertheless, his conception of poetry as consisting in the presentation of graceful and instinctive attitudes, regardless of whether they are morally good . . . or true . . . , is clearly related to Hazlitt's conception of poetry as delighting in power" (p. 153).

11. Rollins, vol. 2, no. 195: to George and Georgiana Keats, 14 February–3 May 1819. See pp. 74–75. For the "Letter to Gifford" see Hazlitt, vol. 9, pp. 13–59. The passage excerpted by Keats is on pp. 36–38.

12. For an excellent discussion of the theatrical element in Keats's poetic vision, see "Keats: Watcher and Witness" in Charles J. Rzepka's *The Self as Mind: Vision and Identity in Wordsworth, Coleridge, and Keats* (Cambridge, Mass.: Harvard University Press, 1986) 165–242. Rzepka suggests that the early Keats positions himself as a spectator who cultivates "a theatrical, self-annihilating empathy" that distracts the seer's attention "entirely from his embodied self" (169), but that from *The Eve of St. Agnes* onward Keats becomes aware that such a posture must be active rather than passive; for the poet finds it necessary to define and manipulate his audience. He realizes that he is not merely spectator but also the manager of his *theatrum mundi*: "The issue in 'The Eve of St. Agnes' . . . can best be stated as the problem of defining, selecting, or controlling one's audience, and the social context of one's art and artistic self-representation, so as to make the image of the poet (or poet-lover) prevail as an objective, agreed-upon reality" (204). I concur with Rzepka in viewing Keats's poetic development as a movement from the posture of passive, self-annihilated spectator to active, self-conscious artist—but I would add that the self-conscious poet nevertheless understands the need to maintain his invisibility, to conceal his manipulations.

Charles I. Patterson gives a useful review of critical reactions to the poem in *The Daemonic in the Poetry of John Keats* (Urbana: University of Illinois Press, 1970), pp. 185–89. As he points out, there has been considerable disagreement about the poem's principal characters. Is Lamia a poet of the Keatsian dream or a false enchantress? Is Lycius Lamia's victim or her exploiter? Is Apollonius in the right when he destroys Lamia or does he demonstrate the heartlessness of cold philosophy? Is there any one character or position in the poem that we are to identify with? Rather than taking sides in these disputes, I shall point out the ubiquitous presence of mixture in "Lamia"—mixed characters, mixed motives, mixed actions and situations. It is the presence of mixture that makes our decisions about the poem difficult.

13. See Ralph Cohen, "Historical Knowledge and Literary Understanding," *Papers on Language and Literature* 14 (1978): 227–49, for a reading of the "Ode on Melancholy" that compares it to Milton's "Il Penseroso" and Warton's "The Pleasures of Melancholy" as prior poems dealing with similar subject matter. In Keats's poem Cohen observes procedural innovations that only become clear when they are seen against the background of the earlier poems: "The pleasures of melancholy led to religious and sensitive musings in the poems of Milton and Warton. In *Ode on Melancholy* pleasure must be sacrificed to attain melancholy, not sacrificed by discipline or self-control but sacrificed by engaging in the most sensuous human activities: 'Veiled

Melancholy' can be seen 'of none save him whose strenuous tongue / Can burst Joy's grape against his palate fine' (27–28). Melancholy can be achieved only at the expense of losing the most intense sensuous pleasures that make life desirable. Thus the attaining of melancholy is a warrant that one has lived intensely at the same time that such intense living is over" (pp. 242–43).

14. For four good examples of this approach, see Walter Jackson Bate's *John Keats* (Cambridge: Harvard University Press, 1963), pp. 580–85; David Perkins's *The Quest for Permanence: The Symbolism of Wordsworth, Shelley, and Keats* (Cambridge: Harvard University Press, 1959), pp. 294–301; Reuben Brower's *The Fields of Light: An Experiment in Critical Reading* (New York: Oxford University Press, 1951), pp. 38–41; and Helen Vendler's "Peaceful Sway Above Man's Harvesting," in her *The Odes of John Keats* (Cambridge, Mass. and London: The Belknap Press of Harvard University Press, 1983). In "To Autumn" Vendler suggests that "we sense Keats's less combative attitude. His native pugnacity and ardor give the earlier odes their vivid energies; but in moulting, and substituting for his wings a pair of patient sublunary legs, he slowed his pace; in becoming a chrysalis again, he watched, and waited, and took notes through his two loopholes of vision" (p. 278).

Chapter 6. Byron: The Surface Self

1. *Byron's Letters and Journals,* ed. Leslie A. Marchand, 3, 1813–14 (Cambridge: the Belknap Press of Harvard University Press, 1974), p. 233: entry for Monday, 6 December 1814.

2. *Lady Blessington's Conversations of Lord Byron,* ed. Ernest J. Lovell, Jr. (Princeton: Princeton University Press, 1969), p. 331.

3. M. H. Abrams excludes Byron from his discussion of Romanticism in *Natural Supernaturalism: Tradition and Revolution in Romantic Literature* (New York: W. W. Norton, 1971), because Byron "in his greatest work . . . speaks with an ironic counter-voice and deliberately opens a satirical perspective on the vatic stance of his Romantic contemporaries" (p. 13). See also "On Byron," *Studies in Romanticism,* 16 (1977), 563–87. This exchange between George M. Ridenour, for the Romantic Byron and Jerome J. McGann for the anti-Romantic, was stimulated by Ridenour's reaction to McGann's *Don Juan in Context* (Chicago: University of Chicago Press, 1976).

4. Critics disagree over the question of Byron's identity, or lack of it. Three of the best arguments for Byron's personal hollowness are Paul West's *Byron and the Spoiler's Art* (London: Chatto and Windus, 1960), John Wain's "Byron: the Search for Identity" in his *Essays on Literature and Ideas* (London: Macmillan, 1963), and Philip W. Martin's *Byron: a poet before his public* (Cambridge: Cambridge University Press, 1982). Two approaches that trace the evolution of Byron's poetic identity are Jerome J. McGann's *Fiery Dust: Byron's Poetic Development* (Chicago: University of Chicago Press, 1968) and Robert F. Gleckner's *Byron and the Ruins of Paradise* (Baltimore: Johns Hopkins Press, 1967).

5. *Byron's Letters and Journals,* 3, 225: entry from Byron's journal, Saturday, 27 November 1813.

6. Canto 3, stanza 33. The poetry is quoted from *Lord Byron: The Complete Poetical Works*, ed. Jerome J. McGann (Oxford: Clarendon Press, 1980), except for *Don Juan*, where I cite Leslie Marchand's edition (Boston: Houghton Mifflin, 1958).

7. For an analysis of Byron's employment of Wordsworth, Shelley, and Rousseau in *Childe Harold's Pilgrimage*, Canto 3, as a diversion from his sense of personal hollowness rather than as an approach to authentic Romantic identification with nature, see Philip Martin's discussion of the canto in *Byron: a poet before his public*. Wordsworth himself seems to have felt that Byron's enthusiasm for nature was derivative. In his *Memoirs*, Moore tells of a visit Wordsworth paid to him in October 1821: Wordsworth "spoke of Byron's plagiarisms from him; the whole third canto of "Childe Harold" founded on his style and sentiments. The feeling of natural objects which is there expressed, not caught by B. from nature herself, but from him (Wordsworth), and spoiled in the transmission. "Tintern Abbey" the source of it all; from which same poem too the celebrated passage about Solitude, in the first canto of "Childe Harold," is (he said) taken, with this difference, that what is naturally expressed by him, has been worked by Byron into a laboured and antithetical sort of declamation" (ed. John Russell [Boston: Little, Brown, 1853], 3, 161).

8. There is disagreement over the literary merit of Byron's heroic poetry. For a defense of the Turkish Tales see Robert F. Gleckner's *Byron and the Ruins of Paradise* and Jerome J. McGann's *Fiery Dust: Byron's Poetic Development*. For a sympathetic approach to the Byronic hero, see McGann's *Don Juan in Context*, chaps. 2, 3, and 4; also Peter L. Thorslev Jr.'s *The Byronic Hero: Types and Prototypes* (Minneapolis: University of Minnesota Press, 1962). Attacks on Byronic heroism include John Jump's chapter on "Heroes and Rhetoric, 1812–1818" in his *Byron* (London and Boston: Routledge, 1972), and Andrew Rutherford's chapter on the Turkish Tales, "Romantic Fantasy," in *Byron: A Critical Study* (Stanford: Stanford University Press, 1961). The most interesting criticism of the Turkish Tales is Philip W. Martin's chapter in *Byron: a poet before his public*, which sees the heroic poetry as providing a sense of gentility for the rising middle-class Regency public at the same time that it gives Byron a sense of independence from middle-class values. Daniel P. Watkins suggests that the Turkish Tales reject "crude idealism" (139), constituting "a praxis that is fundamentally hopeful, if only because it is doggedly committed to exposing social contradictions and injustices. His poems enable us to understand more fully the ideological and political dimensions of social reality" (142–43). See his *Social Relations in Byron's Eastern Tales* (Rutherford: Fairleigh Dickinson University Press, 1987). Although I have my reservations about this view of the Turkish Tales, Watkins's position seems much stronger in relation to Byron's history plays. Watkins argues that the plays criticize idealism and Romantic individualism by rendering a historical analysis of ideology and class struggle: see "Byron and the Poetics of Revolution," *Keats–Shelley Journal* 32 (1985): 95–130, "Violence, Class Consciousness, and Ideology in Byron's History Plays," *ELH* 48 (1981), 799–816, and "The Ideological Dimensions of Byron's The Deformed Transformed," *Criticism* 25 (1983): 27–39.

9. The sense in which Ocean is taken by the narrator of *Childe Harold's Pilgrimage* is shared by Byron himself, as is suggested by a letter of 26 September 1813 to Anabella Millbanke: "You don't like my 'restless' doc-

trines—I should be very sorry if *you* did—I can't *stagnate* nevertheless—if I must sail let it be on the ocean no matter how stormy—anything but a dull cruise on a level lake without ever losing sight of the same insipid shores by which it is surrounded" (*Byron's Letters and Journals*, 3, 119).

10. For a superb analysis of *Don Juan* which regards "the two master symbols of the poem" as "fire and ocean" (p. 181), see Alvin B. Kernan's chapter on the poem in *The Plot of Satire* (New Haven: Yale University Press, 1965). Where I shall approach the Byronic ocean as an opposition between surface and depth, Kernan emphasizes the aspect of onward flow.

11. See Jerome J. McGann's anti-Romantic analysis of the poem, *Don Juan in Context:* chap. 6, "Form," is particularly important. McGann argues that Byron proceeded not on organic models of poetry but by the order he discovered in Horace, who offered a tradition "rhetorical and functional" (p. 109). The poem becomes a series of rhetorical experiments that reveal the multiple contexts and uses of language—so that variety, not organic unity, must become the central linguistic technique of the poem. For critical accounts that argue for the unity of the poem, see Ernest J. Lovell's "Irony and Image in *Don Juan*" in *The Major English Romantic Poets: A Symposium in Reappraisal*, ed. Clarence D. Thorpe, Carlos Baker, and Bennett Weaver (Carbondale: Southern Illinois University Press, 1957), George Ridenour's *The Style of Don Juan* (New Haven: Yale University Press, 1960), and Robert F. Gleckner's chapter on "*Don Juan* and *The Island*" in *Byron and the Ruins of Paradise*.

12. For an interesting stylistic comparison of *Don Juan* and *The Prelude*, see pp. 89–99 of Jerome J. McGann's *Don Juan in Context*. McGann suggests that Wordsworth's need to integrate mind and body, to "transform landscape into either interior or apocalyptic categories" (p. 90), creates problems of stylistic transition that often are poorly solved in *The Prelude*. Since Byron is not committed to integration, he "can manage such shifts and transitions because the whole point of the style of *Don Juan* is to explore the interfaces between different things, events, and moods. *Don Juan* is a poem that is, in fact, always in transition—not in the Wordsworthian sense of 'something evermore about to be,' but in the Byronic sense that 'there woos no home nor hope, nor life, *save what is here*' (*Child Harold* IV, 105, my italics). And for Byron, 'what is here' is a vast spectacle of incongruences held together in strange networks between the poles of sublimity and pointlessness. Transitions between styles, lines, stanzas, and tones not only do not present a problem for Byron, they are the locus of all his opportunities" (p. 95).

13. For a good discussion of *Don Juan* as a meaningless poem, see Brian Wilkie's "Byron and the Epic of Negation" in his *Romantic Poets and Epic Tradition* (Madison and Milwaukee: University of Wisconsin Press, 1965).

14. For the most sustained analysis of Byron's relations with his audience see Philip W. Martin's *Byron: a poet before his public*. In addition, see Andrew Rutherford's short history of Byron's lifetime reception in his Introduction to *Byron: The Critical Heritage* (New York: Barnes and Noble, 1970), pp. 3–12. Edward Bostetter offers a history of the composition and reception of *Don Juan* in his Introduction to *Twentieth Century Interpretations of Don Juan* (Englewood Cliffs, N.J.: Prentice Hall, 1979), as does Elizabeth French Boyd in her chapter "Against the Wind" in *Byron's Don Juan: A Critical Study* (1945; reprint, The humanities Press, 1958). The most complete history of Byron's composition of *Don Juan*, and of his relations with his publishers and

the friends who read the manuscript of *Don Juan* is volume 1 of Truman Guy Steffan's *Byron's Don Juan, The Making of a Masterpiece* (Austin: University of Texas Press, 1957, 1971). An analysis of Byron's calculations of audience response that I find particularly astute is Ian Jack's "Byron: Too sincere a poet" in his *The Poet and His Audience* (Cambridge, Cambridge University Press, 1984).

15. For an analysis of the economics of *Don Juan* which identifies Byron with the misers rather than the men of generosity, see Frank D. McConnell's "Byron's Reductions: 'Much Too Poetical'," *ELH* 37 (1970): 415–32.

16. Jerome J. McGann acutely discusses normal Romantic symbolic techniques and Byron's evasion of them in chap. 6 of *Don Juan in Context*. As McGann says, "To know by symbols is to make up for what Wordsworth calls 'the sad incompetence of human speech' (*The Prelude*, IV, 592). Byron opposes a discourse ruled by symbols, which drive into silence and ecstatic revelation, with a discourse of 'conversational facility' (XV, 20). The structure of *Don Juan* is based upon the structure of human talk, which is dialectical without being synthetic" (p. 111).

17. See Robert F. Gleckner, "Gambling and Byron's Poetics," *Nineteenth Century Studies* 1 (1987): 1–11, part of a special issue on "Entertainment, Amusement, and Diversion in the Nineteenth Century." Gleckner suggests that for Byron gambling provides "a resurrection of the power to feel" (p. 10).

18. Although I recognize the tragic undertones in *Don Juan*, it seems to me that the narrator's ebullience, his pleasure in his manipulations, dominates. But several critics emphasize the tragic tone of the poem. For Alvin Kernan it is part of a mingling of genres—comic, satiric, and tragic. The tragic element emerges "When viewed from the angle of the solitary man"; for "the movement of life which flows through Don Juan darkens to a tragic setting in which while Life rolls on, the individual is fated to stillness and obliteration"—*The Plot of Satire* (p. 213). Ridenour sees a dark Don Juan that continually exfoliates repetitions of the Fall, and Robert F. Glecker carries this interpretation farther in *Byron and the Ruins of Paradise*. However, Gleckner later revised his position, arguing that "this poem" is "at once 'poetic' and anti-satiric, lyric and prophetic, epic and comic, serious and burlesque, all genres subsumed in no genre, sui generis" (p. 201). See his "From Selfish Spleen to Equanimity: Byron's Satires," *Studies in Romanticism* 18 (1979): 173–205.

Chapter 7. Shelley: The Deep Self Surfaced

1. Citations from Shelley's poetry and prose are from *Shelley's Poetry and Prose*, selected and edited by Donald H. Reiman and Sharon B. Powers (New York and London: W. W. Norton and Company, 1977). For the passage from "On Life," see p. 476.

2. For a detailed comparison of Byron and Shelley, see Charles E. Robinson's *Shelley and Byron: The Snake and Eagle Wreathed in Fight* (Baltimore and London: The Johns Hopkins University Press, 1976).

The most comprehensive and ambitious account of mobility in Shelley is Jerrold E. Hogle's *Shelley's Process: Radical Transference and the Development of His Major Works* (New York: Oxford University Press, 1988). See also

Hogle's "Metaphor and Metamorphosis in Shelley's 'The Witch of Atlas,'" *Studies in Romanticism* 19 (1980): 327–53 and his "Shelley's Poetics: The Power as Metaphor," *Keats-Shelley Journal* 31 (1982): 159–97. Other accounts of mobility in Shelley include Daniel J. Hughes' "Kindling and Dwindling: The Poetic Process in Shelley," *Keats-Shelley Journal* 13 (1964): 13–28, and his "Coherence and Collapse in Shelley, with Particular Reference to *Epipsychidion*," *ELH* 28 (1961): 260–83. See also Jerome J. McGann's "Shelley's Veils: A Thousand Images of Loveliness," in *Romantic and Victorian*, ed. W. Paul Elledge and Richard L. Hoffman (Cranbury, N.J.: Fairleigh Dickinson University Press, 1971), 198–218. See also my *The Transforming Image: A Study of Shelley's Major Poetry* (Urbana: University of Illinois Press, 1980).

3. For a comprehensive stylistic account of reflexivity in Shelley, see the chapter on "Reflexive Imagery" in William Keach's *Shelley's Style* (New York and London: Methuen, 1984). In particular, see his discussion of *Alastor* (pp. 81–87).

4. For a reading of Shelley that begins by attending to his dark interior impulses, see Christine Gallant's *Shelley's Ambivalence* (New York: St. Martin's Press, 1989). Gallant views Shelley's ambivalence as surfacing "in his life and his poetry. It showed itself in his buried envy, and concomitant desire to spoil goodness, that persisted towards his friend Byron and to a lesser degree, Keats; and it emerged in his narcissistic desire to dominate and have power over others, as may be seen in his relations with most of the women in his life. In his writing, it led to his seeming blindness to the contradictions between his ideals and his actions. It also resulted in the strain of self-pity in his poetry. . . . Shelley was a moral man; and he was aware of his own inconsistencies at deeper, less conscious levels. Gradually he worked through the position of bad faith as it showed itself on all fronts, and I would argue that one can see this within the poems he created" (12).

5. For an account of the Emilia Viviani episode see chapter 26, "The Tuscan Set: 1821" in Richard Holmes's *Shelley: The Pursuit* (London: Weidenfeld and Nicholson, 1974).

6. In this connection, I find Jerrold Hogle's view of Shelley extremely persuasive. *Shelley's Process* views Shelley's writings as "less a univocal 'body of thought' and more an opening to an interplay of changing voices, a succession of externalized figures for the self spreading into further possible figurations and analogues. . . . I want to point my readers toward the Shelley who stares out, with a sense of being incomplete and unbounded, at the possibilities for extending himself in space, time, and writing and then starts redrawing his possible self-image again and again without finality and without the longing for an Absolute Center with which he has been often associated" (8).

7. Daniel J. Hughes makes a similar point in "Coherence and Collapse in Shelley, With Particular Reference to *Epipsychidion*," *ELH* 28 (1961): 260–83. He observes that the structure of *Epipsychidion* "is best understood as a constantly collapsing one, a quest for coherence which, as soon as it is attained, collapses again. (Coherence is to be understood here as a sustained hypostasis; collapse as a conscious loss of the image once stabilized—not as a formal breakdown of structure.) This alternation of coherence and collapse is true of the macrocosm of the whole and it is true of the microcosm of the individual passage, line, and image. The poem moves forward in a continuous excitement of self-discovery, finally arriving at the deprivation and

'failure' implicit in it from the beginning. But only by exhibiting what it could *not* do can the poem show what it has done: it has exhibited, as few poems in the language can, the ultimate reach of poetry, for the poem is ultimately about poetry itself and the process by which it is created" (pp. 264–65).

8. For an excellent study of Shelley's attention to and employment of genre, see Richard Cronin's *Shelley's Poetic Thoughts* (London: Macmillan, 1981).

9. See Ronald Tetreault, *The Poetry of Life: Shelley and Literary Form* (Toronto: University of Toronto Press, 1987). In his chapter on *The Revolt of Islam*, "Epic Form" (pp. 95–120), Tetreault suggests that the poem fails in part because Shelley's hero Laon exhibits a false "confidence centered in the arrogance of his masculine ego. He sees the revolution as depending exclusively on himself and his words," and his revolutionary rhetoric embodies undertones of violence overlooked by Laon, and, apparently also by Shelley himself. The result is that Shelley's "epic of revolutionary love and life betrays itself through violent hatred and death" (see pp. 112–20). Tetreault does not connect Laon's inadvertently aggressive rhetoric in this epic forerunner of *Prometheus Unbound* with Prometheus's progressive understanding and renunciation of the violence in his curse, but I think the case certainly could be made.

10. Milton Wilson was the first to suggest that the Phantasm of Jupiter is a self-projection of Prometheus. See *Shelley's Later Poetry: A Study of His Prophetic Imagination* (New York: Columbia University Press, 1959), 63–64. Earl R. Wasserman concurs in *Shelley: A Critical Reading* (Baltimore and London: The Johns Hopkins University Press, 1971), 258–61. In his chapter "Dark Mirrors: 'Prometheus Unbound,'" Lloyd Abbey argues that "suddenly to see oneself outside oneself, in a Doppelganger image which reveals all that one has refused to acknowledge, can be at once pathetic, tragic, and farcical. That situation occurs, not once, but repeatedly, in 'Prometheus Unbound,' and focuses the meaning of the drama as a whole" (p. 52). *Destroyer and Preserver: Shelley's Poetic Skepticism* (Lincoln and London: University of Nebraska Press, 1979).

11. For a suggestive account of the self-divisions within Prometheus as a foreshadowing of the Nietzschean Will to Power, see Hogle's *Shelley's Process*, the section of chapter 3 titled "The Will to Knowledge and the Feminist Critique in *Prometheus Unbound*," pp. 103–11.

12. For the feminist implications of *Prometheus Unbound* see Hogle's *Shelley's Process*, "The Will to Knowledge and the Feminist Critique in *Prometheus Unbound*," pp. 103–11. It also should be remarked that throughout, Hogle's book urges a feminist interpretation of Shelley. For a skeptical account of Shelley's feminism see "The Limits of Rivalry: Revisioning the Feminine in a Community of Shared Desire," chapter 4 of Marlon B. Ross's *The Contours of Masculine Desire: Romanticism and the Rise of Women's Poetry* (New York: Oxford University Press, 1989), 112–54. Ross argues that Shelley's poetry "becomes a record of eloquent struggle against masculine desire, even as it hesitantly takes on the contours of that desire. Even as he attempts to remake masculine rivalry into a community of shared desire, he appeals to tropes of masculine potency that disrupt the community he seeks to assemble" (121). For the most critical view of Shelley's feminism see Barbara Charlesworth Gelpi's "A Feminist Approach to Teaching

Shelley" in *Approaches to Teaching Shelley's Poetry*, ed. Spencer Hall (New York: The Modern Language Association, 1990), 157–61. Gelpi concludes that "Shelley's perspective is not feminist" (161).

13. Not only does *Prometheus Unbound* invite comparison with *Don Juan*, it also exhibits a special relation to Blake's *Jerusalem*. Both Shelley's and Blake's poems are cosmic accounts of self-development that work to affirm the value of open expressiveness. But the telling difference between Shelley and Blake is indicated by the final figurations of their poems. *Jerusalem* concludes with the vision of the translucent Man Albion moving forward in the process of brotherly conversation, having recreated himself as a deep self capable of redeeming the world by bringing it within himself. On the contrary, Shelley's poem ends with the vision of a transformed cosmos ecstatically moving forward in the process of erotic celebration, Shelley's Prometheus having disappeared so that the surface of things can take on feeling and significance as the world discloses the redeemed human spirit. In brief, *Jerusalem* is a poem of the interior deep self whereas *Prometheus Unbound* is a drama of the deep self surfaced. It is not without interest that Shelley's transformed world, as represented by his lovers the Earth and Moon, displays sexual union as the central image of human redemption— whereas Los ultimately banishes the feminine principle from Albion's world, opening the way for Blake's apotheosis of brotherly conversation.

BIBLIOGRAPHY

Abbey, Lloyd. *Destroyer and Preserver: Shelley's Poetic Skepticism.* Lincoln and London: University of Nebraska Press, 1979.

Abrams, M. H. *Natural Supernaturalism: Tradition and Revolution in Romantic Literature.* New York: W. W. Norton, 1971.

Adams, Hazard. *William Blake: A Reading of the Shorter Poems.* Seattle: University of Washington Press, 1963.

Adams, Hazard. "*Blake, Jeruslaem* and Symbolic Form." *Blake Studies* 7: 1975, 143–166.

Altieri, Charles. "Wordsworth's Wavering Balance: The Thematic Rhythm of The Prelude." *The Wordsworth Circle* 4: 1973, 226–40.

Averill, James H. *Wordsworth and the Poetry of Human Suffering.* Ithaca and London: Cornell University Press, 1980.

Basler, Roy P. *Sex, Symbolism, and Psychology in Literature.* New Brunswick: Rutgers University Press, 1948.

Bate, Walter Jackson. *John Keats.* Cambridge: Harvard University Press, 1963.

Bernhardt-Kabisch, Ernest. "Wordsworth: The Monumental Poet." *Philological Quarterly* 44: 1965, 503–18.

Blake, William. *The Complete Poetry and Prose of William Blake.* Edited by David V. Erdman; commentary by Harold Bloom. Berkeley and Los Angeles: University of California Press, 1982.

Bloom, Harold. *Blake's Apocalypse: A Study in Poetic Argument.* Garden City, N.Y.: Doubleday and Company, 1963.

———. *The Anxiety of Influence: A Theory of Poetry.* Oxford: Oxford University Press, 1973.

Bloom, Harold, et al. *Deconstruction and Criticism.* New York: Seabury Press, 1979.

Bostetter, Edward. *The Romantic Ventriloquists.* Seattle and London: University of Washington Press, 1963.

Bostetter, Edward, ed. *Twentieth Century Interpretations of Don Juan.* Englewood Cliffs, N.J.: Prentice Hall, 1979.

Boyd, Elizabeth French. Byron's Don Juan: A Critical Study. 1945. Reprint. The Humanities Press, 1958.

Brower, Reuben. *The Fields of Light: An Experiment in Critical Reading.* New York: Oxford University Press, 1951.

Buchan, A. M. "The Sad Wisdom of the Mariner." *Studies in Philology* 62: 1964, 669–88.

Bush, Douglas. *Mythology and the Romantic Tradition in English Poetry.* Cambridge: Harvard University Press, 1937.

Byron, George Gordon. *Byron's Letters and Journals.* Edited by Leslie A. Marchand. 12 vols. Cambridge: the Belknap Press of Harvard University Press, 1973–1982.

Byron, George Gordon. *The Complete Poetical Works.* Edited by Jerome J. McGann. Oxford: Clarendon Press, 1980– .

Byron, George Gordon. *Don Juan.* Edited by Leslie A. Marchand. Boston: Houghton Mifflin, 1958.

Byron, George Gordon. *Lady Blessington's Conversations of Lord Byron.* Edited by Ernest J. Lovell. Princeton: Princeton University Press, 1969.

Coburn, Kathleen. "Coleridge and Wordsworth and 'the Supernatural'." *University of Texas Quarterly* 25: 1955–56, 121–30.

Cohen, Ralph. "Historical Knowledge and Literary Understanding." *Papers on Language and Literature* 14: 1978, 227–49.

Coleridge, Samuel Taylor. *Coleridge: Shakespearean Criticism.* Edited by Thomas Middleton Raysor. London: J. M. Dent and Sons Ltd., 1960.

Coleridge, Samuel Taylor. *Collected Letters of Samuel Taylor Coleridge.* Edited by Earl Leslie Griggs. 6 vols. Oxford: the Clarendon Press, 1956–1971.

Coleridge, Samuel Taylor. *The Complete Poetical Works of Samuel Taylor Coleridge.* Edited by Ernest Hartley Coleridge. 2 vols. Oxford: the Clarendon Press, 1912.

Coleridge, Samuel Taylor. *Inquiring Spirit: A New Presentation of Coleridge from his Published and Unpublished Prose Writings.* Edited by Kathleen Coburn. London: Routledge & Kegan Paul, 1951.

Coleridge, Samuel Taylor. *Letters, Conversations and Recollections of S. T. Coleridge.* Edited by Thomas Allsop, 1864.

Coleridge, Samuel Taylor. *The Literary Remains of Samuel Taylor Coleridge.* Edited by Henry Nelson Coleridge. 4 vols. London: W. Pickering, 1836–39.

Coleridge, Samuel Taylor. *The Notebooks of Samuel Taylor Coleridge.* Edited by Kathleen Coburn. New York: Pantheon Books, 1957– .

Cronin, Richard. *Shelley's Poetic Thoughts.* London: Macmillan, 1981.

Curran, Stuart and Wittreich, Joseph. *Blake's Sublime Allegory.* Madison: University of Wisconsin Press, 1977.

Damrosch, Leopold, Jr. *Symbol and Truth in Blake's Myth.* Princeton: Princeton University Press, 1980.

Devlin, D. D. *Wordsworth and the Poetry of Epitaphs.* Totowa, N.J.: Barnes and Noble Books, 1981.

Evert, Walter H. *Aesthetic and Myth in the Poetry of Keats.* Princeton: Princeton University Press, 1965.

Ferguson, Frances. *Wordsworth: Language as Counter-spirit.* New Haven: Yale University Press, 1977.

Fisher, Peter F. *The Valley of Vision: Blake as Prophet and Revolutionary.* Toronto: University of Toronto Press, 1961.

Foakes, R. A. *The Romantic Assertion.* New Haven: Yale University Press, 1958.

Ford, Newell F. *The Prefigurative Imagination of John Keats: A Study of the Beauty-Truth Identification and its Implications.* Stanford: Stanford University Press, 1951.

Fox, Susan. "The Female as Metaphor in William Blake's Poetry." *Critical Inquiry* 3: Spring 1977, 507–20.

Frosch, Thomas. *The Awakening of Albion*. Ithaca and London: Cornell University Press, 1974.

Frye, Northrop. *Fearful Symmetry: A Study of William Blake*. Princeton: Princeton University Press, 1947.

Gallant, Christine. *Blake and the Assimilation of Chaos*. Princeton: Princeton University Press, 1978.

Gallant, Christine. *Shelley's Ambivalence*. New York: St. Martin's Press, 1989.

Gillham, D.G. *Blake's Contrary States: The Songs of Innocence and of Experience as Dramatic Poems*. Cambridge: Cambridge University Press, 1966.

Gleckner, Robert F. *The Piper and the Bard*. Detroit: Wayne State University Press, 1959.

Gleckner, Robert F. "Blake and the Senses." *Studies in Romanticism* 5: 1965, 1–15.

Gleckner, Robert F. *Byron and the Ruins of Paradise*. Baltimore: The Johns Hopkins Press, 1967.

Gleckner, Robert F. "Most Holy Forms of Thought: Some Observations on Blake and Language." *ELH* 41: 1974, 555–77.

Gleckner, Robert F. "From Selfish Spleen to Equanimity: Byron's Satires." *Studies in Romanticism* 173: 1979, 205.

Gleckner, Robert F. "Gambling and Byron's Poetics." *Nineteenth-Century Studies* 1: 1987, 1–11.

Hall, Jean. *The Transforming Image: A Study of Shelley's Major Poetry*. Urbana: University of Illinois Press, 1980.

Hall, Spencer, ed. *Approaches to Teaching Shelley's Poetry*. New York: The Modern Language Association, 1990.

Hazlitt, William. *The Complete Works of William Hazlitt in Twenty-One Volumes*. Centenary Edition. Edited by P. P. Howe. London and Toronto: J. M. Dent & Sons, Ltd., 1930.

Hogle, Jerrold E. "Metaphor and Metamorphosis in Shelley's 'The Witch of Atlas'." *Studies in Romanticism* 19: 1980, 327–353.

Hogle, Jerrold E. "Shelley's Poetics: The Power as Metaphor." *Keats-Shelley Journal* 31: 1982, 159–97.

Hogle, Jerrold E. *Shelley's Process: Radical Transference and the Development of His Major Works*. New York: Oxford University Press, 1988.

Holmes, Richard. *Shelley: The Pursuit*. London: Weidenfeld and Nicholson, 1974.

Hughes, Daniel J. "Coherence and Collapse in Shelley, with Particular Reference to *Epipsychidion*." *ELH* 28: 1961, 260–83.

Hughes, Daniel J. "Kindling and Dwindling: The Poetic Process in Shelley." *Keats-Shelley Journal* 13: 1964, 13–28.

Jack, Ian. *The Poet and His Audience*. Cambridge: Cambridge University Press, 1984.

Jenkyns, Richard. *The Victorians and Ancient Greece*. Oxford: Basil Blackwell, 1980.

Johnson, Kenneth R. *Wordsworth and The Recluse*. New Haven: Yale University Press, 1984.

Jones, Edgar. "A New Reading of Christabel." *The Cambridge Journal*, November 1951, 106.

Keach, William. *Shelley's Style*. New York and London: Methuen, 1984.

Keats, John. *The Letters of John Keats*. Edited by Hyder Edward Rollins. 2 vols. Cambridge: Harvard University Press, 1958.

Keats, John. *The Poems of John Keats*. Edited by Jack Stillinger. Cambridge: the Belknap Press of Harvard University Press, 1978.

Kernan, Alvin B. *The Plot of Satire*. New Haven: Yale University Press, 1965.

Klancher, Jon P. *The Making of English Reading Audiences, 1790–1832*. Madison: The University of Wisconsin Press, 1987.

Langbaum, Robert. *The Mysteries of Identity: A Theme in Modern Literature*. New York: Oxford University Press, 1977.

Larrissy, Edward. *William Blake*. New York: Basil Blackwell, 1985.

Levinson, Marjorie. *Wordsworth's great period poems: Four essays*. Cambridge: Cambridge University Press, 1986.

Liu, Alan. *Wordsworth: The Sense of History*. Stanford: Stanford University Press, 1989.

Lovell, Ernest J. "Irony and Image in *Don Juan*." In *The Major English Romantic Poets: A Symposium in Reappraisal*, edited by Clarence D. Thorpe, Carlos Baker, and Bennett Weaver. Carbondale: Southern Illinois University Press, 1957.

Magnuson, Paul. *Coleridge's Nightmare Poetry*. Charlottesville: University Press of Virginia, 1974.

Martin, Philip W. *Byron: a poet before his public*. Cambridge: Cambridge University Press, 1982.

McConnell, Frank D. "Byron's Reductions: 'Much Too Poetical'." *ELH* 37: 1970, 415–432.

McGann, Jerome J. *Fiery Dust: Byron's Poetic Development*. Chicago: University of Chicago Press, 1968.

McGann, Jerome J. "Shelley's Veils: A Thousand Images of Loveliness." In *Romantic and Victorian*, edited by W. Paul Elledge and Richard L. Hoffmann. Cranbury, N.J.: Farleigh Dickinson University Press, 1971.

McGann, Jerome J. *Don Juan in Context*. Chicago: University of Chicago Press, 1976.

McGann, Jerome J. *The Romantic Ideology: A Critical Investigation*. Chicago and London: The University of Chicago Press, 1983.

McGann, Jerome J. and Ridenour, George M. "On Byron." *Studies in Romanticism* 16: 1977, 563-587.

Mellor, Anne K. *English Romantic Irony*. Cambridge: Harvard University Press, 1980.

Mellor, Anne K. "Blake's Portrayal of Women." *Blake: An Illustrated Quarterly*. A special issue on Blake's portrayal of women. Vol. 16 (Winter 1982–83): 148–55.

Mellor, Anne. *Blake's Human Form Divine*. Berkeley: University of California Press, 1974.

Mitchell, W. J. T. *Blake's Composite Art: A Study of the Illuminated Poetry*. Princeton: Princeton University Press, 1978.

Muir, Kenneth, ed. *John Keats: A Reassessment*. Liverpool: Liverpool University Press, 1959.

Nethercott, Arthur H. *The Road to Tryermaine: A Study of the History, Background, and Purpose of Coleridge's "Christabel"*. Chicago: University of Chicago Press, 1939.

Paley, Morton D. *The Continuing City: William Blake's Jerusalem*. Oxford: Clarendon Press, 1983.

Patterson, Charles I. *The Daemonic in the Poetry of John Keats*. Urbana: University of Illinois Press, 1970.

Perkins, David. *The Quest for Permanence: The Symbolism of Wordsworth, Shelley, and Keats*. Cambridge: Harvard University Press, 1959.

Pettet, E. C. *On the Poetry of Keats*. Cambridge: Cambridge University Press, 1957.

Prickett, Stephen. *Coleridge and Wordsworth: The Poetry of Growth*. Cambridge: Cambridge University Press, 1970.

Radley, Virginia L. "Christabel: Directions Old and New." *SEL* 4: 1964, 531–41.

Ragussis, Michael. *The Subterfuge of Art: Language and the Romantic Tradition*. Baltimore: The Johns Hopkins University Press, 1978.

Rajan, Tilottama. *Dark Interpreter: The Discourse of Romanticism*. Ithaca and London: Cornell University Press, 1980.

Reed, Mark. "The Speaker of the Prelude." In *Bicentenary Wordsworth Studies in Memory of John Allan Finch*, edited by Jonathan Wordsworth and Beth Darlington. Ithaca: Cornell University Press, 1970.

Reiman, Donald H. "Coleridge and the Art of Equivocation." *Studies in Romanticism* 25: 1986, 324–50.

Ridenour, George. *The Style of Don Juan*. New Haven: Yale University Press, 1960.

Robinson, Charles E. *Shelley and Byron: The Snake and Eagle Wreathed in Fight*. Baltimore and London: The Johns Hopkins University Press, 1976.

Ross, Marlon B. *The Contours of Masculine Desire: Romanticism and the Rise of Women's Poetry*. New York: Oxford University Press, 1989.

Rutherford, Andrew. *Byron: A Critical Study*. Stanford: Stanford University Press, 1961.

Rutherford, Andrew. *Byron: The Critical Heritage*. New York: Barnes and Noble, 1970.

Rzepka, Charles J. *The Self as Mind: Vision and Identity in Wordsworth, Coleridge, and Keats*. Cambridge: Harvard University Press, 1986.

Schapiro, Barbara. *The Romantic Mother: Narcissistic Patterns in Romantic Poetry*. Baltimore and London: The Johns Hopkins University Press, 1983.

Schulz, Max F. "Coleridge Agonistes." *JEGP* 61: 1962, 268–77.

Schulz, Max F. "Coleridge and the Enchantments of Earthly Paradise." In *Reading Coleridge: Approaches and Applications*, edited by Walter B. Crawford. Ithaca and New York: Cornell University Press, 1979.

Shelley, Percy Bysshe. *Shelley's Poetry and Prose*. Edited by Donald H. Reiman and Sharon B. Powers. New York and London: W. W. Norton and Company, 1977.

Sherry, Charles. *Wordsworth's Poetry of the Imagination.* Oxford: the Clarendon Press, 1980.

Sikes, Herschel M. "The Poetic Theory and Practice of Keats: The Record of a Debt to Hazlitt." *Philological Quarterly* 38: 1959, 401–13.

Simpson, David. *Irony and Authority in Romantic Poetry.* Totowa, N.J.: Rowman and Littlefield, 1979.

Siskin, Clifford. *The Historicity of Romantic Discourse.* New York: Oxford University Press, 1988.

Sperry, Stuart M. *Keats the Poet.* Princeton: Princeton University Press, 1973.

Steffan, Truman Guy. *Byron's Don Juan. The Making of a Masterpiece.* Austin: University of Texas Press, 1957, rev. 1971.

Stillinger, Jack. *The Hoodwinking of Madeline and Other Essays on Keats's Poems.* Urbana: University of Illinois Press, 1971.

Strickland, Edward. "Metamorphoses of the Muse in Romantic Poesis: Christabel." *ELH* 44: 1977, 641–68.

Tannenbaum, Leslie. *Biblical Tradition in Blake's Early Prophecies: The Great Code of Art.* Princeton: Princeton University Press, 1982.

Tayler, Irene. "The Woman Scaly." *Midwestern Modern Language Association Bulletin* 6: Spring 1973, 74–87.

Tetreault, Ronald. *The Poetry of Life: Shelley and Literary Form.* Toronto: University of Toronto Press, 1987.

Thompson, E. P. *The Making of the English Working Class.* London: Victor Gollancz, 1963.

Thorslev, Peter L. *The Byronic Hero: Types and Prototypes.* Minneapolis: University of Minnesota Press, 1962.

Todorov, Tzvetan. *Mikhail Bakhtin: The Dialogical Principle.* Minneapolis: University of Minnesota Press, 1984.

Twitchell, J. B. *The Living Dead: A Study of the Vampire in Romantic Literature.* Durham, N.C.: Duke University Press, 1981.

Van Ghent, Dorothy. *Keats: The Myth of the Hero.* Princeton: Princeton University Press, 1983.

Vendler, Helen. *The Odes of John Keats.* Cambridge, Mass. and London: The Belknap Press of Harvard University Press, 1983.

Wain, John. *Essays on Literature and Ideas.* London: Macmillan, 1963.

Waldoff, Leon. *Keats and the Silent Work of the Imagination.* Urbana and Chicago: University of Illinois Press, 1985.

Wasserman, Earl R. *The Finer Tone: Keats' Major Poems.* Baltimore and London: The Johns Hopkins Press, 1953.

Wasserman, Earl R. *Shelley: A Critical Reading.* Baltimore: The Johns Hopkins University Press, 1971.

Watkins, Daniel P. "Violence, Class Consciousness, and Ideology in Byron's History Plays." *ELH* 48: 799–816, 1981.

Watkins, Daniel P. "The Ideological Dimensions of *The Deformed Transformed.*" *Criticism* 25: 27–39, 1983.

Watkins, Daniel P. "Byron and the Poetics of Revolution." *Keats-Shelley Journal* 32: 95–130, 1985.

Watkins, Daniel P. *Social Relations in Byron's Eastern Tales*. Rutherford: Fairleigh Dickinson University Press, 1987.

West, Paul. *Byron and the Spoiler's Art*. London: Chatto and Windus, 1960.

Wilkie, Brian. *Romantic Poets and Epic Tradition*. Madison and Milwaukee: University of Wisconsin Press, 1965.

Wilson, Milton. *Shelley's Later Poetry: A Study of His Prophetic Imagination*. New York: Columbia University Press, 1959.

Wordsworth, Jonathan. *The Music of Humanity: A Critical Study of Wordsworth's "Ruined Cottage"*. London: Thomas Nelson and Sons, 1969.

Wordsworth, Jonathan. "The Five-Book *Prelude* of Early Spring 1804." *JEGP* 76: 1977, 1–25.

Wordsworth, Jonathan and Gill, Stephen. "The Two-Part *Prelude* of 1798–99." *JEGP* 72: 1973, 503–525.

Wordsworth, William. *The Borderers*. Edited by Robert Osborn. Ithaca and London: Cornell University Press, 1982.

Wordsworth, William. *Home at Grasmere*. Edited by Beth Darlington. Ithaca: Cornell University Press, 1977.

Wordsworth, William. *The Poetical Works of William Wordsworth*. Edited by Ernest de Selincourt and Helen Darbishire. 5 vols. 2d edition. Oxford: at the Clarendon Press, 1952–59.

Wordsworth, William. *The Prelude 1799, 1805, 1850: Authoritative Texts Context and Reception Recent Critical Essays*. Edited by Jonathan Wordsworth, M. H. Abrams and Stephen Gill. New York: W. W. Norton and Company, 1979.

Wordsworth, William. *The Prose Works of William Wordsworth*. Edited by W. J. B. Owen and Jane Smyser. 3 vols. Oxford: at the Clarendon Press, 1974.

Wordsworth, William. *The Ruined Cottage and The Pedlar*. Edited by James Butler. Ithaca: Cornell University Press, 1979.

Wornhoudt, Arthur. *The Demon Lover: A Psychoanalytical Approach to Literature*. New York: Exposition Press, 1949.

INDEX